Thomas Dallam, James Theodore Bent

Early Voyages and travels in the Levant

Thomas Dallam, James Theodore Bent

Early voyages and travels in the Levant

ISBN/EAN: 9783337207915

Printed in Europe, USA, Canada, Australia, Japan

Cover: Foto ©Andreas Hilbeck / pixelio.de

More available books at **www.hansebooks.com**

The Hakluyt Society.

REPORT FOR 1892.

THE TRAVELS OF PIETRO DELLA VALLE IN INDIA, edited by Mr. Edward Grey, in two volumes, have been issued to members during the year. More recently, a volume containing Mr. Markham's translation of the JOURNAL OF COLUMBUS' FIRST VOYAGE, together with documents relating to the voyages of John Cabot and Gaspar Corte-Real, has also been issued.

Mr. Theodore Bent's EARLY VOYAGES TO THE LEVANT, comprising the Diary of Thomas Dallam, and extracts from the Diaries of Dr. John Covel, is now ready for issue; and there will shortly appear, in two volumes, a collection of EARLY VOYAGES TO HUDSON'S BAY IN SEARCH OF A NORTH-WEST PASSAGE, edited by Mr. Miller Christy. These contain carefully annotated transcripts of the rare first editions of the North-West Foxe and Capt. James's Voyage.

The President has translated the LETTERS OF AMERIGO VESPUCCI, and other documents relating to the career of the Florentine navigator, with Notes and an Introduction. The volume is now ready for the press.

Dr. Robert Brown's LEO AFRICANUS is also ready for press.

Among other works undertaken for our Society, Mr.

Miller Christy has in hand JENS MUNK'S VOYAGE TO HUDSON'S BAY, translated from the Danish. This work will complete our series of voyages to the North-West in the first half of the seventeenth century.

The Council having decided on sending a set of its publications, as complete as possible, to the Chicago Exhibition, the books (80) were suitably bound and sent to Chicago. They were placed in the British Section (Liberal Arts, Group clv), in a case specially made to hold them. This set has since been purchased by an American book collector at the price fixed, 310 dollars.

Our list of Subscribers, with a total of 289, shows an increase on previous years. The balance at the bank was £239 18s. 5d. at the end of 1892.

The following Members of Council retire: Mr. Bouverie Pusey, Mr. Ernest Satow, and Capt. Sir J. Sydney Webb; and the following gentlemen are proposed for election: Capt. Nathan, R.E., Mr. F. Ducane Godman, F.R.S., and Mr. C. P. Lucas.

Statement of the Accounts of the Hakluyt Society for the year 1892.

Dr.

		£	s.	d.
Jan. 1.				
To Balance	...	266	6	8
,, Subscriptions and Arrears	...	280	7	0
,, Sales	...	72	7	0
		£619	0	8

Cr.

	£	s.	d.
By Insurance	2	10	0
,, Rent	20	0	0
,, Printing and Binding ...	281	3	9
,, Agent, Commission ...	16	15	0
,, ,, Gratuity for 1891 and 1892	10	0	0
,, Prætorius for Maps ...	10	0	0
,, Autotype Co., for Portraits of Della Valle and Admiral Button ...	9	5	6
,, Index for Della Valle	5	5	0
,, Mr. Miller Christy, for Transcriptions	10	0	6
,, Messrs. Tweedie, Law Expenses	6	0	6
,, Advertising in *Literary Circular*	8	0	6
,, Cheque Stamps ...	0	2	6
,, Balance	239	18	5
	£619	0	8

Examined and found correct,

CLEMENTS R. MARKHAM.

WORKS ISSUED BY

The Hakluyt Society.

———o———

EARLY VOYAGES AND TRAVELS IN

THE LEVANT.

No. LXXXVII.

PORTRAIT OF DR. COVEL,
From the Painting in Christ's College, Cambridge.

EARLY
VOYAGES AND TRAVELS
IN
THE LEVANT.

I.—THE DIARY OF
MASTER THOMAS DALLAM,
1599-1600.

II.—EXTRACTS FROM THE DIARIES OF
DR. JOHN COVEL,
1670-1679.

*WITH SOME ACCOUNT OF THE LEVANT COMPANY
OF TURKEY MERCHANTS.*

Edited, with an Introduction and Notes,
BY
J. THEODORE BENT, F.S.A., F.R.G.S.

LONDON:
PRINTED FOR THE HAKLUYT SOCIETY,
4, LINCOLN'S INN FIELDS, W.C.
M.DCCC.XCIII.

LONDON:
PRINTED BY CHAS. J. CLARK, 4, LINCOLN'S INN FIELDS, W.C.

COUNCIL

OF

THE HAKLUYT SOCIETY.

CLEMENTS R. MARKHAM, ESQ., C.B., F.R.S., *Pres. R.G.S.*, PRESIDENT.
MAJOR-GENERAL SIR HENRY RAWLINSON, K.C.B., D.C.L., LL.D., F.R.S.,
 Associé Étranger de L'Institut de France, VICE-PRESIDENT.
LORD ABERDARE, G.C.B., F.R.S.
VICE-ADMIRAL LINDESAY BRINE.
ROBERT BROWN, ESQ., M.A., PH.D.
MILLER CHRISTY, ESQ.
THE RIGHT HON. SIR MOUNTSTUART E. GRANT DUFF, G.C.S.I., *late Pres. R.G.S.*
F. DUCANE GODMAN, ESQ., F.R.S.
ALBERT GRAY, ESQ.
C. P. LUCAS, ESQ.
A. P. MAUDSLAY, ESQ.
CAPTAIN NATHAN, R.E.
ADMIRAL SIR E. OMMANNEY, C.B., F.R.S.
E. A. PETHERICK, ESQ.
S. W. SILVER, ESQ.
COUTTS TROTTER, ESQ.
PROF. E. B. TYLOR, D.C.L.
CAPTAIN W. J. L. WHARTON, R.N.

, *Honorary Secretary.*

CONTENTS.

PORTRAIT OF DR. COVEL, photographed from the painting at Christ's College, Cambridge, by kind permission of Vice-Chancellor J. Peile . . . . *frontispiece*

                                                                           PAGE

INTRODUCTION i

LIST OF ENGLISH AMBASSADORS TO THE PORTE IN THE SIXTEENTH AND SEVENTEENTH CENTURIES . xlii

ADDENDA ET CORRIGENDA xliii

DALLAM'S TRAVELS (1599-1600) 1

DR. COVEL'S DIARY (1670-1679) 99

INDEX . . . 289

INTRODUCTION.

§ 1.—OF THE FORMATION OF THE LEVANT COMPANY OF TURKEY MERCHANTS.

HE two manuscript diaries which are published in this volume give us the experiences of men who resided in Constantinople during the earlier days of the Levant Company. When Master Thomas Dallam went with the present of a marvellous organ from Queen Elizabeth to the Sultan Mahomed III in 1599, our Company of Turkey Merchants had scarcely organised themselves. When Dr. Covel went as chaplain to the embassy in 1670, the Company was still struggling to gain for itself those rights—or capitulations, as they are called—which formed the basis of the prosperity of the Company during the ensuing century and a half. Consequently, I think, a succinct account of the rise of this Company will form a suitable introduction to the perusal of the diaries themselves.

INTRODUCTION.

In the development of our system of commerce the Company of Turkey Merchants played a most important part, second perhaps only to the great East India Company, and its history is the history of one of those pillars on which British prosperity has been constructed. It was a marked feature of the sixteenth century, when all those Companies—the African Company, the Muscovy Company, the East India Company—all had their rise, and by them was laid the foundation of our subsequent mercantile successes. The Levant Company lived an active life of 244 years; and, besides the amount of wealth it accumulated for this country, it did infinite service in the development of art and research, geography and travel, the suppression of slavery, and the spread of civilisation in countries which would still have been unapproachable had not the continued efforts of the 244 years been towards civilisation and humanity.

The history of the capitulations or treaties with which foreign nations sought to establish themselves in the greatest centre of commercial enterprise before the opening out of other routes to India is a very interesting one, and dates back to remote ages, when commercial bodies were formed in the city of Constantine, at the time when the power of the Greek emperors was on the wane. As far back as the ninth and tenth centuries of our era, the emperors of the East granted to the Warings or Varangians from Scandinavia capitulations or rights of exterritoriality, which gave them permission to own wharves, carry on trade, and govern themselves in the Eastern capital: these rights established numerous *imperia in imperio* during the succeeding centuries in Constantinople. The Venetians obtained them early in the eleventh century; the Amalfians in 1056, the Genoese in 1098, and the Pisans in 1110, and henceforward they became so general, that the Greeks of the later empire complained that there were no wharves for themselves, and that they could not compete with these indefatigable foreign traders; much as we hear complaints now amongst our own artisans of the influx of German and Belgian workmen into England.

When the Turks took Constantinople they did little to interfere with the existing order of things: the Genoese and Venetians got their capitulations renewed; the right to have disputes with their fellow-countrymen decided by their own authorities; the right to have questions between them and Ottoman subjects decided only in presence of a Venetian interpreter; exemption from the tax imposed on Christians in lieu of military service; and the right to appoint their own magistrates in Constantinople. Being a nomadic race, the Ottoman Turks cared little for commerce: their ships were the caïques of the Greeks; their emperors wrote their decrees in red ink, as their Greek predecessors had done; and to the foreign traders who flocked to Constantinople they gave the same privileges that the Greek emperors had done, and, as far as they were concerned, the *status quo* was maintained.

Meanwhile trade was passing westwards; the time

was come when the Portuguese, the French, and finally the English were to succeed the Italian republics as the commercial nations of the world.

In 1536 Sieur Foret arranged a capitulation for the French between Sultan Solyman I and Francis I, and the essential articles of this treaty have been often redrawn and embodied in many treaties with the different European Powers, and still remain as the foundation of the many treaties under which foreigners now live in Constantinople: matters of dispute between Frenchmen were to be decided only by their own authorities; questions between Frenchmen and Turks were to be decided only in the presence of the French dragoman; they could appoint their own magistrates, and were exempt from the *harach*. This was the first of what we may call the modern capitulations, by which the Western nations have obtained their footing in Constantinople; they are by no means an invention of the Turks, but a distinct inheritance from the old Byzantine days, which they were compelled to adopt, and which has turned out to be as great a boon to the Mussulman as to the foreigner who obtained it.

In proportion to the exigencies of the Turk and his want of money, the system of capitulations has increased in strength. Encroachments have occurred; fresh clauses have had to be introduced to meet the subtleties of the Turk; the so-called *avanias*, of which we shall hear more in Dr. Covel's diary, had to be combated; but, nevertheless, the progress has been continuous, and no Company has contributed more to the success of the foreigner on Turkish soil than the "Turkey Merchants" of England.

During the reign of Elizabeth, our infantile commercial adventures were beginning to make themselves felt. Early in the sixteenth century there had been a few isolated cases of voyages to the Levant in search of wealth. From 1511 to 1534 we hear of certain "tall ships belonging to London, Southampton, and Bristol, which made voyages to the East, trading with Sicily, Crete, Chios, and sometimes Cyprus, Tripoli, and Beyrout in Syria"; but there appears to have been no systematic commerce carried on in English bottoms in those days, most of the trade between the Levant and England being conducted by the Venetians. So far back as 1513 we had a consul established at Chios, and in 1534 (Hakluyt, vol. ii, p. 98) we read of an exciting voyage made by *The Holy Cross* and *The Matthew Gonson* to Crete and Chios, both ships coming back much the worse for wear. In 1550 Captain Bodenham, with "the great Barke *Aucher*", went to Chios, and three years later Anthony Jenkinson went to Aleppo, and got trading privileges "on a footing with the most favoured nations". This was the actual foundation of our future capitulations, and the first commencement of our Levant Company.

Up to this time the carrying trade between England and the Levant had been carried on, on ships called argosies, by the Venetians. Sir Paul Ricaut, son of a London merchant, who was born in 1620, was secretary to Lord Winchilsea, and consul at

Smyrna for eleven years; he wrote, by the direction of Charles II, a work entitled *The Present State of the Greek and Armenian Churches.* He also wrote a book entitled *The Present State of the Turkish Empire*, a very interesting work, the first edition of which, Pepys tells us, was destroyed in the Great Fire of London. In this work he tells us that the ships known as argosies were so called because they were built at Ragusa for the Venetian merchants. "These vast carracks called argosies, which are so famed for the vastness of their burthen and bulk, were corruptly so denominated from Ragosies, ships of Ragusa." The Ragusans, as merchants, were much to the fore in those days, prior to the great earthquake, and had, as we see from Dr. Covel's diary, an ambassador of their own at Constantinople.

> "Your mind is tossing on the ocean;
> There, where your argosies, with portly sail,—
> Like signiors and rich burghers on the flood,
> Or, as it were, the pageants of the sea,—
> Do over-peer the petty traffickers,
> That curt'sy to them, do them reverence,
> As they fly by them with their woven wings."
>
> (Shakes., *Merchant of Venice*, Act i, Scene 1.)

One of these argosies was wrecked off the Isle of Wight about 1575, and it is said that the Venetians refused to bring merchandise into such dangerous seas after this catastrophe. Perhaps this argosy may be the very one which suggested to Shakespeare the shipwreck of the Venetian merchantman. At any rate, this fact obliged individual action on the part of the English merchants of the day, and at once necessitated the formation of a distinct Company, if the trade with the Levant was to be continued.

Another point also contributed to the starting of an independent trade with the Levant, namely, a quarrel with Venice concerning the duties on currants (*State Papers, Domestic*, 11th April, 1606). In 1575 Venice had granted a patent to one Acerbo Velutelli, a native of Lucca, which gave him the sole right of importing to England currants and oil from Venetian dominions. Velutelli contrived to get these articles conveyed to England on English ships, and, by exacting an export duty for his own benefit, enriched himself and impoverished the Venetian traders. Venice then imposed a fine of 5*s*. 6*d*. on currants and oil conveyed to England in other than Venetian bottoms. Elizabeth retaliated by a similar fine on their importation, and for a time trade in these commodities was at a standstill.

Yet another, and that a political, cause promoted our intercourse with Turkey. Queen Elizabeth was just entering into her vital contest with Philip II of Spain, and to secure the alliance and co-operation of the Sultan was one of her favourite schemes at this critical juncture. Until the reign of Amurath III the English had been altogether strangers to Turkey; but in 1579 three merchants were sent to Constantinople—William Harebone, Edward Ellis, and Richard Staple—to spy out the land, as it were, and, if possible, obtain for English merchants the same social and commercial privileges that other nations enjoyed. Two years later Queen Elizabeth formed a treaty charter with Amurath III for five years, in which he styles himself "the most sacred Mussulman-like Emperor", and she also granted letters patent to a small Company entitled "The Company of Merchants of the Levant", consisting of Sir E. Osborne, Thomas Smith, Stephen and William Garret—" because they had found out and opened a trade in Turkey, not known in the memory of any man now living to be frequented by our progenitors."

The first of the Company's ships to trade with the Levant was sent out in 1582. It was called *The Great Susan*, and William Harebone, the first ambassador from England to the Ottoman Porte, was carried out by her. He established factories at Constantinople, obtained capitulations from the Porte, and regularly inaugurated our trade there. Harebone was considerably assisted by the great Vizier Sokolli and the Sultan's tutor, the learned historian Seadedin, in his negotiations. (Von Hammer.)

At the same time it is evident that commercial objects were not paramount in Queen Elizabeth's mind, but a desire to obtain the Sultan as an ally against her formidable enemy. In her letters to the Sultan she takes advantage of the well-known horror the Mahommedans have of image-worship, and styles herself, "the unconquered and most puissant defender of the true faith against the idolaters who falsely profess the name of Christ".

In 1587 her agent in Constantinople presented a petition to Sultan Amurath III, for assistance against the Spanish Armada, imploring him to send help "against that idolater, the King of Spain, who, relying on the help of the Pope and all idolatrous princes, designs to crush the Queen of England, and then to turn his whole power to the destruction of the Sultan, and make himself universal monarch."

Christendom, luckily for the reputation of Elizabeth, never saw an alliance between the Crescent and the Cross of so peculiar a nature brought to any ultimate result. The Sultan promised, but did nothing. Turkey was already on the decline, and her internal troubles occupied her sufficiently. Ranke, vol. i, p. 433, speaks of "the advances made by the English Government to the Turks in the time of Elizabeth", and this factor had no doubt as much to do with the formation of the Levant Company as anything else.

In 1586 a charter was granted to fifty-three individuals, with power to trade in the Levant; and though, of course, the ambassador resided at Constantinople, in those days the principal mart of English trade was Aleppo, where Michael Locke was at that time consul, whose account of the condition of affairs in that city is quaint and interesting. He also speaks of the trade of Chios being great some years before, and alludes to it as "the great store of sundry commodities", and further states that in 1593 tin was the principal article of export from England. He founded a factory at Aleppo which was one of the most flourishing in the Levant for 150 years. The outlet of this commerce was Scanderoon, and we find all the vessels which traded to the East, including the ship *Hector*, which took Master Dallam out, going to Scanderoon before Constantinople.

Sir Edward Barton was the first resident ambassador at Constantinople. Harebone had evidently been only sent out as a plenipotentiary extraordinary to inaugurate the intercourse with the Levant. Hakluyt (vol. ii) gives us an account of the present which Sir Edward Barton took out on the ship *Ascension* in 1593 for the Sultan Amurath III: "12 goodly pieces of plate, 36 garments of cloth of all colours, 20 garments of cloth of gold, 10 garments of satin, 6 pieces of fine Holland, and certain other things of good value." To his powerful wife, the Sultana Safiye, Queen Elizabeth sent a "jewel of her Majesty's picture set with rubies and diamonds; 3 pieces of gilt plate ; 10 garments of cloth of gold ; a very fine case of glasse bottles, silver and gilt; and 2 pieces of fine Holland." With Mahomed III, who succeeded his father, Amurath III, in 1595, Sir E. Barton seems to have been on most intimate terms, carrying on the traditional alliance, and hopes of possible hope of support which had been started in his father's reign.

Mahomed III was the eldest son of Amurath, one of his 103 children. He was a son of his Venetian wife and favourite, the Sultana Safiye, a lady of the House of Baffo, who had been captured by a Turkish corsair in her youth. Mahomed III put nineteen of his brothers to death on his accession, the grossest instance of fratricide even in Turkish annals. He was at the outset of his reign chiefly engaged in wars in Hungary, and in these Sir Edward Barton accompanied him. They ended in the victory of Cerestes, and, on his return to Constantinople, Sir E. Barton, worn out by the rigours of the campaign, died. In Sultan Mahomed III's letter to Queen Elizabeth, in 1596, he thus alludes to Sir E. Barton: "As to your highnesse's well-beloved Ambassador at our blessed Porte, Edward Barton, one of the nation of the Messiah, he having been enjoined by us to follow our imperial camp without having been enabled previously to obtain your highness's permission to go with my imperial Staff, we have reason to be satisfied, and to hope that also your highness will know how to appreciate the services he has thus rendered to us in our imperial camp."

Mustapha, the first Turkish envoy to England in 1607, also alludes to Sir E. Barton: "Mr. Barton was in the army . . . . when Raab, *alias* Severin, was won from the Christians."

Sir E. Barton came of a Yorkshire family, and was sent out to Constantinople as ambassador in 1593, with the title of "Agent for her Majesty with the Grand Seignior". Subsequently, however, he received his stipend from the Levant Company. He died at Chalki, one of the Prince's Islands, in 1597, and was buried at the monastery there. His tombstone (which Dr. Covel saw, *vide* p. 281) was displaced and put over the door of the monastery wrong way up, until Lord Strangford had it put in its present position, and the following inscription is still legible :—

"Eduardo Barton, Illustrissimo Serenissimo Anglorum Reginæ Oratori viro præstantissimo, qui post reditum a bello Ungarico quo cum invicto Turcorum imperatore, profectus fuerat diem obiit, pietatis ergo, ætatis anno xxxv. Sal. vero MDXCVII XVIII Kal. Januar."

Mr. Henry Lello was appointed to succeed Sir E. Barton. From the Venetian Baily's report we learn about his reception by the Sultan. He calls him Sir Henry Billoe (Von Hammer), but this is an obvious mistake. Sir Henry Lello wrote regularly to England an account of affairs as they progressed at Constantinople. His term of office is chiefly marked by a prolonged quarrel with the French ambassador, to which Dallam refers in his MS. (*vide* p. 81), to settle which the Baily of Venice, one of the Capello family, was chosen arbiter.

Sir Henry Lello's correspondence is now in the Record Office, and from one of his letters we learn officially how the Sultan received the present which Dallam took out. I herewith transcribe a considerable portion of it as bearing very good testimony to the accuracy of Master Thomas Dallam's MS. :—

"*S. P. Foreign, Turkey, No.* 4.

"*Henry Lello to Sr Robt Cecil,* 2 t *Oct.* 1599.

"Right Honorable,—I omitted the last curier, for that I could not then, nor yet cannott, advize yor honno^r of that good succes of my ymployment heere wth the G^r Signior, as I expected, by the meanes of the french Ambassador, who, with his great bribes (receyvinge now the Pope's pay), sparethe nothinge to hinder all my desingnes in mallice, seinge the reputation of Her Majesty is so great in this port, and cheefly for the consulledge of forrestiers, wch the Grand Signior lyttle after the arrivall of the shipp graunted should come under Her Majesty's banner, nothwithstandinge the same was formerly graunted by his father and him sealfe, proffering all other reasonable demaunds wch her Majesty should desire, countinge hir frindshipp before that of any other Christian Prince, rejoysinge greatly to see the shipp to come into port, and more hir princely presents, espetially the instrument and plate, whereof hee made greàt accompt, and at the tyme apoynted mee to come present the same; he made demonstration therof by spekinge himsealf to me wch hath not ever bin used (as is reported) to any Cristian prince's ambassador, the manner whereof in breefe I doe hereby advize yor honnor.

"Althoughe he kept his court out of the Cittie, yett cam hee home of purpose for mee to delliver her Majestie's letter and present, and to kisse his hand, at wch tyme I apoynted to attend upon me xii gentlemen on horsebacke, vested in cloth of gould and silver, a gentlem̄ usher, ii pages in white damaske, 20 menn in livery gownes, xii merchaunts, desently apparelled merchauntlike in blacke, and my sealf attired as richly as I might.

"The captains of the Chowses and Spahees (Chiauses and Spahis) were sent to accompany and entertayne mee to the G^r Signior his pallace, where first in open court before the G^r Signior, his Pashas, or Counsellors, I declared to them her Ma^tye's pleasure, salutations, and requests.

"Conferring about divers late accidents, espetially of her Majestie's forces against Spaine, and of the peace made betweene him and the French Kinge, wch thay all seemed to dislike, we spent a smale tyme untill the banquett ordayned for mee was provided; which being furnished, only I, Halul Pasha, the Cheefe Vizier, and a first Pasha, late general of *Scelestia* (Silistria), sate at one Table, the other Pashas satt apart by them sealves; at another, a lyttle distant from us, satt the ii *Cadiliskers*, or cheefe Judges of all this empire, and apart from them ii of the high Tresorors; by them satt alone the highe chaunsellors, every one served accordinge to his degree, but our Table furnished wth the allowance and dayenties as are usually served to the G^r S^r, in great variety and abundance; wch finished, order was sent by the G^r S^r that before our entrance unto him bothe I and my gentlemenn should be clothed in vests out of his Tresorie, wch were there scarcely found, yet had I ii, and ten for my gentlemenn; and so, in company of the Vizeires, I entered into the presence chamber, where the Grand Sigio^r satt uppon a cushion of red sattin most richly ymbrodred wth pearls, and all his chamber floored with Redd sattin Ritchly ymbrodered wth gould; and, omyttinge the sumptuousnes of the sight, coming to deliver my Ambassadge unto him, I first salluted him in her Highnes' name; secondly, declared to him the good intelligence betweene her Highnes and his father,[1] and of the bennefitt therof to both their dom̄nions and subieckts; thirdly, I ymformed him of Her Majesty's pleasure for my Confirmation in former charge of Ambassador, requiringe therein not only his Highnes' consent, but princely favour in all future occations; and, lastly, recom̄ended unto him the affayres of her merchaunts traffickinge in his dom̄nions, wher unto hee him sealf answered as afore, sainge he did much reioyce at Her Majesty's frindshipp, and prayed God that shee might allwayes have the victory over her enemyes as hether unto. Lastly, he tould me I should receyve sattisfaction of all I desiered, Licensinge me to departe. I was accompanied with Chiauses and other his officers to my house, having binn both outward and homward Salluted wth divers tiers of artillery from the Shipp, for wch and the favour of the Grand Signo^r shewed me that day ministred many dayes after occation to speak of my Entertainment.

"But this while thinkinge my sealf sure of all things, the French ambassador, with his bribe of 6,000 chickins,[2] did not only over throughe our former graunt of counsolledge of forresteeres, but all other demandes I made, besides the confirmation of our ould Capittulations, the Vizeer denienge me audience to shew reason for my just demands."

[Then follows a long account of his difficulties owing to the interference of the French ambassador, and certain details concerning the war in Hungary; and the letter closes as follows :—]

---

[1] Queen Elizabeth and Amurath III.   [2] Sequins.

"I comitt yor honno^r to Gode's most mercifull protection this 21th of October 1599.

"Yo^r honno^{rs} most dewtifull
"Ever to comand,
"HENRY LELLO."

Addressed—

"To the right Honble Sir Robert Cecill, knight, principal secr^{rie} to the Queen's most Ex^t Mag^{tie} and Her Highnes' honorable privie Counseill."

§ 2.—OF THE DALLAM FAMILY.

Such was the state of affairs in Constantinople when Master Thomas Dallam, whose diary we here produce, went to present a complicated organ, which he had made, as a gift from Queen Elizabeth to Sultan Mahomed III. His MS. diary was written just after the publication of Richard Hakluyt's volumes of travels, or else it would in all probability have been included in them. From the foregoing remarks it will easily be seen why so handsome a gift was sent out with so much trouble ; the Queen was anxious for the Sultan's friendship and allegiance against her Catholic enemies. To further the interests of the infantile Levant Company such a present would be exceedingly useful, and, in choosing Dallam as the bearer of this present, Queen Elizabeth evidently selected, as subsequent events showed, the most skilled man in his craft that she could.

Some interesting notes with regard to this present may be gathered from the State Papers, Jan. 1596. For some time there had been a discussion about sending a present to the new Sultan of Turkey.

The Levant merchants apparently thought it would imperil their own safety and their factories in Constantinople if Sir E. Barton's papers were not made out by the Queen, and if the present did not come from her Majesty herself. Hence, out of compliance with their wishes, Sir E. Barton, though the Company's nominee, was accredited as ambassador from Queen Elizabeth, and the present, which the Levant merchants no doubt paid for, purported to be from the Queen of England to the Sultan.

In the State Papers, January 31st, 1599, just a month before Dallam set out on his voyage, the following entry is made: "A great and curious present is going to the Grand Turk, which will scandalise other nations, especially the Germans." This great and curious present was the organ which Dallam had built, and which he was about to take out in person.

Of the previous history of Thomas Dallam we know little. From the tombstone of his son in New College, Oxford, we gather that he came from the village of Dallam, in Lancashire, not far from Warrington. From the papers of the Blacksmiths' Company we learn that he came up to London, and was apprenticed to that Company, and admitted as a liveryman of the same. In those days the Blacksmiths' Company had supervision over many Companies, including the organ-builders, and in this branch of the craft Thomas Dallam was employed.

From Dr. Rimbault we learn many details concerning this celebrated family of organ-builders and the instruments they constructed. Of this particular one, which Dallam made, and which was set up in Whitehall for Queen Elizabeth's approval prior to its being shipped off to Constantinople, there appears to be no other record; but, immediately on his return from the East, Thomas Dallam seems to have worked hard at his trade, and he and his sons constructed most of the principal organs of the seventeenth century.

In 1605-6 Dallam was engaged for fifty-eight weeks in constructing the organ of King's College, Cambridge, for which purpose he closed his workshop in London, and for this work he received the sum of £371 17s. 1d. This organ was destroyed in the civil wars, but the case still remains. In 1607 he got £1 15s. for tuning the same organ, and a like sum for the sale of surplus tin, and his name frequently occurs in the College records till 1641. In 1613 Dallam made "new double organs" for Worcester Cathedral, and got £211. This organ was likewise destroyed in the rebellion.

On 29th of September 1626, Thomas Dallam was made a steward of the annual feast of the Blacksmiths' Company, but did not put in an appearance, and was fined £10 for neglect of duty. In the following year he petitioned in court to be let off his stewardship, and his petition was granted him on payment of certain small fines.

Almost immediately after his return from Constantinople Thomas Dallam must have married, for his eldest son, Robert, was born in 1602, and was brought up by his father in the organ-building trade under the auspices of the Blacksmiths' Company. Together, between 1624 and 1627, they put up an organ in Durham Cathedral, which was eventually sold to the Church of St. Michael-le-Belfry, York, where it remained till 1885, and was finally disposed of to Mr. Bell, organ-builder, York, for the sum of four pounds.

Robert Dallam also built an organ for Jesus College, Cambridge, for £200, and several others. Finally, we hear of him as engaged to build an organ for New College, Oxford; and he died at Oxford, May 31st, 1665, and, from his tomb in that College we learn certain particulars about the family, the concluding lines of which would seem rather to refer to his father than himself, for we have no record of his having travelled in distant lands. It runs as follows:—

"Hic jacet D^{mnus} Robertus Dallam Instrumenti Pneumatici (quod vulgo organum nuncupant) peritissimus artifex filius Thomæ Dallum de Dallum in comitat: Lancastriæ mortuus est die Maii ultimo

"anno $\begin{cases} \text{Domini 1665} \\ \text{ætatis suæ 63.} \end{cases}$

"Qui postquam diversas Europæ plagas hâc arte (quâ præcipue claruit) exornasset solum hoc tandem, in quo requiescit cinere suo insignivit."

Ralph Dallam, another son of Thomas, also an organ-builder, constructed the organ which was put up in St. George's Chapel after the Restoration, and also built organs in Rugby, Hackney, and Lynn

Regis, and died whilst making the organ in Greenwich Chapel in 1672.

George Dallam, another son, lived in Purple Lane in 1672, and in 1686 added a "chaire organ" to Harris's instrument in Hereford Cathedral.

Thus it will be seen that Thomas Dallam, the writer of the diary, was the progenitor of a distinguished family of organ-builders, whose work was in great request in the seventeenth century. We have also to thank him for the graphic account of the Imperial Court at Constantinople during the reign of Mahomed III, and incidents in seafaring life at that period, which add considerably to our knowledge of the state of nautical affairs as they existed in the days of Raleigh and Drake.

§ 3.—OF THE FURTHER PROGRESS OF THE LEVANT COMPANY.

It was understood from the first that the Levant Company should pay and appoint the consuls, ambassadors, and other officials of their Company, though difficulties arose on this point between the Government and the Company concerning the salary of Sir Edward Barton. Affairs seem to have gone on smoothly till 1600, when the monopoly was removed, and the Company had to struggle on as best it could against competition which proved almost fatal to it at the very outset of its career.

Accordingly, in 1605, we find petitions from the Company to James I, complaining that they could no longer pay the salaries of the ambassadors and consuls, and that they feared that the Turks might seize their factories and buildings in the Turkish towns. Lord Salisbury entered into consultation with Chief Justice Popham on the subject, and the result was that, on the 14th December 1606, letters patent were granted by James I which may really be said to have established the Company on a permanent basis. The five years' terminable licences were made perpetual, and privileges were granted to several persons and their sons, and such others as should be after admitted. The Company was to have the monopoly of all the Levant trade: in fact, the English traffic of nearly all the Mediterranean was handed over exclusively to the Company, which was to be open to all merchants who could pay £50 towards the expenses of carrying on the trade, the salary of the ambassadors and consuls, and the presents which, from time to time, were necessary to be given to the Sultan to keep him favourably disposed, and the first year's "imposition", or tax of £5,322, was handed over to the Company to assist in tiding over a time of difficulty.

Thomas Glover, who had been one of Thomas Dallam's companions on board the ship *Hector* on his journey out, was ambassador at this time, with power to appoint consuls and regulate the trade for the Company. It does not appear what emolument he got from the Company, but it was doubtless considerable, as he was forbidden to trade on his own account, and, under his skilful management, the successful career of the Levant Company was inaugurated.

It was absolutely necessary in those early days of mercantile enterprise to give the monopoly of the Levant trade to one Company; only a rich and united body, with the privileges accorded to them by their capitulations, could carry on such trade. It was necessary, for the safety of the ships, that they should sail in large numbers for mutual protection from Dunkirkers, corsairs, and other hostile craft, and hence very strict penalties were imposed on private individuals who sought to carry on trade under the protection of the Company without actually belonging to it. The celebrated case of Bates, who refused to pay a tax to the Company on currants, and drove them off in his own cart from the wharf, was tried shortly after this, and when it was decided in the Company's favour, their monopoly was clearly established.

In the reign of James I the Company received the name of "The Governor and Company of Merchants of England trading to the Levant Seas", and the arms of a ship with three masts in full sail between two rocks. Their crest was a demi sea-horse salient; their supporters two sea-horses; and their motto, "Deo Respublicæ et amicis."

In 1612, Mr. Paul Pindar, another of Thomas Dallam's companions on board the ship *Hector*, succeeded Sir Thomas Glover as ambassador for the Company to the Porte.

In 1623, Sir T. Roe was ambassador. He got a

salary of £1,800 per ann. from the Company, besides a portion of the consulage and other advantages, but at the same time he was forbidden to carry on a trade of any kind. During this period the Levant Company continued to make satisfactory progress, and the only thing to remark is the controversies which, during the reigns of James I and Charles I, raged between the regulated Companies, namely, the Levant Company and Merchant Adventurers, against the East India Company, which, as then constituted, they considered as the monopoly of a few which told against the monopoly of larger corporate bodies.

In 1643 further privileges were granted to the Levant Company. In an ordinance of both Houses, upholding the Levant Merchants, dated 9th of March 1643, the following points occur :—

"'That for the better supportation and encouragement of the Fellowship of merchants of England, trading to the Levant Seas, which, besides the building and maintaining of divers great ships, both for defence and burthen, the venting of kerseys, sages, perpetuanas, and several other commodities hath been found very serviceable and profitable to the State, by advancing navigation, and transporting into foreigne parts for severall years together above 20,000 broadclothes per annum, besides other commodities whereby the poor people are sett at worke, and the whole kingdome receive benefit. The Lords and Commons do ordaine :—

"'That the Fellowship of Merchants trading to the Levant Seas shall continue a corporation ; that they shall have free choice and removal of all ministers by them maintained at home and abroad, whether they be dignified and called by the name of Ambassadors, Governours, Deputies, Consulls, or otherwise.

"'That they shall have power to levie monies on the members of their corporation, or on strangers ; on goods shipped in English bottoms, or on English goods in strange bottoms, which shall goe into or come from the Levant Seas, for and towards necessary charge, maintenance, and supply of their ministers, officers, and government.

"That no person shall send ships into these parts limited by their corporation, but such as are free brothers, or otherwise licensed, each person to pay, if a mere merchant, £50, if above twenty-one years of age, or £25 if under that age; and they shall have power to fine persons disobeying their orders in a sum not exceeding £20, or imprisoning their persons till the said sum be paid."

About this time the Levant Company suffered somewhat from the conflicting state of parties in England. Sir S. Crowe was appointed in 1642 as ambassador of the Levant Company; he was a staunch loyalist, and, during his tenure of office abroad, his goods in England were confiscated by the Parliamentarians. On hearing this, Sir S. Crowe imprisoned many of the English factors in Constantinople, and appropriated their goods. The Parliamentarians forthwith obliged the Company to send out another representative, Sir J. Bendish, who, after some difficulty, succeeded in establishing himself as the ambassador of England, and Sir S. Crowe was sent home. On arriving in London, he was impeached at the suit of the Company, condemned, and kept in prison till 1653.

The regulations of the Company with regard to their *employés* were very strict in those days; none of the consuls under their authority might marry without the consent of the directors, and the factors or merchants at Constantinople and elsewhere in the Levant frequently received admonitions from the governing body at home against "sensuality, gambling,

Sabbath-breaking, neglect of public worship", and other irregularities of life in which the merchants, far from the influence of their strait-laced relatives at home, were prone to indulge.

In 1661 the Earl of Winchilsea went out on *The Plymouth* as ambassador for the Company. Captain Hayward was in command of the vessel, with whom Pepys (p. 50) made merry at the Rhenish Wine House. Lord Winchilsea is described as "a jovial Lord, extremely favoured by Vizier Kiuprili". Two Kiuprilis, father and son, were practically the rulers of Turkey from 1658 to the death of the latter in 1676. Both the Kiuprilis were men of exceedingly good powers of organisation, and raised Turkey to comparative power, despite the weakness of her princes. The Sultan Mahomed IV, about whom Dr. Covel in his MS. tells us so much, was a man of weak character, devoted only to the chase, and left the organisation of the empire to his Vizier. From him Lord Winchilsea obtained further capitulations, an account of which is given us by his secretary, Paul Ricaut, in a pamphlet entitled *The Capitulations and Articles published by Paul Ricaut, Esquire, Secretary to his Excellencie the Lord Ambassador, in* 1663, and addressed to the Governors of the Levant Company. In this pamphlet he says: "The first capitulations took place 80 years before, in Queen Elizabeth's reign, and have been enlarged in the time of allmost every ambassador, with such alterations as the state of affaires, and the abuses, and the iniquities of the times suggested." The principal grievance which this set of capitulations rectified was "that English ships should be exempt from search for foreign goods". Mahomed IV, in his address to Charles II, on the occasion of the granting of these capitulations, speaks in high-flown language of "the Queen of the aforesaid Kingdom" who commenced the Levant trade.

A curious and ludicrous instance of the fanaticism of the times occurred in 1661. An individual called "John the Quaker" arrived at Constantinople, and began to preach at the street corners repentance to the Turks in his own native tongue. Naturally enough, the Mohammedans looked upon him as a lunatic, and consigned him to a mad-house, where he languished for eight months, until his nationality was discovered, and he was taken before Lord Winchilsea. On entering the ambassador's presence, true to the regulations of his creed, John refused to remove his hat, whereupon he was bastinadoed; and, on his clothes being examined, a letter was discovered in his pocket addressed to the Sultan, politely telling that monarch that he was the scourge employed by God to punish wicked Christians.

There was a distinct revival at this juncture in the condition of the power of the Ottoman Turks at Constantinople; under the severe rule of the elder Kiuprili, and the firm but temperate jurisdiction of his son Ahmed, both internal and external affairs prospered favourably. Ahmed Kiuprili conducted the wars with Austria with a fair amount of success. He won Crete for the Turks, in 1669, from the

Venetian general Morosini; the wars with Sobieski, under his guidance, were, with certain fluctuations, favourable to the Turks. He, in 1675, instituted the levy of 3,000 boys from the Christian population to fill the ranks of the Janissaries; and three days after the peace of Zuranna, by which the Turks regained much of their lost military prestige, he died, very shortly after the events related in such minute detail by Dr. Covel in our second manuscript, and very shortly after the ratification of further capitulations with the Levant Company at Adrianople; the incidents concerning the obtaining of which Dr. Covel relates so graphically.

§ 4.—OF DR. JOHN COVEL.

The writer of the second MS. we have before us is mentioned by Evelyn in his *Diary* (ii, 338) as "Covel, the great Oriental traveller". Evidently he intended either to publish a work himself, or that his diary should be published shortly after his death, for he divided part of his MS. into chapters, put in illustrations, and collected together everything connected with himself, every scrap of letter and paper that would be of use, even down to his *testamur* when he took his B.A. in 1657; but this mass of MS. has remained hidden in the British Museum, and has never yet seen the light of day. It is easy to see why any publisher would recoil from bringing out so prolix a work, for the Doctor is wearisome in the extreme. Before we leave Deal, in his first chapter, at the outset of his travels, we are treated to at least thirty closely-written pages on the wonders of the deep, which he picked up there; soon follows a long dissertation on sea-sickness, and its supposed causes; and whenever he came near any place of archæological interest, such as Carthage, Ephesus, Constantinople, etc., he gives us enough information to fill a good-sized volume on each spot. Consequently, it has been found necessary to eliminate much in Dr. Covel's exceedingly bulky diaries.

His narrative is, however, extremely interesting on many points: during the six-and-a-half years he resided at Constantinople, from 1670 to 1677, he noticed everything; his sketches of life, costumes, and manners are minute and life-like. Sir George Wheeler says, in his volume of travels: " Dr. Covel, then chaplain to his Majesty's ambassador there, amongst many curiosities shewed us some Turkish songs set to musick; which he told us were, both for sense and music, very good : but past our understanding." Being, as he was, intimately connected with the embassy, he had ample opportunity for studying the politics of the time. Dr. Covel was present at the granting of the capitulations of 1676, which gained for the Levant Company privileges which established it, for the ensuing century and a half of its existence, on an unapproachable foundation.

John Covel was born at Horningsheath, in Suffolk, in 1638, and educated at Bury St. Edmunds and

Christ's College, Cambridge, in the hall of which his portrait, by Valentine Ritz, is still to be seen. He studied medicine in early life with a view to being a physician, which will account for his intimate knowledge of botany and drugs; but eventually, being elected to a Fellowship at his College, he changed his line in life and took Holy Orders.

Covel was distinguished for his erudition, and was a scholar of no mean repute, as his MS. shows; and on the Restoration, in 1661, he was deputed to make a Latin oration in the hall of Christ's College, to celebrate the return of the Stuart family to the throne of England. He composed a long poem also to celebrate this event, a few stanzas of which I give here:

> "The Horrible winter's gone,
>   And we enjoy a cheerful spring;
> The kind approach of the Sun
>   Gives a new birth to every thing.

> "The trees with blossoms are crowned now,
>   Which then did penance in snow;
> And there with busy noise the Bee
>   Practise mysterious chemistry.

> "Just so, great Prince, when you arrived,
>   Each drooping heart revived;
> Your glorious rays and divine influence
>   Gave us new life and sense.

> "Too rigid Fate
>   Had blasted Church and State;
> And, with a boisterous storm,
>   Put all things out of form.

"Oh, may your glories ever shine !
Always rising still more bright.
What never stops at any height
Can never decline."

In 1669 Covel was appointed as chaplain to the ambassador at Constantinople, Sir Daniel Harvey, by the Levant Company, and Charles II gave him a dispensation to go to Constantinople and hold his Fellowship at the same time : it runs as follows :

"Given at our Court at Dover, 19th day of May, in the 22nd year of our reign. Our will and pleasure is that you dispense with the absence of the said John Covel, so that he receive and enjoy (by Himself or his assignees) all and singular the profits, dividends, stipends, emoluments, and dues belonging to his fellowship in as full and ample manner to all intents and purposes as if he were actually resident in the College."

During his residence at Constantinople he witnessed many important sights, notably the great *fêtes* at Adrianople in honour of the circumcision of Prince Mustapha, and the marriage of the Sultan's daughter, which were the most noted *fêtes* of the century in Turkey,[1] and also the granting of the capitulations during the time of the plague. The next nine years of Covel's life were spent in travel. In 1679 he returned to England, and immediately afterwards took his D.D., and was chosen as Margaret preacher of Divinity at Cambridge. In 1681 he got one of his college livings of Kegworth, and was soon afterwards appointed as chaplain to the Princess of Orange, and resided at the Hague.

---

[1] Von Hammer.

In October 1685 the Prince of Orange intercepted a letter written by Dr. Covel to Skelton, the English ambassador, giving an account of Prince William's tyrannical behaviour to his wife. Dr. Covel was forthwith dispatched home again in great disgrace; he never spoke of what had transpired, and it was long a mystery. There is, however, a letter to Princess Mary amongst his papers, in which he speaks of the scurrilous reports which alleged that he tried to make mischief between the King and the Prince, and between the Prince and your Royal Highness, and concludes, "in the words of the Royal Martyr, your most glorious grandfather, that as He hath given us afflictions to try our patience, so He would give us Patience to bear our afflictions."

Dr. Covel was twice Vice-Chancellor of the University of Cambridge, the first time in 1689, when King William visited the University, and his letters show a considerable degree of anxiety as to how the King, whom he had maligned as Prince, would receive him. In reply to these anxieties, King William sent a curt answer, stating "that he could distinguish between Dr. Covel and the Vice-Chancellor of the University".

Dr. Covel, was not fortunate with his voluminous writings; he got into another scrape with the Court in a book entitled *The Interpreter of Words and Terms;* it was ordered to be destroyed, being, as it was supposed, "in some points very derogatory to the supreme power of this Crown". He also wrote on gardening and fruit-trees; but his *magnum opus* was a work on the Greek Church, which he published shortly before his death, which remained for long the standard work on the subject. It is entitled: *Some Account of the present Greek Church, with Reflections on their present Doctrine and Discipline, particularly on the Eucharist and the rest of their seven Pretended Sacraments.* In his Preface he apologises for the long delay, owing to his "itinerant life", and having been "chained to a perpetual college bursar's place". It is evident from his diary that, when at Constantinople, Dr. Covel gave himself up to this study very closely, in fact, he was deputed to do so, for the controversy was then at its height which was started by M. Arnold, Doctor of the Sorbonne, as to whether the Greeks held the doctrine of transubstantiation or not, and a union between the Eastern and Western Churches was much feared by the Protestants. The eccentric Marquis de Nointel, who was the French ambassador to the Porte at that time, was most eager to bring this about, and as he was on very friendly terms with Sir John Finch, it was suspected that he used his influence to win over the English ambassador; hence Dr. Covel had an important task to perform, and no wonder he writes so bitterly on the ignorance and corruption of the Greek clergy. To show his zeal, the Marquis de Nointel celebrated Midnight Mass on Christmas Eve, 1673, in the cave of Antiparos, with a broken-off stalactite as his communion-table, on which may still be read the words he carved :—

"Hic ipse Christus adfuit
Ejus natali die mediâ nocte celebrato
MDCLXXIII."

The ambassador was accompanied by five hundred people—his domestics, merchants, Greeks, and Turks —and he was so impressed by it, that he repeated the experiment on two subsequent occasions. The proposed union of the Churches, however, never came to anything, and by the time Dr. Covel's book came out the controversy was at an end and forgotten.

Dr. Covel was appointed Master of Christ's College in 1688, and retained this position until his death in 1722, at the ripe age of eighty-four.

The good work that Sir John Finch did for the Company in getting the capitulation of 1676, as Dr. Covel relates, in the teeth of the plague at Adrianople, did much for the security of trading and property in the Levant. Attached to these capitulations is the following clause: "That two ships' loads of figs and currants should be allowed to be annually exported from Smyrna for the use of the King's kitchen." Sir John Finch was the son of the Speaker of the House of Commons, and was brought up as a physician, together with his bosom companion Thomas Baines; they studied together in England, and in Padua, and when Sir John was appointed as Minister to Tuscany, he got Charles II to attach his friend as physician to the legation, and also to bestow on him the honour of knighthood. When Sir John Finch was moved to Constantinople Sir Thomas

Baines accompanied him in the same capacity; they were together with Covel during the trying time of the plague at Adrianople, and frequent allusion is made to them both in the diary. They were known in Constantinople as the ambassador and the chevalier, the two inseparable friends, whose attachment to one another was as romantic as that of Damon and Pythias. Sir Thomas Baines died in Constantinople in 1680, and, in great grief, his friend had his body embalmed and sent home to be buried in Christ's College. Two years later, immediately on his return to England, Sir John Finch himself died, and, by special request, was buried in the same tomb as his friend, with the same marble slab over them, on which Henry More wrote a touching epitaph. Jointly, they endowed two scholarships and two fellowships for Christ's College, and are still jointly thanked as benefactors of that very College over which their friend and companion in adversity, Dr. Covel, ruled for forty years after their deaths.

§ 3.—OF THE SUBSEQUENT HISTORY OF THE LEVANT COMPANY.

From the life of Dudley North, afterwards Sir Dudley, son of Lord North, and ambassador for the Company to the Porte, which life was written by his son, we get an interesting insight into the life and times of those Merchant Adventurers in the seventeenth century, who were undoubtedly the founders of our national fortunes and national pre-eminence.

Dudley North was born in 1641, and went out to Smyrna as supercargo, and was apprenticed to a Turkey merchant when eighteen years of age, with a capital of £400. For many years he lived a most frugal life, making himself master of the Turkish language, and keeping himself aloof from the extravagant and luxurious lives which the English merchants in the Smyrniote factories lived in those days. When they "procured a pack of hounds, and hunted in the country, after the English way", young North resisted the temptation to buy a horse, and went out hunting on an ass. He was a young man sure of eventual success. On his subsequent removal to Constantinople, and employment in the factory of Messrs. Hedges and Palmer, he lived in the building itself, and looked after the bookkeeping, and gained his first credit by getting in the outstanding debts of the firm. He made himself master of the "rules of Turkish justice", and at once set about to institute five hundred claims in the law courts. These claims he conducted himself in the Turkish Courts in the Turkish language, and won a great many of those which his employers had hitherto looked upon as hopeless.

He soon set up business on his own account, and as it rapidly increased, he sent for his brother Montagu, from Aleppo, and together the brothers built up for themselves the fabric of a colossal fortune.

The brothers North appear to have dealt largely in jewels, with which they tempted the women of the Seraglio, and to have lent money at from 20 to 30 per cent. to impecunious Pashas. Dudley North became treasurer of the Levant Company in Constantinople, did excellent work in the survey of the city, and eventually concluded his successful career by being appointed ambassador for the Company to the Porte. He was a man of strong business capacity, and "his first care", says his son, "on setting up for himself, was to get a fire-tight room to secure his goods from fire, and a sofa-room in which to entertain the Turks."

About this time we hear ever more and more, in the Levant Company's dealings with the Turks, of the *avanias*, or unauthorised demands made by the Turks on foreign merchants. Sir Dudley North at once took up this question, and wrote himself an interesting account of these encroachments on the capitulations granted to the Turkey merchants. The *avanias* had their origin in small matters of etiquette; gradually they spread to commerce and merchandise, and in 1685 came the great edict, which obliged every foreigner who had married a Turkish subject, himself to become a subject of the Porte, and these men were forbidden to leave the country without the Sultan's consent.

This edict has given rise to the still numerous Levantine families to be found in the Turkish Empire, families bearing English, French, and Italian names, and tracing their origin to those nations, but practically absorbed in the Ottoman Empire. It was a great blow to many artisans and merchants who had married and settled in the Levant. No less than forty French watchmakers, who had married Greek wives and settled in Galata, were obliged to become Turkish subjects in spite of the remonstrances of the French ambassador, and the case of Mr. Pentloe settled the question with regard to the English. He had married a Greek lady, and on his death left a will appointing two English merchants as his executors, obliging them to realise his property, and send his widow and her two children to England. Accordingly, the executors proceeded to carry out his wishes, but the Turkish Government seized Mrs. Pentloe and her children on embarkation, and threw the two executors into prison, from which they did not emerge for some considerable period; all Mr. Pentloe's money was confiscated, and our ambassador could get no redress. This iniquitous *avania* was not repealed for a hundred years afterwards, and may be taken as the origin of most of the so-called Levantine families, great numbers of which are to be found in Constantinople, Smyrna, Salonika, and other trade centres in the Turkish Empire.

The progress of the Levant Company was steady, and prosperity attended their commerce. Notwithstanding, in 1681 we find the Turkey merchants petitioning Parliament against the East India Company, and begging for permission to have "exercise of trade in the Red Sea, and all other dominions of the Grand Signior, and to forbid the East India Company to import raw or wrought silks"; and further stating that as their freights were "raw silks, gaules, grograms, yarn, cotton, etc., and as they, not being a joint-stock Company, did not export much gold", that the East India Company ought to be restricted from importing such things as they considered they only had the monopoly of. To this petition the East India Company drew up an exhaustive reply, and Parliament set the petition on one side.

For the first three decades of the last century the prosperity of the Levant Company may be said to have been at its height. In the years 1716 and 1717 they exported to Turkey "43,000 cloths, and a very great quantity of lead, tin, sugar, etc." In 1718, for the greater protection of merchants, "general ships", which sailed together in large squadrons, were appointed, and the manufacturers had nothing to do but to convey their goods to the wharves, consign them to the shipowners, and pay the freight. These general ships, as they were called, used to leave England about July 1st, so as to have good weather in the open seas, and reach Turkey about the right time for the winter markets; then they returned home with raw silks, mohair, and other products of the East.

For some cause or another, in 1753 the condition of the Levant Company was not so satisfactory. In this year they sent a petition to Parliament for the remodelling of their charter on more favourable conditions. In this petition they stated that a quarrel between Sir Kenelm Digby and the Venetian admiral in the Bay of Scanderoon had cost the Company £20,000; that the indiscretion of a young man at Aleppo had imperilled the lives of all Europeans, and incurred enormous losses on the Company; that they had to pay an indemnity of £12,000 for prisoners taken in war, and other similar misfortunes had fallen upon them. Consequently, Parliament thought fit to grant them their petition : they were to have unmolested choice of the ministers maintained by them at home and abroad, ambassadors, governors, deputies, consuls, etc. ; nobody except free brothers of the corporation could send ships into those parts, and very stringent rules were made on this point, full powers being given to the Company to fine, imprison, and send home in custody any individuals who infringed this rule ; they were allowed to make their own laws and by-laws, though these had to receive the sanction of the Board of Trade ; and, with various little assistances from Government in minor points, the Company of Levant Merchants again became exceedingly flourishing, and continued to be so until the end of its days.

At the end of the last century it would appear that the Company consisted of eight hundred members, each and all calling themselves " Turkey Merchants". The wages of their officials, that is to say, the ambassador, secretaries, chaplains, consuls, and physicians at Constantinople, Smyrna, Aleppo, Alexandria, Algiers, Patras, etc., came to £15,000 per annum. Many of our consulates in the East, as they now stand, were built by them, and the fine embassy at Constantinople cost the Company £10,000. The Porte gave the ground for this building out of gratitude to England for driving the French out of

Egypt, and the opening of it was hallowed by the liberation of many Christian slaves, mostly Maltese, who came in a body to the ambassador to tender their heartfelt thanks.[1]

In 1803 it was that the British Government first assumed the appointment and payment of the ambassador and his secretaries ; this was the first step towards the disestablishment of the Company. The Eastern Question was then beginning to make itself felt, the Balkan States were in arms against Turkey, and, the interests of trade being naturally subordinate to foreign policy, the Levant Company had to give way.

In 1825, when the disintegration of the Turkish Empire appeared imminent, the Levant Company came to an end. Mr. Canning's communication to them ran as follows : " It results solely from considerations of public expediency, and in no degree from any disrespect, or disposition to impute any blame to their past administration." The fact was obvious : the new order of things had to supersede the old ; the political atmosphere was full of ideas of free trade ; and the aristocratic, exclusive Company of Turkey Merchants had to give way, and they did so gracefully. The deed of surrender was drawn up in 1825, "of all the several grants, privileges, liberties, powers, jurisdictions, and immunities granted and conferred by their charters"; and in solemn conclave the Company of merchants dissolved them-

---

[1] Clarke, *Travels*.

selves, after honourably providing pensions for their officials, and handing over a substantial balance to the treasury.

During its life of 244 years the Levant Company had had a most exemplary and noble career, beneficial not only to its members, but to the English nation, building up for her her commerce, and making her name respected in the East. It would take a volume to enumerate the deeds of their great men, and how they have not only contributed to our commercial success, but have embellished our literature with admirable studies both of the past and of the present. Sir Paul Ricaut and Sir James Porter wrote admirable works on the policy and government of the Turkish people. Montague, Covel, and Pococke gave some of the earliest accounts of the people of the East in our tongue.

Under the influence of the Company, considerable attention was paid to archæology : Spon and Wheeler, Chishull, Shaw, and last, but not least, Lord Elgin, who rescued the marbles of the Parthenon from being damaged in the bombardment of 1827. The Company's doctors used to make a special study of the plague. *Russell on the Plague* was quite the standard work of its time, and Dr. Maclean also made a special study of that dread disease ; and to the efforts of these men we may almost say that we owe the gradual diminution and eventual eradication of the malady.

The rescuing of slaves from corsairs, the liberation of oppressed Christians, whether they happened to be English, Greeks, or Armenians, will be for ever one of the noblest and proudest of our actions. Without the influence of the Levant Company, Greece would probably have never succeeded in establishing her independence, and the Mussulmans would have effectually eradicated the Christian populations of the East; and it is a question for grave thought, as to whether our free and enlightened Government, during the half-century that it has had control over our actions in the East, has been as active and as influential as the Company of Turkey Merchants, who could draw the sword as well as the purse-strings, and were not hampered by the parsimonious feelings of those who have to draw up an economical budget to present to the people whose goodwill they wish to retain.

LIST OF ENGLISH AMBASSADORS TO THE PORTE IN THE 16TH AND 17TH CENTURIES.

Mr. WILLIAM HARBORNE	1588.
Mr. EDWARD BARTON	1588—1597.
Mr. HENRY LELLO	1597—1607.
Sir THOMAS GLOVER	1607—1611.
Mr. PAUL PINDAR	1611—1619.
Sir JOHN EYRE[1]	1619—1621.
Sir THOMAS ROE[2]	1622—1628.
Sir PETER WYCH	1628—1639.
Sir SACKVILLE CROWE[3]	1639—1647.
Sir THOMAS BENDYSH[4]	1647—1661.
The EARL OF WINCHILSEA	1661—1668.
Sir DANIEL HARVEY	1668—1672.
Sir JOHN FINCH[5]	1672—1681.
LORD CHANDOS	1681—1687.
Sir WILLIAM TRUMBULL	1687—1691.
Sir WILLIAM HUSSEY	1691 (June-Sept.)
LORD WILLIAM PAGET	1693—1702.

---

[1] Mr. John Chapman was sent out in September 1621, arriving in Constantinople December 12th, with orders for Eyre to return directly and leave Chapman in charge of the Embassy till the arrival of his successor.

[2] Sir Thomas Phillipps was appointed in October 1625 to succeed Roe, but, for some reason, he did not go.

[3] He arrived in Constantinople 13th October 1638, but did not assume office till the middle of 1639, owing to the Grand Seigneur's absence.

[4] In 1653 Mr. Richard Lawrance was sent out by Cromwell to replace Bendysh, but, apparently owing to the latter's influence, the Grand Seigneur refused to receive Lawrance, and Bendysh remained as Ambassador till 1661.

[5] Though appointed in 1672, Finch did not reach Constantinople till 1674.

ADDENDA ET CORRIGENDA.

P. xxiii, *for* "Sir J. Bendish" *read* "Sir T. Bendysh".

Pp. xxxiii-v, Sir Dudley North was *not* Ambassador, but Treasurer, of the Levant Company.

Pp. xxxix-xl, Mr. Albert Gray adds: "An Act of Parliament (6 Geo. IV, c. 33, Royal assent 10 June 1825) was passed which, after reciting the Letters Patent of James I, and the subsequent Acts relating to the Levant trade, recites that it would be beneficial that the exclusive rights and privileges of the Company should cease and determine, and that 'the said Governor and Company are willing and desirous to surrender up the said Letters Patent into His Majesty's hands'. In pursuance of this Act a deed was forthwith executed surrendering the Letters Patent to the Crown. One section of the Act is now of some historical importance. It provided that 'all such rights and duties of jurisdiction and authority over His Majesty's subjects resorting to the ports of the Levant for the purposes of trade or otherwise, as were lawfully exercised and performed' by the Company's consuls, should thenceforth be exercised or performed 'by any consuls or other officers respectively as His Majesty may be pleased to appoint for the protection of the trade of His Majesty's subjects in the ports and places, etc.' This was the first statutory assignment to Royal consuls of jurisdiction in places outside the dominions of the Crown. From this Act sprang in due time the Foreign Jurisdiction Act of 1843 (now replaced by that of 1890), under which British subjects and British protected persons enjoy the protection of British courts of law in almost every independent Oriental country from Morocco to Corea, and by means of which the foundations of law and order are being laid in the great protectorates of Africa."

P. 11, "North Cape" is Cape Finisterre, known of old to the seamen of the Mediterranean as the *North Cape*.

P. 16, "Morottome" is probably Marabout, on the coast of Africa, near a "fort in ruins". See Admiralty Chart, sect. vii, 252.

P. 63 *note, for* "Paul Pinder" *read* "Paul Pindar".

P. 84, "Chorlaye in Lancashier", is the town of Chorley, on a hill on the Chor, nine miles south-south-east of Preston.

Pp. 95, 96, "Grande Malligam" is Malaga. "Alama" may be identified with Almeria, a large seaport of Spain, *not* with Alhama, as stated in the note.

P. 96, "Mount Chegos" is probably Serra de Monchique, north of Cape St. Vincent, *not* Los Guigos, behind Algeciras, as stated in the note.

P. 102, "Virginia men" alludes to ships bound for America; "Streightsmen" to those bound for the Mediterranean.

P. 106, "Les Scenes" refers to the cluster of islands known as the *Chaussée de Sein*, off the coast of Brittany (cf. *Sailing Directions*, Glossary, p. 34, ed. for the Hakl. Soc.).

P. 133, "Romania" was the name originally given to the whole of the western Roman Empire. This term, together with Roumelia, has now become much circumscribed.

P. 133, *Maniotes* were the inhabitants of Mani, the southern portion of the Peleponnesus. This term has probably the same origin as Romani.

P. 140, line 15, *for* "work" *read* "word".

P. 141, *Agnus castus* is the oleander.

P. 143, "Magla" should be Nagara, exactly on site of ancient Abydos.

P. 153, "Kalenderis" are, as stated by Dr. Covel, a sect of dervishes.

P. 153, "Jamurluck" is a tunic.

P. 154, "Bellonius." This is Pierre Belon, a well-known French archæologist, who wrote *Thesaurus Græcarum antiquitatum*, Antwerp, 1589.

P. 196, "Mr. Cook." This must be the Mr. Coke who was present at the solemnities, and wrote the following :—
"A True Narrative of the Great Solemnity of the Circumcision of Mustapha, Prince of Turkey, eldest son of Sultan Mahomed, present Emperor of the Turks. Together with an account of the Marriage of his Daughter to his great Favourite Mussaip at Adrianople. As it was sent in a letter to a Person of Honour.

"By Mr. Coke, Secretary of the Turkey Company; Being in Company with his Excellency the Lord Embassador, Sir John Finch. London, 1676." Reprinted in *Harleian Miscellany*.

PART I.

MASTER THOMAS DALLAM'S DIARY.

1599.
In this Book is the Account of an Organ Carryed to the Grand Seignor and Other Curious Matter.

Nessecaries for my voyege into Turkie, the which I bought upon a verrie short warninge, havinge no frend to advise me in any thinge.

Imprimis for one sute of sackcloth to weare at sea	.	1	2	0
Item for another sute of Carsaye[1]	.	.	1	18	0
Item for tow wastcotes of flanell	.	.	0	8	0
Item for one hatt .	.	.	.	0	7	6
Item for an arminge sorde	.	.	.	0	6	0
Item for a chiste .	.	.	.	0	9	8
Ite for 3 shirtes .	.	.	.	0	18	6
Ite for one doson of bandes	.	.	0	12	8
Item for half a doson of bandes	.	.	0	10	0
Item for one bande .	.	.	.	0	2	6
Item for sixe shirtes more	.	.	.	1	14	0
Item for one doson of hand chirthers (handkerchiefs)	.	0	10	0
Item for one pare of garters .	.	.	.	0	4	0
Item for one doson of poyntes[2]	.	.	.	0	1	0
Item for another doson	.	.	.	0	2	0

---

[1] *Carsaye=Kersey*, a kind of stuff. The ordinances for upholding the Levant Company merchants, 9th March 1643, speak of the "venting of Kerseys, sayes (silks), perpetuanas (a stuff so called for its durability), and several other articles.
[2] Points were laces for fastening up clothes; *e.g.*,
"*F.* Their points being broken,—
P. Down fell the hose." (Shaks., *Hen. IV*, ii, 4.)

LIST OF NECESSARIES.

	£	s	d
Item for 2 pare of stockins	0	12	0
Item for one pare of lininge britchis	0	1	4
Item for one pare of pumpes and pantables[1]	0	3	6
Item for 3 pare of showes	0	7	0
Item for a girdle and hangers[2]	0	2	8
Item for a gowne	1	10	0
Item for a pare of virginals	1	15	0
Item for a pare of fustion britchis	0	2	6
Item for a hatbande	0	4	2
Item for another hatbande	0	1	0
For a seller and glassis	0	11	6
Item for Rosa solis[3] and a compostie[4]	0	6	0
Item for oyle and vineger	0	2	0
Item for prunes	0	1	3
Item for Resons of the son (sun-dried raisins)	0	1	4
Item for cloves, mace, and peper	0	1	6
Item 2 pounde of suger	0	3	0
Item for nutmuges	0	1	0
Item for gloves	0	3	0
Item for knives	0	5	0
Item for 30ll of tin in bars	0	18	0
Item for a grose of Spownes (spoons)	0	9	0
Item for otemeale	0	0	10
Item for carreing my chiste to Blacke wale	0	1	6
Item for my passige to Graves end	0	0	6
Item my staying there 4 dayes—it coste me	0	12	0
Item at Deale Castell	0	1	0
Item at Dartmouthe	0	4	0

---

[1] Pantables = pantofles. "Swearing by the pantables of Paris." (Sidney, *Arcadia*.)

[2] The hangers were that part of the sword-belt to which the weapon was suspended. "Sir, French rapiers and poniards, with their assigns, as girdle, hangers, and so." (*Hamlet*, v, 2.)

[3] *Rosa solis* = a cordial.
> "We abandon all ale
> And beer that is stale,
> Rosa solis and damnable hum;
> But we will rack
> In the place of sack
> 'Gainst *Omne quod exit in um*."
>   (*Witts Recreations*, 1654.)

[4] Compostie = compost, a mixture. "Compostes and confites." (*Babees Boke*, p. 121.)

At Plimmouthe, stayinge thare seven Dayes it coste me . 0 15 0
At Argeare[1] in Barbarie 0 4 0
At Zante in Gretia . . . . .
At Scandaroune in A[2] . . . .

From the Landes end of England to the straites mouthe is 4 hundrethe leagues.

Betwixte the straites mouthe and Argeare in Barbarria is one hundrethe and fiftie leages.

From Argeare to Cisillia is 2 hundrethe leages.

From Cesillia to Zante is 90 leages.

From Zante to Scandaroune is 2 hundrethe and fiftie Leages.

          400 L.
          150
          200
          090
          250
          1090 Leages.

---

  [1] Algiers.   [2] Asia Minor.

DALLAM'S TRAVELS
WITH AN
ORGAN TO THE GRAND SIGNIEUR.

A brefe Relation of my Travell[1] from
The Royall Cittie of London towardes
The Straites of Mariemediteranum, and
what hapened by the waye.

HE shipp whearin I was to make my voyege to Constantinople, Lyinge at Graves ende, I Departed from Londone in a pare of ores, with my chiste and suche provision as I had provided for that purpose, the nynthe of Februarie 1598 (1599), being Frydaye.

Comminge to Graves ende, I wente aborde our shipp, Called the Heckter, and thare placed my chiste, my bedinge, and a pare of virginals,[2] which the martchantes did alow me to carrie, for my exersize by the waye. Other comoditis I carriede none, savinge one grose of tin spounes, the which coste me nyne shillinges; and thirtie pounde of tin in bares, which coste me 18s. The shipe beinge verrie

---

[1] These words are in a later hand.
[2] Virginals were spinetts, so called from being played by young girls. The term "a pair of virginals", "a pair of organs", was common, and only denoted one instrument. Cf. the phrases "a pair of stairs", "a pair of bellows", still exist.

unreddie, and no cabbins appoynted for passingeres, I was constrainede to go into the towne for my Lodgingc and Diette, till the thirtenthe Daye in the After nowne, at which time anker was wayed and we under sayle, untill we came to Deale Castell.

Cominge to Deale Castell, thare we came to an anker, for the wynde sarved not to pass by Dover. Thar our ship stayed fouer dayes for a wynde. In the meane time we wente a shore into the towne of Deale, and also to Sandwiche, to make our selves merrie. When the wynde came fayer, it was in the nyghte, and diverse of us that weare passingers, and also som saylers, weare in the towne of Deale, wheare som of our company had dranke verrie moche, espetialy one of our five Trumpeters, who, beinge in Drinke, had Lockid his Chamber dore; and when he that came from the ship to call us went under his chamber wyndoe and caled him, he Came to the wyndoe and insulted him; whear upon we wente all a waye a borde our ship, and lefte that Dronkerde be hinde. Thar the wynde sarvinge well, we sayled merraly by Dover, and so a longe the Sleve.[1]

But beinge aboute 30 leages at sea, sodonly thare cam a contrarie wynde, the which did prove a marvalus greate storme for the space of eyghte and fortie houres. In the nyghte we did not only louse our pinis caled the Lanerett,[2] who was to goo with us to the gulfe of Venis, but we also loste our selves, not knowinge whear we weare by Reason the fogge was so greate that we could se no son. When it began anythinge to cleare, we founde our selves to be harde upon the ponie stones[3] betwyxt Ingland and Ierlande, a

---

[1] "The Sleeve" is a literal translation of the French "La Manche".
"Along the Celtic sea, called oftentimes 'the Sleeve'."
(Drayton, *Polyolb.*, xxiii.)
[2] Lanneret = a hawk.
[3] Probably the dangerous "Pommier Rocks" in the Casquets.

verrie dangerus place. Than our mariners did Labur to gitte into the mayn otion againe, but the storme not altogether seacinge, but the foge more Increasinge, we wear the next Daye at a non plus againe, not knowinge wheare we weare, but beinge under sayle, and the foge verrie thicke. Upon a sodon we saw the seae breake a gainste the shore, the which was verrie greate Rockes, and we weare so neare the shore that it was not possible to caste aboute in time to save ourselves from shipwracke, but it pleased almyghtie God so to defend us from harme that we weare juste befor the harbur at Dartmouthe, a verrie straite entrie betwyxte greate Rockes that ar on bothe sides of that entrie. Than weare we all verrie joyfull, and entred in thare verrie willingly. Thare we stayed four dayes. In the meane time the Mr.[1] and Martchantes sent postes aboute to all the haven townes upon that coste to inquier of our pinis, the Lanerett. In the End word was brought that presently, after the storme, 3 or 4 sayle of Dunkerkes[2] had her in chace, and in the storme her topmaste was broken, so that, to save her selfe from beinge taken, she Ron a shore at Falmouthe. Havinge thar goten a new topmaste, she sente word by the mesinger that she would meet us in Plimmouthe sounde. This worde beinge broughte, Anker was wayed, and we under sayell; when we cam Ryghte before Plimmouthe a peece was discharged to call our pinis; but even at that time the wynd came contrarie, so that we moste needes also goo in thare, and cam

---

[1] The captain.
[2] *Dunkirks.* The Dunkirkers were at that time the pirates of the Channel, and their privateers did much damage to English trade.

" This was a rail
Bred by a zealous brother in Amsterdam,
Which being sent unto an English lady,
Was ta'en at sea by Dunkirkers."
(*The Bird in a Cage*, O. Pl., viii, 267.)

to an anker in Catt water, wheare we founde our pinis. Thare we stayed sevene dayes for a wynde.

The 16th day of Marche, beinge verrie could wether, the wynde came fayer, and as we weare under sayle in Plimmouthe-sounde, thare came in a litle carvell[1] with salte, who no sonner was come to the shore, and hearinge the name of our shipe, but they caused a parlie to be sounded be a trumpett, whearupon sayle was storouk, and tow sailers of that carvell came aborde our shipe, advisinge our Mr. not to goo to seae with oute good store of companye; for they wente to seae in a man of ware from Plimmouthe, caled the Plow, and theye weare taken by seven sayell of Dunkerkes, who Did straitly examon them if they could tell weare the Heckter was, or whether she weare gone her voyage or no, but they protested that they never hard of suche a shipp. Som of these men thei put to death, to feare otheres. Whate they did with the Reste of theire men they knew not. They touke theire ship from them, and gave sixe of them that litle carvell to bringe them home.

When our Mr. and captaine had harde these men speake, he toulde them that he would not staye one hour for any more companye than God alreddie had sente him, the which was only our pinis and tow shipes that weare goinge for New found Land, and for there owne saftie mad haste after us. Saylinge forthe before a faire wynde, our ship sayled so well that we could spare the pinis our mayne saile, and yeate the nexte morninge our pinnis was verrie far behind. Aboute 8 of the clocke, one in our maine tope discried 3 sayle, the which did ly close by our fore porte a little after; he saw four more, which lay the same cource, and these weare the seven sayell which we weare tould of. Than we

---

[1] *Carvel, caravel,* Italian form of ship in the Middle Ages. Word extant in modern Greek καράβι.

began to Louke aboute us, our goneres made Reddie there ordinance, our faightes[1] oute, and everie man his bandaleare[2] and muskett. We hade the wynde of them, and needed not to have spoken with them, but our Captaine thoughte it not fitt to show our selves fearfull or cowardly; Leaste the wynde should sodonly turne, or scante upon us, and our flyinge would incurridge our enemyes to com the more bouldly upon us. Than he caled the botson and bid him beare towardes them, the which he willingly wente aboute; so we bore Towardes them, and when we came so neare them that we myghte well disarne the hulke of there amberall and of their vizamberall, and they cam bouldly upon us, our Mr. bide the botswayne stow them a brood side; for our mayne sayle was so brode, that they could not se the stoutnes of our ship; for may hape, cothe he (mayhap, quoth he), they may take our ship to be one of the Quen's, and yf we doo hapen to heale them, or theye us, they which make answer maye say our ship is caled the Seven stars, for the quene as yeate hathe none of that name; but assowne as they sawe the brode side of our ship, thinking us in dede to be one of the Quene's ships, they presently turned them aboute to flye away. Than we gave chace to them, havinge almoste loste sighte of our pinis, and all other shipes savinge those which we gave chace unto. They made all the sayle they coulde, and yeat with in halfe an hour we weare come with in shott of them. Than our captain bid the Mr. goner give them a chace peece[3] shout at the amber-

---

[1] Faightes = fightes. Waste-cloths formerly hung about a ship to conceal the men from the enemy. Shaks., *Merry Wives of Windsor*, Act ii, Scene 2: "Clap on more sails: pursue, up with your fights." Close fights = close quarters.

[2] Bandeleer = leathern cases or belts containing charges for firelocks, used before modern cartouche-boxes were invented.

[3] Chase peeses = chase-guns, which were placed during an engagement at the chase-ports at the bows.

all, but hitt him not, so the Mr. goner gave him a shott cloce by his fore bowe[1] ; yeat would they nether strike sayle, nor show any flagge, but made away with all the sayle they had, drablings[2] and topgalands, but all would not serve their turne, for we came nearer and nearer unto them. Than our Mr. bid the goner shoute throughe the amberall his maynsayle, and so he did verrie near her drablinge. Than the Amberall, vise amberall, Rear amberall, and one more shoute the mayn topp ; but at that time they hade the wyndie side of us, though we weare com unto them, yeat no man would once show himselfe. Than the booteson of our ship stod upon our spar decke,[3] with his sorde drawne in his hande, commandinge them to come under our Lee side. The which verrie unwillingly they dide, yeate no man would show himselfe. Now we beinge verrie neare the coste of Spayne (or France) he tackte about againe to goo his Ryghte cource, and all this seven sayell did follow us ; than our Mr. caled unto the amberall him selfe, comanding them to caste oute the bote and com abord us (or eles he would sinke them) ; after so callinge twyse unto them, one that semed by his spetche to be a Ducheman, answered, we woll, we woll, but Longe it was before the boote came forthe, yeat at laste there bote came forthe, and the captaine of that shipe, with 4 saylers to Row the bote, wente a borde the wise amberall, and there stayed halfe an houre. Than those thre captaines came a borde our shipe ; now all this whyle we weare saylinge our courc, and all these seven shipes durst do no other but follow us. When these thre captaines came aborde us, one of

---

[1] Written on the opposite blank page of the MS. is: " We gave them 3 chase peeces before they woulde strike."

[2] Drablings=the drabler, or a piece of canvas laced on the bonnet of a sail to give it more drop.

[3] Spardecke. This is a loose term applied to the quarter-deck, gangways, and forecastle.

our company saw one of them have under his arme a good
long mony bage full of somthinge, and so they wente with
the Mr. of our ship into his cabin, and talked a good whyle.
In the meane time the sayleres which broughte these
captaynes a borde, standinge on our hatchis, and our
saylers Loukinge upon them, one of our men sayde, surly I
should know this fellow, for he is an Inglishman. That
man presently answered, swearinge a greate othe, and sayde
that he was no Inglishman, nether could speak one worde
of Inglishe; and yeat he spoke as good Inglishe as any of
us. Than one of our maysteres mates, our pursser and
boteson touke theyr boote, and foure of our owne sayleres,
and wente a borde thre or foure of those shipps; and in
that meane time, our Mr. and the 3 captaines havinge well
talked of the mater, our Mr. cam forthe of his cabbin and
strode upon the sparr decke, causing all our company to be
caled before him, did Reed a letter which semed to be but
newly wrytten; the efeckte of that letter was as yf it had
bene made as a pass from the kinge of France, with sartayne
wynes which the captaynes sayde weare a borde ther
shipes. But whyle he was a Reeding that Letter, our
mysteres mate, purser, and bootson came frome the shipps
and sayd they weare men of warre, Laden with nothinge but
men, soulders, musketes, Raperes and dagers, sheldes and
buckeleres, and ment nothinge so moche as to have taken
us; but our maister havinge alreddie taken the prise in his
cabbin, seemed to be verrie angrie with his mate and the
purser for sayinge so, he havinge a letter to show the contrarie; so he discharged the captayn and let the shipes go,
the which greved the sayeleres and the Reste of our company verrie moche. Yf he had done, as he myghte verrie
well have done, broughte these seven sayle as a prise into
Inglande, it would have bene the braveste sarvis that ever
any Inglishe marchante shipe did, and tharby have Reaped
greate cridit as any ever did.

[At our cominge home out of Turkie it was well knowne that those seven saile, after they escaped from us, and before our coming home, they had taken and Robed upon the seae, betwyxt London and New Castell, thre score sayle of Inglishe and other contrie ships.]

MARCHE 1599.

The 20th Day, the wynde sarvinge well, we paste the Northe Cape, and entered the bay of Portingale. The 23 we Recovered the Soothe Cape. Than we weare becalmed for a time. The 24 thare came an Infinite company of porposis aboute our ship, the which did leape and Rone (run) marvalusly. The 25 we saw 2 or 3 greate monstrus fishis or whales, the which did spoute water up into the eayere, lyke as smoke dothe assend out of a chimnay. Sometime we myghte se a great parte of there bodye above the water. The calme did yeat continue. The 27, havinge a verrie fayer wynde, the which did blow a good gale aboute 12 or one of the clocke, we entered the straytes of Marie-medeteranum in Dispite of our enymyes. At the entrie it is butt 3 Leages at the moste from shore to shore. In my thinkinge it seemed not to be above 3 myles, but the Reason of yt is because the Lande is verrie hie on bothe sides, Spayne on our Lefte hand, and Barberie of the Ryghte. On Spayne side we did se a verrie fayer towne or cittie, caled Tarrefe,[2] the which stood verrie pleasantlye close to the seae. On Barbarie side Thar is a myghtie mountayn of Rockes, the which theye do call Ape hill.[3] 7 Leages further, on Spayne side, thar is a verrie stronc (strong) towne Caled Jebbatore.[4] This towne Lay verrie fayer to our vew. It is verrie well fortified, and of greate strengthe. Thare dothe also Ly a greate number of the king of

---

[1] The paragraphs inserted between brackets are written, in the original, on the opposite blank page.

[2] Tarifa.   [3] Still known as Ape Hill.   [4] Gibraltar.

Spayens gallies and men of warr, to keepe the straites. On the easte side of the towne tharis a greate mountayne, wheare on a great parte of the towne dothe stande. This mountayne is verrie upryghte on bothe sides, but on the easte sid it is so uprighte that no man can go to the top of it. It standes cross wyse to the seae. On the fore end tharis a stronge bullworke, by which means the towne is more secure.

We sett oute from Plimmouthe the 16th of Marche, havinge than verrie could wether, and no sine of any grene thinge on trees or hedgis; and the 27, at the entringe of the straites, the wether was exsedinge hoote, and we myghte se the feeldes on bothe sides verrie grene, and the tres full blowne, the which unto me was a verrie greate wonder to finde suche an alteration in a 11 dayes. Ryghte over againste Jeblatore, on Barbarie side, thar is a towne verrie fayer to our vew, caled Shutte.[1] This towne is waled aboute, and the feldes about it verrie pleasante, and of good soyle.

Thoughe on bothe sides of seae tharis hudge mountains and Raged Rockes, on the Easte end of this towne a litle tharis a Large and stronge bullworke (or forte), and the Lyke is on the weste side. The kinge of Spayne Dothe also houlde that toune, beinge in Barberie.

A litle further on the Coste of Spayne thar is a Towne caled Marvels,[2] but I could not well disarne it for the fogge which at that time Laye upon the seae. The nexte towne is caled grand Malligan,[3] and than Sallabrin,[4] which towne is fortie Leages easte of Jeblatore.

The 28 of Marche we sayled still a longe by the shore of Spayne, wheare we myghte se upon hudg mountaynes great store snowe that Dothe ly thare contenually, and yeate in the vallies below it is verrie hote.

---

[1] Ceuta.   [2] Marbella.   [3] Malaga.   [4] Salobreña.

AT ALGIERS.

The 29th daye we sayled by the shore of Africa.

The 30th daye we entered into a harber in Barberia, Caled Argeare.[1]

When we weare upon the sea before the towne it made a verrie fayer show. It Lyethe cloce to the seae, upon a verrie upryghte hill. The towne in proportion is Lyke a top sayle. It is verrie strongly waled about with tow wales and a dich.

The housis be bulte of Lyme and stone. The greateste parte of the towne, or housis in the towne, have flatt Roufes, covered artifitialy with playster of paris. A man beinge on the topp of one house may goo over the greateste parte of the towne. Diverse of the streetes ar verrie narrow and uneasie goinge in them, for the towne standes upon Rockes. Above the towne, upon the top of the hill, thar is a castell, the which may comande the Roode, or a parte of the seae before the towne. Almoste a myle from that castell into the contriewardes thare is an other castell, the which is gardede or kepte by a sartaine number of souldieres; but, as farr as I could Learne, it is but only to keepe the heade of there springes of water, which com to there fountaines in the town, for the Turkes Drinke nothinge but water; and they saye that hors and man maye goo under, or in the earthe, from that castell to the towne. I and 3 or 4 more wente yeat a myle further into the contrie, wheare we saw another castell, the which, as we did thinke, was made for the same use. We went so farr into the contrie at the Requeste of Mr. Chancie, who was our fysition and surgin for the seac. He wente to gather som harbs and Routes. This dai being the Laste Day of Marche, it was a wonder to us to se how forwarde the springe was: trees and hedgis wear full blowne, corne, wheate, and barly shott, yong oringis and apples upon the

---

[1] Algiers.

trees; and cominge againe into the towne, we mett Mores and other people drivinge assis laden with grene beanes, to be sould in the markett. As they went a Longe the streete, they often would cale to the people, and say, balocke, balocke, that is to saye, bewarr, or take heede. We saw diverse Moores com in riding, all naked, savinge a litle clothe before them like a childe's apron. Som of them did carrie a darte, otheres a bowe and arros.

There be also a greate number of Jewes, but the greateste nomber be Turkes.

The toune or cittie is verrie full of people, for it is a place of great trad and marchandise. They have tow markeett dayes in the weeke, unto the which do com a great number of people out of the mountaines and other partes of the contrie, bringinge in great store of corne and frute of all sortes, and fowle, bothe wylde and tame. Thar be great store of partridgis and quales, the which be sould verrie cheape, a partridge for less than one pennye, and 3 quales at the same price. Thar be also great store of henes and chickins, for they be hatchte by artificiall meanes, in stoves or hote housis, without the helpe of a hen. The maner of it I cannot at this time playnly discribe, but heareafter I may, yf God permitte.

They have also greate store of Camels, assis, asnegoes,[1] oxon, horsis, and som dromedaries. Thar be a greate number of Turks that be but Renied[2] cristians of all nations. Som, but moste are Spanyardes, Italians, and other Ilands adjoyninge, who, when they be taken, ar compelled so to doo, or els to live in moche more slaverie and myserie. But, in prosis of time, these Renied cristians do become most berberus and villanus, taking pleasur in all sinfull

---

[1] *Assinego*, a Portuguese word to signify "ass". "Thou hast no more brain than I have in mine elbow; an assinego may tutor thee." (*Troilus and Cressida*, ii, 1.)

[2] Cf. French, *renier* = renegade.

actions; but that which is worste of all they take moste delite in, and that is, Theye proule aboute the costes of other contries, with all the skill and pollacie thei can, to betraye cristians, which they sell unto the Moors and other marchantes of Barbarie for slaves.

Thare ar in this toune great store of hote houses, or bathes, the which they call bangowes,[1] and also cooke's housis, that dress meate verrie well.

The next day after we came into the Roode, the kinge sent worde to our captaine that he should come unto him and bringe with hime the presente which he had to carrie unto the Grand Sinyor; so our captaine wente unto him and tould the kinge That the presente which he carried to the grand sinyor was not only a thinge of greate substance and charge, but allso it was Defficulte curios, and would aske a longe time to put it together, and make it fitt to be sene. When the kinge understode whate our captaine had saide, he would give no cridite unto his wordes, but kepte him as a prisner, and caused me and my mate to be sente for. When we came before him, and wear examined, he found us to be in the same tale that our captaine had toulde; and than was our captane Released and we discharged, and the kinge sente our captaine for a presente a borde our shipe tow buls and thre sheepe, the which weare verrie leane, for they do thinke the worste thinges they have is tow good for cristians. They ar all in generall verrie covitus, and use all the pollacie they can to gitt from the cristians, lawfully or unlawfully, as moche as they maye.

The Turkishe and Morishe weomen do goo all wayes in the streetes with there facis covered, and the common reporte goethe thare that they beleve, or thinke that the weomen have no souls. And I do thinke that it weare

---

[1] Bagno.

well for them if they had none, for they never goo to churche, or other prayers, as the men dothe. The men ar verrie relidgus in there kinde, and they have verrie faire churchis, which they do call mosques.

Of the Further Procession of our Navigation.

We departed from the Cittie of Argier the fourthe of Aprill, saylinge still near the Coste or shore of Africa. 20 leages from Argere Thare is a faire towne caled Teddell,[1] but we sailed afar of from it. We also passed by a litle towne calede Budgge,[2] under a hudge mountaine, risinge hie, and picked lyke a suger lofe. Som of our navigateres saide that at this place St. Augustine did sometime keepe a scoule or exersise. It is 30th leagues from Argere towardes the easte on the same side.

The seventhe of Aprill beinge Easter eve, we saw verrie strainge lyghtninge in the skie, or in the eire. It was verrie wonderfull and strainge, for we myghte se the eayre open and a fier lyke a verrie hote iron taken out of a smythe's forge, somtimes in liknes of a roninge worme, another time lyke a horsshow, and agine lyke a lege and a foute. Also the Thunder clapes weare also exseding greate. The seventhe daye we passed by a place caled Morrottome. The 18th, by a hudge mountaine, which is an Ilande in the seae, close by the shore. This ilande is called Simberrie.[3] Upon that shore, over againste it, was somtime the Cittie of Carttag, but some wryteres caled it Carthage. Aboute five leagues further we sawe the cape, or forte, caled Debone.[4] At the weste sid of it thar is a greate and large Tovne, caled Tonis,[5] by some peopell Thunes. Thare dothe lye

---

[1] Dellys.
[2] Bougie.
[3] Zembra el Jamoor, over against Carthage.
[4] Cape Bon.
[5] Tunis.

some parte of the Turkes gallis. The 14th we sayelled by a famous iland Caled Sissillia,[1] cloce by the shore of it. This ilande, they saye, is threscore leages in lengthe; a verrie frutfull and pleasante iland. It dothe yelde greate store of corne and all maner of frute. At the weste End Thare Dothe alwayes ly at the leaste nyne gallies, and at the weste end ten or more.

Neare unto the easte ende of this Cissillie there is a verrie heie mountayne, the which they do cale Montabell, but the ryghte name of it is mounte Ettna. In the Daye time we that sayle by it maye se the topp of it covered with snow, but in the nyghte we did see manye flashis of fiere, to our thinkinge about the mydle of the mountaine. This brave ilande is under the kinge of Spayne. We did leave it upon our lefte hand. Than, upon our ryghte hande, we saw another ilande, which is caled Malta, and that is likewyse under the kinge of Spayne, and is now kept for the quantati (*sic*) the Master of the Roodes,[2] so that the Turkes can hardly pass that waye. A litle before we cam so farr as Malta, we gave chace to a shipe, beinge the 15th daye. After the mayster of that shipp parsaved by our flage whate we weare, and did se that thre suche as him selfe was not able to contende with us, he caste out his boote and came a borde us, and broughte with him for a presente diverse Comodities: som turkie carpites, some quiltede Coveringes of watchat[3] silke, and tow or thre great peecis of salte fishe that wear 7 or 8 foute longe and one foute square. It was strainge fishe unto us. We never tasted it,

---

[1] Sicily.　　　[2] Grand Master of Knights of Rhodes.
[3] *Watchet silk*, so called from the colour of the dye of woad, Saxon *Wadchet*.

"Who like a mighty king doth cast his Watchet robe
Far wider than the land, quite round the globe."
(Drayton, Bk. xx, p. 1044.)

for after he that broughte it had talked privetly with our
mayster, he gave him leve to Departe, and to take all his
presente with him; but it muche greved our sayles (sailors),
for som offesers of our shipp wente aborde that shipp
whyles he was talkinge with our mayster, and they founde
by the pursseres bouke that theye had ten thousand
Dolleres worthe of Spaynishe goodes a borde. But our
Mr. having recaved som secrite bribe, he sayed that the
shipe and good came from Sio,[1] wheare Mr. Willyam Auld-
ridge was consell, with other idle reasons, and tharfore he
would not take anythinge from him; and so the ship
went awaye. Than we paste by Malta. The 17th daye
we gave chace to another shipp of Massillia,[2] and borded
here, but had litle or nothinge from her. Than we crost
the gulfe of Venis.

The 19th we discried lande in Gricia.

The 20th daye we paste by Saffranee, leavinge it on our
lefte hande. At this porte of Saffranee[3] thare be tow
tounes, and a moste singuler good harber. Neare unto it is
the iland caled Sante, but rether Zante. The same Daye we
came to an anker before the greate toune of that ilande, the
which theye Do call Zante, by the name of the ilande;
thar is also a good harbur. The teune or Cittie of Zante
is Cittiwated cloce to the scae, and is a good myle in
lengthe; behinde it, upon a verrie hie and stepie hill, Dothe
stande a large platforme of a castell, whearin Dothe live the
governer of that castell and towne; he is caled the Providore.[4] Within the wales of this castell is diverse other
dwelers, and many housis; within that place the Providore

---

[1] Chios.   [2] Marseilles.
[3] *Saffrance* = Sovrano, or Windward, the modern Bay of Argostoli in Cephalonia.
[4] Each of the Ionian Islands was governed by a *Proveditore* from Venice until the downfall of the Republic in 1797.

dothe tow dayes in the weeke hould a courte, and heare diverse causes, as well of the Grekes as of the Venition and Italians; for this ilande is under the Ducke of Venis, but he houldes it under the greate Turke, and Dothe paye tribute yearlye or quarterly for it. The greateste parte of the people in this ilande be Greekes, and theye doo labur harde in planting and triminge the corron (currant) gardins, ollive gardins, and vinyards. Hear growethe verrie litle corne, but from hence comethe the moste of our Corrance and beste ayle (oil); thar is also good wyne. There provision of breade, beefe, gotese, shepe, and swyne and pullin (fowls), they have it from Castle Turne[1] in Morea, the which place is neare the playnes of Arcadia, whear plentie of catle ar. The Providore, and those which ar nexte unto him in office, whome they do cale sinyors of healthe, would not suffer us to com on shore because we came from Argeare, whear Turks do live, and we broughte from thence som Turkes in our shipp; yeate, at the End of six dayes, we had proticke,[2] which is, Leve to com a shore. The order thar is, that all Those which doo com out of any parte of Turkie, havinge not a letter of healthe from sóm Venition or Ittalion, muste remayne ether a borde the ship, or in the prison which they do cale the lazerett, for ten Dayes; yf in the meane time any man hapene to be sicke, they muste all reste thare for ten dayes more, and so still for ten Dayes untill the have there healthe.

Whyleste we laye thus for sixe dayes upon the seae before the towne, I touke greate notis of a little mountayne, the which, as I thought, did ly close to the seae, and semed to be a verrie pleasante place to take a vew of the whole iland and the seae before it. It showed to be verrie greene and playen ground on the tope of it, and a whyte thinge lyke a rocke in the mydle tharof. I touke suche

---

[1] Castel Tornese. [2] Pratique.

pleasur in behouldinge this hill that I made a kinde of vow or promise to my selfe that assowne as I sett foute on shore I would nether cate nor Drinke untill I had bene on the tope tharof; and in the meane time did labur with tow of my companyons, and perswaded them to beare me company. One of there names was Myghell Watson, my joyner; the other's name Edward Hale, a Cotchman. The day beinge come that we should go a shore, I chalinged my associates with there promise, and gott there good wils to go with me before we wente into the towne. This hill is called by the Greekes Scopo (*i.e.*, outlook). It is from the town more than a myle, but I gave our sayleres somthinge to carrie us in the coke boote, as we thoughte to the foute of the hill; but when we weare sett a shore we found it to be almoste tow myles unto it. When we cam to the foute of it, by greate fortune we hapened on the ryghte waye, the which was verrie narrow and crouked. It was arlye in the morninge, and we weare toulde, 2 or 3 dayes before, that no man muste carrie any weapern with him when he wente a shore, and tharfore we wente only with cudgels in our handes. So, assendinge the hill aboute halfe a myle, and loukinge up, we sawe upon a storie of the hill above us a man goinge with a greate staffe on his shoulder, havinge a clubed end, and on his heade a cape which seemed to hus to have five horns standinge outryghte, and a greate heard of gootes and shepe folloed him.

My frende Myghell Watson, when he saw this, he seemed to be verrie fearfull, and would have perswaded us to go no farther, tellinge us that surly those that did inhahite thare weare savidge men, and myghte easalye wronge us, we hauinge no sordes or dageres, nether any more Company; but I tould him that yf thei weare divers, I would, with Godes help, be as good as my worde. So, with muche adow, we gott him to go to that storie wheare we sawe the man with his club; and than we saw that that man was a heardman. Yeate, for all this, Myghell Watson swore that he would goo no farther, com of it what would. Edward Hale sayd somthinge fayntly that he would not leave me, but se the end. So we tow traveled forwarde, and when we cam somthinge neare the topp, we saw tow horsis grasinge, with packe sadls on ther backes, and one man cominge downe the hill towardes us, having nothinge in his handes. Cothe I to my fellow: Nede, we shall see by this man what people they be that inhabit heare. When this man came unto us he lay his hand upon his breste, and boued his head and bodye with smylinge countinance, makinge us a sine to go up still. Yeat than Ned Hall began to diswade me from goinge any further; but I tould him it would not stand with my othe to go backe untill I had bene as farr as I could go. Cominge to the top thare was a prittie fair grene, and on one sid of it a whyte house bulte of lyme, and some square, the whyche had bene the house of an ancoriste, who, as I harde after wardes, Died but a litle before our cominge thether, and that she had lived five hundrethe years. Ryghte before us, on the farther side of the greene, I saw a house of som 20 pacis longe, and waled aboute one yarde hie, and than opene to the eaves, which was aboute a yarde more. And I se a man on the inside reatche oute a coper kettell to one that stood with oute the wale. Than saide I to Ned Hale: I will go to yender house and gitt som drinke, for I have greate neede. The wether was verrie hote, and I was fastinge. But Ned Hale tould me that I had no reason to drinke at there handes, nether to go any nearer them. Yeate I wente bouldly to the sid of the house, whear I saw another man drinke, and made a sine to him within that I woulde drinke. Than he touke up the same ketle which had water in it, and offer it me to drinke. And when I did put out my hande to take it, he would not give it me, but sett it further of, and than cam near the wale againe, and lifte up a carpit which lay on the ground, and thar was six bottels full of verrie good wyne, and a faire silver cupe, and he filed that silver boule full of a redeishe wyne, which they do cale Rebola, and he gave it me to drinke; and when I had it in my hande I caled to my frende Nede Hale, who stood a far of, for he was a fraide to com neare. Hear, Nede, cothe I, a carrouse to all our frendes in Inglande. I pray you, cothe he, take heede what you dow. Will you take what drinke they give you? Yeae, truly, cothe I; for it is better than I have as yeat disarved of. When I had give God thankes for it, I drank it of, and it was the beste that ever I dranke. Than he filled me the same boule with whyte Rebola, the which was more pleasante than the other. When I had muche comended the wyne, and tould Ned Hale that he was a foule to refuse suche a cup of wyne, than he come neare the house, and desiered to have som water; so he had the kettle to drinke in. When this was all done, I was so well pleasede with this entertaynmente, that I knew not how to thanke this man. I had no mony aboute me but one halfe Dolor of Spanyshe mony, and that mony is best accepted of in that countrie. I offered to give that peece of silver to this man, but he would not by any means take it. Than I remembered that I had tow severall (Seville?) knyfes in my pocket. I toke one of them and gave it him, and the blad gilded and graven. When he had taken it oute of the sheathe and louked upon it, he caled with a loude voyce: Sisto, Sisto! Than another man Came runninge, unto whom he showed but only the hafte of it, and than they began to wrastell for the knife; but he that I gave it unto kepte it, and leape ower the wale to the side whear I was, and, bowinge him selfe unto me, he toke me by the hande, and led me aboute by the ende of that house, and so into a litle cloyster, throughe the whyche we passed into a Chappell, whear we found a preste at mass and wex candls burninge. He pute me into a pue, whear I satt and saw the behaveour of the people, for thare weare about 20 men, but not a woman emongste them; for the wemen weare in a lower chapell by them selves,[1] yeate myghte they heare and se. Ned Hale cam after, but hauinge loste sighte of me, at his cominge into the chappell he kneled Downe neare unto the wemen, but saw them not; but they saw him, and wondred at his behaveour; for, after I had kneeled Downe, I stode up in my pue to louk for him, and than I saw tow wemen put oute there heades and laughed at him—as indeed they myghte, for he behaved him selfe verrie foolishly. Nether he nor I had ever sene any parte of a mass before, nether weare we thinge the wyser for that. This chapell was verrie curiusly paynted and garnished round aboute, as before that time I had never seene the lyke. Sarvis beinge ended, we Departed out of the chapell; but presently one cam after us, who did seme verrie kindly to intreat me to goo backe againe, and he leed us throughe the chappell into the cloyster, wheare we found standing eyghte verrie fayre wemen, and rychly apparled, som in reed satten, som whyte, and som in watchell Damaske,[2] there heads verrie finly attiered, cheanes of pearle and juels in there eares, 7 of them verrie yonge wemen, the eighte was Anchante (ancient), and all in blacke. I thoughte they hade bene nones, but presently after I kenewe they wear not. Than weare we brought into that house wheare before I had dranke. Clothe beinge layde, we weare requested to sitt downe, and sarved with good breade and verrie good wyne and egges, the shels of them collored lyke a damaske Rose,[3] and these mad lyke an alla compana (*alla campagna*[4]) Route, for they keep it in the earthe,

---

[1] The γυναικεῖον, or woman's quarter in a Greek church.
[2] *Vide* note 3, p. 17. [3] Easter eggs.
[4] Eggs for a country festivity.

because nothinge will thar take salte. My fellow, Need Hale, would nether eate nor drinke anythinge but water, yeat I did eate one egge, bread and chese, and I dranke tow boules of wyne. Whylste we satt there, the Jentelwemen came in, and thre of them came verrie neare us, and louked earnestly upon us. I offered one of them the cup to drinke, but she would not. Than I offered to give him that tended upon us my halfe Dollor, but he would not take any monye. These wemen standing all together before us, I thoughte they had bene Dwelleres there, because no mony would be taken. I presented my other knyfe, of 2s. price, unto the ould Jentlewoman, the which she was unwilling to take, but at laste she tooke it, and than they all flocked together, and, as it semed to me, they wondered muche at it. When thei had well louked upon it, they came altogether towardes me and bowed there bodies, to show ther thankfulnes. So Ned Hale and I Touke our leves and wente awaye verrie merrily; but when we came to the place wheare we lefte our fainteharted frend Myghell Watson, who all this whyle has layen in a bushe, when we had tould him the wonderes that we had sene, and of our kinde entertainmente, he would not beleve us, for he was a shamed, and desiered us to make haste to the towne that he myghte git som vittals; but we mad the less haste for that, and wente to se another monestarie. Near unto the place upon this mountaine growed many sweete floweres, in stead of heathe, time, and other good earbes, and fine springes of watere. Cominge to the towne of Zante, we Inquiered out the house wheare our marchants and other passingeres weare, which was at the sine of the Whyte Horse; but Myghell Watson, for shame, would not go in with us. When our martchantes saw us, they began to be verrie angrie, sayinge that they had soughte alaboute, and thoughte that we had bene drowned, or com to som evell fortune; but I bid them hould ther peace, and lett me tell them my adventurs. When I had toulde them all the storie, they wondered at my bouldnes, and some Grekes that weare thare sayde that they never hard that any Inglishe man was ever thare before. It was than aboute 12 of the clocke, and nyne of these Jentlmen would needes go presently thether to se That which I had done, and bcause I would not go againe, beinge wearie, for it was 4 myles thether, they hiered a gide, and yeate, when they came to the mountaine, they myste of the Ryghte way, and did climbe upon the Rockes, so that som of them gott fales and broke there shins ; but at laste they got thether, and the waye for them by me beinge preparede, thei weare bid verrie welcom ; but there gide hade Instrucktede them with that which I never thought on, the which was, that at ther firste cominge they should go Into the chappell, and thar offer som mony, as litle as they would, and than theye should have all kinde entertainmente. So, verrie late in the evininge, they Returned safly againe, and gave me thankes for that which theye had sene.

The 30th day I wente with 3 more, havinge a Greke to show us the way into the Castle.

MAYE.

The firste day of maye we saw there greatest traverses[1] or sportes that they have in all the yeare, for that day dothe meete at the toune of Zante all the able men of the Greeks with there best horsis and artillerie, which is nothinge but staves to Rvne at the Ringe, or at quintan.[2] They borroed our five trompateres to sounde whe[n] they Run at

---

[1] "Many shiftes and subtle traverses were overwrought by this occasion." (*Proceedings against Garnet*, 1606.)
[2] A game with a beam and sack of sand.

Ringe the prizis; the maner of it was so simple, that it is not worthe keping in memorye. In the fore noune they Run Quintan for a prize, the after noone at Ringe.

The second of Maye we departed from Zante.

The Turkes which weare passingeres in our shipp, and came with us from Argeare in Barbaria, and were to goo wythe us to Scandarowne, did somwate hasten us on of our voyege, and, the wynd beinge fayer, we sett sayle the second of Maye. The sam daye we sailed verrie neare an Ilande called Travallie,[1] in the which we did se a Castle, and in that Castell, or in som monestarie near unto it, thar be alwayes Thirtie fryeres, and no wemen in that Ilande, nether any more housis: it is low ground and levell, and litle above one myle in lengthe.

The third Daye we Entered in betwyxte Neagraponte, the mayne land of Grece, and a fine Iland called Sireego.[2] They saye that in this Iland faire Hellin was borne, and from thence stolne awaye before the Distrucktion of Troye.

The fourthe and the fifte Daye, havinge but a litle gale of wynde, we sayled cloce by the shore of Candie. This Ilande is fiftie leages in lengthe. We sayled neare unto that highe hill Caled Crete, wheare St. Pale preachede, and an ould Jue That was a pssinger in our ship tould us that on the tope of that hill Dothe stand a brason man houldinge a bowe bente as yf he wear shoutinge againste the easte, and he sayd that it was placed thare by arte magick, before which time few ships could live upon those seaes, the Easterly wyndes weare so furius; but sence that time they have bene as other places or seaes ar. Over aginste Candie we lefte many litle Ilandes, spetialy at the easte end, Melo and Antimelo.[3]

---

[1] Probably the Strophades, the largest of which is still called Convent Island, and has a convent on it of monks only.
[2] Cerigo, anc. Cythera.   [3] Milos and Antimilos.

The sixte Day we had a virrie straite entric betwyxte tow Ilandes at aleven of the clocke, and did Run within a bot lengthe of the shores. They be verrie hudge and upryghte mountaines. That which we lefte on our Ryghte hande is calede Cassa,[1] a place not Inhabbited ; the other upon our lefte hande is caled Scarpanta, and it is Inhabitede. In this Ilande tharbe verrie greate store of foule, that in the nyghte time doo Rouste in the grounde as our counis in Ingland dow.

16 leagues from Thence is the Ile of Roodes, but sence that Ilande was taken by the Turkes, the Roods[2] hathe bene kepte by the Spanyarde at Malta.

The seventhe daye we saw the coste of Carmance.[3]

The 8 and 9 we weare in a maner be calmede. The tenthe, and eleventhe, and 12th we sayled by the Coste of Siprus, havinge it upon our lefte hande. Neare unto the weste ende we saw a towne caled Baffa.[4] Eyghte leagues further, at Cape Gata, we sett a man a shore, who was a Greke, and borne in Siprus, and thare dwelled, but havinge a brother dwellinge in Candie, whom he had not in a longe time seene, he gott passage in a shipe to goo to Candie ; but the wynde would not suffer the ship to tuche thare, but carried that man to Zante, and in 3 monthes space he could not meete wythe any ship to carrye him backe againe to Candie. When our shipe came, he hearinge that we weare to sayle by Candie, he fell at our Maysteres feet, and craved passege in our shipe thether. So he was taken in. Yeat when we sayled cloce by the shore of Candie, our Mr. would not land him thare, but carried him to Siprus, and sett him on shore thare ; the which I thought was the man's hard fortun, and so he thoughte himselfe, for he wepte bitterly, because he had

---

[1] Cassos and Carpathos. [2] *I.e.*, the Knights of Rhodes.
[3] Caramania. [4] Paphos.

spente so muche time, and could not se his brother, whom he so dearly lovede.

Aboute ten leagus from the easte end of this Iland, in Siprus, near unto Cape Grego, thare is a greate and large towne caled Famagusta. It is a harber, or good porte. Thare dothe lye the moste of there gallis and other shipinge.

The 13th daye we sayled Juste to the easte ende of Siprus, for the wynde was verrie smale.

This Iland is the moste pleasante of any that hetherto I did ever see. The shores be lowe, and playne feeldes risinge into the lande still hier and hier, that a man maye se neare twentie myles into the Contrie, wheare we sett the man a shore. We saw great store of wylde swyne; but, out of all question, it is a verrie fruitful contrie.

When we weare about the mydle of Siprus, we sawe the Mounte Lebynus, which is in Assirria, and but tow smale dayes Journaye from Jerusalem. The 14th, havinge a freshe gale of wynde, we recovered the Cape Cansele,[1] the which is neare unto Scandaroune. The 15th we came to an anker in the Roode before Scandaroune, the which is in the verrie bottom of all the straites as farr as any shipp can go. The 16th daye our Mr. Guner, tow of his mates, Mr. Chancie, our surgin, one of our Trumpeteres, my selfe, and my maete, John Harvie, every one of us havinge a muskett, with powder and shott, we wente ashore, and though the mountaynes thare be exsedinge heie so that no ship dare goo within tow myles of the shore, for feare of not havinge a wynde to carrie them out againe, yet betwyxte those mountains and the seae there be desarte placis, thicke woodes, and boges, whearin dothe breed score of wyld foule, and allso wyld beastes, namely swyne and foxes.

---

[1] Ras el Khanzir.

We havinge entred into these woodes, thinkinge to kill som wylde foule, our myndes wear trabled to find oute som pathe waye, for feare of tearinge our cloese, and everie tow or 3 butlengthe[1] (boatlengths) we should finde a man caled a mountaincard, lyinge in a bushe, havinge in his hande ether a bowe and arrowes, or eles a peece, the which weapeins as we supposed they did carrie to kill wyld foule; but we havinge strayed some thre myles into the wildernes, we found a square playne, the which was nothinge but a quagmyer, and in the mydeste thar of was tow myghtie greate buffelawes, beastes biger then our greate oxen. At the firste we saw nothinge but there heades, and they made a great noyse with their snufflinge, and, in the ende, went Runing awaye, which was a wonder to us, for had it bene an ox, or cowe, or horse of oures, theye would thare have bene drowned.

Whylste we stood wondringe at this, we espied a great companye, to the number of aboute 40, of the afore sayde mountayneares, the which weare gathered together, and goinge aboute to catche us by inclosinge us aboute. This company beinge in that place, we knew not how to with stand, but only by flyinge away, and the woodes that weare betwyxte us and the seae weare so heie that we could not see the seae nor the maste of our shipe; but Runninge at a ventur throughe thicke and thine, thorns and bryeres, tearinge our close, at the laste we recovered a fayer playne, wheare we myghte se our shipe, and within a myle of the shore. Than weare we glade, and touke our

---

[1] Dallam's constant use of the word *butt* for *boat* sufficiently explains the following passage in Shakspeare, where *butt* is supposed to have been a misprint:
". . . . where they prepared
A rotten carkasse of a *butt*, not rigg'd,
Nor tackle, sayle, nor mast."
(*Tempest*, i, 2.)

case, wheare we founde a fayre fountaine of verrie comfortable water, for we weare fastinge, and faynte with travell.

After we had couled and Refreshed our selves, we Returned throughe the scatelsteade,[1] plat,[2] or foundationes of the towne or cittie of Scandaroune, so caled by the Turkes, but formerly caled Allicksandretta. There we myghte se greate peecis of wales wheare goodly housis and monestaris had bene, which in the same is now nothing but boges and pondes, wals of housis, and a castle, so sunke into the grounde with water aboute it that no bodie can go unto it. We did se thare, upon the wales of an oulde house, verrie strainge varmente Runing up and downe at great pace, som of them biger than a great toude, and of the same collore, but they had longe tayles lyk a Ratt.[3] Som of them weare longer maede and less of boddie, and so many otheres of diveres fations. An other time my mate Harvie and I wente into the feeldes to washe our lininge, and, whylste it was a driinge, we went to gather some fruite, for thar be great store of good frute that is comon, cominge to a whyte Damson tre. As we were a gatheringe we espied a great Ader that was in the tre upon the bowes, at least 12 or 14 foute from the grounde. He was even Reddie to leape upon one of us. Assown as we turned our backe to run awaye, He leape oute of the tre, and Rune into a thickett of brieres. A greate number of suche smale matteres I will omitte.

The 18th Daye our ship was to be unladen of suche goodes as was appoynted to goo to Alippo[4]; but that

---

[1] Scalastead. Cf. roadstead, the wharf or emporium for disembarkation.

[2] *Platt* = plan. "To draw plattes of Sicily, and describe the situation of Libya and Carthage." (North's *Plut.*, 220 B.)

[3] Lizards.   [4] Cf. Introduction for the English trade in Aleppo.

morninge, as sowne as we weare up, we saw a marvalus goodly show of tentes upon the sid of that mountayne, stritchinge downe unto that fountaine which I spoke of before; the which, when our mayster sawe, he sente a boate ashore to know the cause ; and our marchantes sent him worde that he should not, by any meanes, send any goodes or any man a shore untill he did se all the tentes gone, for thare was the souldieres of Damascus, a parte of the greate Turkes armye, that weare goinge to the warres, and if theye did finde any thinge on the shore that did lyke them, they would tak it as theire owne. So at nyghte we saw these tentes a takinge up, for, by Reason the contrie is verrie hote, theye dow travell by nyghte, and not by daye ; so for four dayes there came everie nyghte a fresche companye, and we kept a borde our shipe. Everie daye thar would com Ridinge to the seae side a great company of brave horsmen, with their lancis. Som hade their neagors to carrie their Lancis and other weapeins. Som sayd that they weare sent for to Constantinople, the which is 20 dayes Jurnaye from Scandaroune.

The 30th daye the Franch Consell which is Resedent at Alippo Dined aborde our shipp.

The same daye, towardes nyghte, our men begann to unlood our ship of such goodes as was for Alippo, for souner theye could not well, by Reason of the abbundance of Jenesaris that passed that waye, and pitched thare tentes within one myle and halfe of the Roode ; and it is a verrie uncomfortable place. Thare is but 3 houstile,[1] one Itallian, one Franche, and one Inglishe. Some litle cottigis thare be made of Reedes, lik a somer house, and tow smale tentes.

---

[1] Hostelries.

June.

The firste of June Thar was letters convayede verrie straingly from Alippo to Scandaroune, the which is thre score and twelve myles distance. After I hade bene thare a litle whyle, I persaved that it was an ordinarie thinge. For, as we weare sittinge in our marchantes house talkinge, and pidgons weare a feedinge in the house before us, thare came a whyte cote pidgon flyinge in, and lyghte on the grounde amongeste his fellowes, the which, when one of the marchantes saw, he sayd : Welcom, Honoste Tom, and, takinge him upe, thare was tied with a thred under his wynge, a letter, the bignes of a twelve penc., and it was Dated but four houres before. After that I saw the lyke done, and alwayes in 4 houres.

The fourthe Daye, in the morninge, thare weare pitched above twentie tentes at the place afore sayde, but the number of brave Jenesaries I could not learne, because I could not be conversante with them, or any that did know it. The moste of them weare horsmen, and everie man had his Lance, and most of them his boye, or slave, to beare his Lance, and everie mane his bowe and quiver of arrowes, and semeterrie by his sid. Not only there maner of shoutinge, but ther bowes and arrowes be strainge.

In the time of our being at Scandaroune, our longe boote wente everie Frydaye to Tharschus,[1] the cittie or towne wheare the appstele St. Pale was borne, for that was ther markett Daye, and she wente to buy vittals. Tharshus is but 16 myles from Scandaroune, and aboute the myd waye, or somwhat nearer to Scandarowne, is the place wheare Jonas[2] was caste out of the whales bellie, as the Turkes and Greekes tould us.

---

[1] Tarsus.

[2] "Jonah's Pillar", a rock in the sea, at the mouth of Scanderoon harbour.

The Mr. guner of our shipe, one of his mates, my mate Harvic, and I, with two saylores which Rowed us thether, we wente to that verrie place, and thare we gathered and filled a sacke full of sampeare,[1] whiche did grow upon those Rockes.

The tenthe of this monthe we departede from Scandaroune towardes Constantinople, the wynde beinge direcktly againste us, bordinge it from shore to shore.

Towardes nyghte we came neare to a fayre towne on our Ryghte hande ; at one end of it thare is a fayre and large castle, and the towne is a great lengthe by the sea side. This towne is caled Yeaass,[2] about six leagues from Tharesus, which the Turkes do cale Bayas, for they do chainge the names of moste townes.

The 12, 13, and 14th we sayled by the coste, and neare the shore of Carmanye, which is in Asia the Less. The wynde beinge nothinge favoarable, we had great leasur to louke upon the shores.

The 15th day we saw Siprus againe.

The 20th daye we Recovered to a Cape, which is one hundrethe leagues from Scandaroune.

The 23 we sayled by Castle Rosee,[3] which is in litle Asia.

The 25 we sawe a farr of the famus Ilande Called the Roodes, the which in times paste hathe bene kepte by Christian Knyghts, but now Inhabited by Turkes.

The 26 we sayled by the shore of the Roods, of the

---

[1] Sampeare = Samphire, the *Crithnum maritimum*, pickled as a salad. " Hangs one that gathers samphire : dreadful trade." (Shaks., *Lear*, iv, 6.)

[2] Ayash, or more probably Korghos, or Corycos. Ayash, ancient Elaeusa, is at present a mass of ruins, Roman and mediæval, about 30 miles west of Messina, joining on to the ancient Corycos, now Korghos, with an island and fortress built during the Crusades, which is probably the " fayre and large castle" alluded to by Dallam.

[3] *Castellorosso*, an island much frequented by Greek mariners.

which we tooke sufficiente vew, for the wynde was directly againste us; we myghte se whear divers fortes hathe bene upon litle mountayns.

This Ilande is 14 or 15 Leagues in lengthe and four leagues in bredthe. The 27 we sayled by the northe ende of the Ilande, and at the northe ende of the Ilande, and at the northe-easte corner of the same, thar is a towne or Cittie, the which for Cittiwation and strengthe I cannot not give it due commendations.

This 27 daye died one Thomas Cable, who was under 20 yearis of age, and son to one of the owneres of our shipe.

As we weare to pass betwyxt the northe end of the Ilande and the shore of Asia, which is but 5 leagues betwyxte, and the wynd direcktly in ye gulfe againste us, and also we wantede freshe water and other vitals verrie scarce, our Mr. and marchantes thoughte it good to touche at the towne.

Cominge to an ankere neare unto the wales of the towne, thare we founde in the Roode a gallioune of the great Turkes, the bigeste ship he hathe, aboute one thousand tun, a verrie carte, a ship of no strengthe; yeat was she Richly laden, and cam from Alicksandria.

We weare no sowner come to an anker but the Turkes began to com aborde us, so that the verie firste day thar came abord us not so few as five hundrethe Rude Turkes, and lykwyse everie day that we stayed thare they seased not.

The nexte daye, beinge the 28 of this monthe, the Captaine basha, governer of the towne, beinge gone abroad with there galles on some greate busines, the Chia[1] his Debitie (deputy), who for the time was Captaine, he, with the chefeest men of the towne, came abord our ship, and

---

[1] *Kiaya* is Turkish for "deputy".

she was trimed up in as handsom maner as we could for the time. Our gonroume was one of the fayereste Roumes in the ship, and pleasant to com into. In the gonroume I had a pare of virginals, the which our Mr. goner, to make the better showe, desired me to sett them open. When the Turkes and Jues came in and saw them, they wondered what it should be ; but when I played on them, than they wondered more. Diveres of them would take me in there armes and kis me, and wyshe that I would dwell with them. When the Captaynes Debutie had well vewed our shipe, the Captaine and Mr. of our shipe, accordinge to the Custam of the contrie, did give unto this man as muche brode clothe for a present, as would make his Captaine a veste or a goune after the Turkie manere; and so they wente awaye. Assowne as they weare gone, the stuerde of our ship and his men, my mate Harvie and I, went on shore to se the towne within. When we came to the gate wheare we should enter, I louked well upon it, and saw a superscription wryten or coutt in stone, but I could not understand it, only the yeare of our Lorde, when this gate was bulte or Reedified, and it was thus sett downe: Ano Dom. 1475.

When we had entered this gate, the firste turninge that we could finde upon our Ryghte hande we turned up a verrie fine streete to go to the wales. We there founde myghtie greate ordenance, bothe of brass and Iron, the which was made by Christians; som great peecis of brass that weare burste when the Turkes lay seige unto the towne.

Ther weare marvalus greate peecis that weare made of hamered Iron, everie stafe[1] at the leaste 3 Inches square, and houped aboute lyke a barrell, the bore so bige as tow man myghte creep in bothe at once. A Greeke that

---

[1] Stave = stave of a barrel.

gided us aboute the Wales tould us that one of these peecis, beinge once discharged, could not be charged a gaine, and made Reddie to be discharged, in less than tow houres.

This towne is Doble waled, betwixte the wales the distance of a pare of shorte butts (boats), and the ditche is verrie Depe, but drie.

To be shorte, havinge paste Rounde aboute the towne with oute any contradicktion or staye, only the time that we Dranke a pitcher of wyne which coste us but one penye, we made haste unto the seaye sid, and so to goe aborde. When we weare with oute the gate, loukinge for our bote, we se it cominge of from our shipe. When it cam to the shore, thare was in it Mr. Maye, our preatcher, and one that was appoynted to be our Imbaseders under butler. Cothe Mr. Maye to me: Ar you Reddie to goo aborde? Yeae, truly! said I; for I am verrie hungrie and wearrie with travell. I praye you, sayde he, go backe againe with me to the gate, that I maye but se the superscription over it, and sett one foute within the gate, and then I will go backe againe with you. So we wente all backe with Mr. Maye to the gate. When we weare thare, he saw a farr of a fountaine of water, made lyke one of our Conducktes, with a fayre, brighte Dishe of steele hanginge in a cheane, for the Turkes drinke nothinge but water. I praye you, cothe Mr. Maye, goe with me to yonder fountaine, that I may drinke som of that water, for it semethe to be verrie good, and I have a greate desier to drinke som of it. So we wente all with him to the fountaine, and everie one of us did drinke a dishe of water. As we weare a drinkinge, thare came unto us tow stout Turkes, and sayd: Parlye Francko, sinyore? which is: Can ye speake Ittallian, sinyor? Soe cothe Mr. Maye. Soe, as theye weare a talkinge, I louked aboute me, and a Turke, settinge upon his stale (stall), who did know me—for he had hard me play on my virginals and kissed me aborde our shipe—he beckened me to com unto him; and when I came som what neare him, in kindnes and som love he bore unto me, made me a sine to be gone; and poynted to the gate, and bid me make haste. So to the gate went I as faste as I coulde Truge, and my mate Harvie and the Reste of my Company followed after as faste as theye could; leavinge Mr. Maye and the under butler talkinge with the Turkes, for theye tow could speake Ittallian a litle, and so could none of us. When we weare gotten withoute the gate we Louked backe towardes the fountaine, but we se nobodye there; for the Turkes had carried Mr. Maye and the other man to prison. By chance we founde our bote and sayleres thare Reddie, and aborde our shipe we wente. When we came aborde, I wente presently to our Mr., and tould him all that had hapened. When I tould him how I had bene aboute the towne, he Imagened that we by that meanes had given som offence; because it is Daingerus for a stranger, beinge a Christian, to Take a vew of that towne, and so thoughte that for our faulte these men weare taken presoners. What wordes did pass betwyxte our Mr. and me I will omitt till God send us into Inglande. No man durste be so boulde as to goo ashore all that Daye, nether did any com abord us.

The nexte morninge a litle Greeke bote cam from the towne abord our shipe wythe a Letter from Mr. Maye, Direckted not onlye to our Mr. and marchantes, but also to the Reste of theyre companye. This Letter was wrytten so pittifully, as yf theye had bene presoneres thare seven yeares: showinge how they weare taken from the fountayne and copled together, lyke as theye hade bene tow Doggs, with a cheane of could Rustie Iron, and lede into a Darke dungeon, thare cheane fastened with a staple unto a poste wheare they muste continually stande, and nether sitt nor knele, and everye tow houres weare shaken over them whippes

made of wyere, threatening most Crouell punishmente; and
tharfore desiered that by all meanes thei would seke som
meanes for theyer spedie Release, or eles that theye myghte
be presently put to Deathe, for theye weare not able to
Induer that myserable lyfe and sharp punishment, which
was lykly to be Inflicted vpon them yf the ship did once
departe. Our Mr. and marchantes weare so wounded with
Reding this letter, and pittinge the presoneres case, and
banishinge all feare, they Resolvede to go ashore. Our
Mr. and five martchants havinge made themselves as brave
as they could, they wente a shore verrie stoutly to the
Captayns house, desieringe to speake with the chial, the
Captain bassha his debutie, who after he had made them to
staye whyle he came unto them to know the cose of theire
cominge, one of our men that could beste speak Ittallian
Tould him that Theye founde them selves verrie muche
aggreved that theyer men should be stayede as presoneres,
and not to be Informed of the Cause; and lyke wyse
wondered how they Durste be so bould as to make stay of
any one of our men, we beinge goinge with so Riche a
presente to the Grand Sinyor, and those tow men which
theye had stayed weare tow spetiall men, one of them our
Divine and preacher, the other the chefe and princepall
man for the presente. This, with other wordes, they sayed
to feare them; also theye sayd that yf he would not
presently deliver those men, they would hier a gallie and
send to the Grand Sinyor, that he might understand how
they wear wronged and hindred in their voyege without
any occation given to our knowledge.

The Answer of the Chial was this:

Yeaster Day I was abord your Shipp presentinge my
Captayn's person in his absence; you gave me not suche
entertainmente as my place Did Requier; you made me no
good cheare, nether Did you give me a presente for my
Captaine.

Our men answeared: The beste Entertainmente that we could give unto yow for the time yow had; good cheare we could mak yow none, for we had nothinge for our selves; our cominge to this place was to haue some Relefe heare, and to furnishe our selves with suche vitals as this contrie yeldethe for our monye. Whereas yow saye that yow had no presente for your Captayne, yow say not truly, for yow had so muche brode Clothe as would make your Captaine a Veste. But than said the chial: I had none for my selfe, and one will I have before yow have your men. Then saide they: Is that all the occation that moved yow to Impreson our men? And will the gifte of suche a presente give you contente That we maye have our men? Yea, surlye, sayde the chia. And so this Quarell was ended. Heare yow maye se the base and covetus condition of these Rude and barbarus doged Turkes, and how litle they do Regard Christians.

This Cittie wale which is nexte unto the seae is marvalus stronge, and so fortified with greate ordinance, not upon the wale, but their nosis Do louke throw the wale, so placed that no ship can pass on that side of the lande withoute leve. Within the town, in most streetes, a man cannot trott a horse, the streetes ly so full of bulletes, made of marble,[1] and of all sizis, from 16 Incchis to 3 Inchis. Many other Thinges conserninge this Cittie and Iland I do omit till my Returne into Inglande; but of all the townes or Citties that in my life I have sene, for strengthe I never saw the lyke.

Now, havinge Redemed our men oute of prison, the next day beinge the 30th, or last day of June, we wayed Anker, hoysed saile, and so to sea.

The firste of July, beinge under saile, we entered the sea

---

[1] Small black and white stones are still used for paving floors, etc., in Rhodes.

Aegebu,[1] passinge by and emongste the Iles of Archipelagua, wheare is a marvalus company of little Ilandes. The second daye we sailed by one of them emongeste the Reste, leavinge it southe. It is caled Lango.[2] Upon the northe side verrie pleasante lowe grounde, wheare semed to be not only store of vines, but plentie of other frute. Also we se a verrie fine toune, whose wales Resiste the waves of the sea. Within the towne verrie fayer buildinges, the which was never done by the Turkes, thoughe they now Inioye (enjoy) the same. It was our happ to caste Anker before the towne alnyghte, but in the morninge we sett sayle. The towne is called Lango (Stanco), by the name of the Ilande.

The third daye, standinge upon the spar-decke of our shipp, I tould no less than 16 Ilandes which weare Rounde about us.

The fourthe day, leavinge Learo[3] southe, we came to the Ilande Samose, wheare that famos felosefer Pathagarus was borne. This Ilande, for the moste parte, is Inhabited with Greekes. The wynde beinge verrie contrarie to our cource, that findinge a faire Roode, we Caste anker thare, wheare we myghte se a litle towne, a myle and better from the shore.

The people in the towne, seeinge our shipp com to an anker, we sawe them Rune into the felds and drive awaye there Cattell with greate speede up into the mountaines. Also in the Rood, halfe a myle from us, was a litle shipp or barke, the which they halled ashore, and carriede awaye the goodes that was in her; but they touke more paynes then theie needed, for we ment them no harme, and one

---

[1] *Ægean* Sea.
[2] Stanco=Kos, contracted form of εἰς τὰν Κῶ. Cf. Stalimna for Limnos, Stamboul, εἰς τὴν πόλιν, etc., etc.
[3] Leros.

hour within nyghte we wayed Anker; but the wynd was so Direcktly in the narrow passage[1] we had to go betwyxt that Iland and another,[2] that we could not pass, but weare forced to put in againe at the southe easte corner of the same ilande, under hudge mountaine.[3] To my thinkinge it is only one parme stone (pumice stone), and of sartaintie all that parte which was nexte unto the sea is a fearme stone, and verrie streighte uprighte.

The nexte Day som of our men went a shore to se yf they could find any freshe water, and to cut doune som fier wood.

One of those men, beinge a verrie bould fellow, stole away from his fellowes, and wente to the towne aforesayde. He presumed partly upon his language, but the reste of his fellowes came aborde without him, and everie one did thinke that he was taken prisoner. The nexte daye, aboute ten of the clocke, he came to the sea sid, and weaved for a boate; so, when he cam aborde, he broughte with him som hens and som breade, and was halfe Drunke with wyne. About tow houres after came to the shore the captaine of that ilande, who was a Turke, and broughte with him a presente, in hope to recave a better.

Heare doth grow a kinde of graine or corne, which theie do call myllio (millet), a small seed muche lyke unto canara-bird seed. The increase of it is at the least one hundrethe and fiftie foulde. They make of it finer bread than of wheate. The eighte Daye Died one John Knill, sarvante to Mr. Wyseman, marchante, who was also one of the owneres of our shipp.

The tenthe daye we wayed anker, and provede to pass our cource, but the wynde would not suffer us, beinge weste

---

[1] The Boghaz.
[2] Between Samos and the Island of Nicaria.
[3] Mt. Kerki, at the west end of Samos.

and by northe, as it was before. When we saw that we could not prevaile againste the wynde, we came rounde to that place whear we did firste anker, thinkinge thare to git som better store of vitals and freshe water; but beinge verrie darke before we could git into the harber, by the necklyience (negligence) of him that sounded, our ship was a grounde, the which turned us to greate feare and muche truble a greate parte of that nyghte; yeat in the ende all was well. But in the morninge, when we did thinke to have gone a shore, we espied 4 gallis and a frigett, which came stealinge by the shore. The gallis stayed a league of, under the shore of Asia the lesse, but the frigett came into the roode to se what we wear, and thar came to an anker; the which when our Mr. persaved, not knowinge what There intent was, he caused anker to be wayed with all speed, and beinge under saile, the frigett went before us, and also the gallis; for than our Mr. purposed to goo that way which before he Durste not adventur; for wheraas we should have lefte this ilande on our Righte hand, now we lefte it on our lefte hand, and ventured to goo be twyxte Samose and the mayne land of Asia the less, the which is a marvalus straite pasege for suche a ship as ours was. Even in the straighteste place these four gallis stayed for us, but when they se our strengthe and bouldnes, they weare afrayed of us. They had placed ther gallis cloce by the shore, so that ether the beake head did tuche the shore or else there ors myghte, and yeat had we hardly roume enoughe to pass betwyxte theire ores and the mayne lande. Our Mr. caused all our company to stand up and make as great a show as we coulde, and when we weare ryghte over againste them, our five trumpetes sounded sodonly, which made them wonder, loukinge earnestly upon us, but gave us not a worde; so we Dashte them oute of countinance who mente to have feared us, and we lefte them by the shore of Samose, beinge the eleventhe day of July.

The 12th daye we discried Scio. The 13th we sayled by the shore of that ilande.

The 14th we cam to an anker in a rood, tow leagues shorte of the greate towne or Cittie of Scio, so called by the name of the ilande.

The 15th day, in the morninge, our longe boate beinge reddie to go ashore for freshe water, which we stod great need of, for in 3 dayes before we had nothinge to eate but rice boyled in stinkinge water, and our bevveredge did also stincke. The boate beinge lanched, thre of our jentlmen passingeres came unto me and asked me yf I would goo a shore to see yf we could buy some freshe vittals, and I sayd: Yeae, with all my harte. Assowne as we weare in the boate, the Mr. was tould of it, and he louked over the ship side, and spoke unto me, for the other myghte have gone with his good will, and nevere com againe, nether woulde he have stayed halfe an hour for them ; but theye did know that he would not leave me behinde. So the Mr. asked me whether I would go, and I tould him but to sett foute on shore, drinke som freshe water, and com aborde with the boate. Than he bid me come aborde againe presently, but the jentlmen had me betwyxte them, and helde me faste; nether did I meane to dow as he bid me. Well, sayd the Mr., I see ye will goo ashore, and the companye that is with yow will draw yow up to yonder towne which you se, and I will tell you before you goo that which yow shall finde true. In no parte of the worlde Dothe grow any masticke[1] but in this ilande, and now is the time for it. The commodities heare ar nothinge but masticke, cotten woll, and wynes. Yow cannot goo to yonder towne but yow muste needes go throughe the gardens wheare these thinges grow ; and yf you be sene to take one sprige of masticke, or one podd of cotten woll, or

---

[1] There are twenty-two mastic-growing villages on Chios.

one bunche of grapes, it is a whole yeares impresonmente, and thare wilbe no redemption for you. Tharfore do not saye but that I gave yow suffitiente warninge, etc.

This iland of Scio is risinge from the sea side som 3 or 4 myle, and this towne which we mente to go unto is tow myle from the sea, and it semed, a farr off, to be a prittie towne, with a castell in the mydeste of it.[1]

When the Mr. had tould us his mynde, for the Daingeres we myghte fale into unawares, than he sayd to me that yf I cam not backe againe with the boat when she had taken in water, he would sett sayle and be gone; but we feared not that, for as sowne as we came to lande, we wente direcktly to the towne. It was upon the Sondaye, and the people seinge our ship com to an anker, and seldum had sene the lyke in that contrie, and lykwyse saw us com a shore, many wemen and childrin came to meet us, who wondred as muche at us as we did at them. We wente on right forwardes, givinge no bodie one worde till we came into the mydle of the towne under the castell wale, and thare standinge still loukinge aboute us, thare came a Greeke unto us, and demanded whom we soughte for, or whither we would goo. To of our company could speake Ittalian well, who Answered that our cominge was to buy som vitals.

This man saide thare was a Consoll in the towne, and we muste repare unto him before we could have anythinge, so he wente with us unto the Consols house. The streetes weare full of people, which flocked together to louke upon us.

When we came to the Consols house, we weare to go up a pare of staires, made lyke a ladder at one end of the house withoute. This lader went up to a stage or scaffould which was on the backesid of his house, that louked righte towardes the sea wheare our shipp lay at an anker. The

---

[1] Doubtless one of the mastic villages to the south of the island, most of which have still castles in their midst.

consoll was apon this stage, sittinge at a table, and with him thare was six verrie gallant jentlwemen, and verrie beautifull. Assowne as we came up, these brave wemen arose and wente awaye, and the Consoll came unto us, imbracinge us one after another, and bid us verrie wellcom. He caused the Table to be furnished with a verrie fine bankett (banquet) of sweete meates, and but tow litle cakes of breade; our drinke was verrie good raspis.[1] Whyleste we satt thare talkinge, the common sorte of the people in that towne came to the garden wales, for on that sid of the house was the Consols garthen, and the wales weare of stone withoute morter, and the people Did so muche desier to se us, that they did climbe upon the wales. The Consoll many times stood up chidinge them, and shakinge his hande at them, threatininge punishmente; but the more he chid, the more the people did climbe upon the wale, and the wale beinge over loden, Downe came the wale, makinge a greate noyes, the lengthe of a pare of butes (boats), and almoste so muche in another place. The which made The Consoll verrie angrie, and he myghte verrie well have wyshte that we had note com thare.

Wheare we satt we myghte se our shipp ryghte before us, and we se the boate goo a bord with water.

In this meane time, the Consoll had sente tow men aboute the towne, to se what vitels they could git for us; at the end of tow houres theye came againe, and tould us that theye could find nothinge that was to be sould at that time, beinge Sondaye, but aboute a bushell of garlicke, the which we wear contented to take, because we would have somthinge; and we saw that we weare trublsom to the Consoll; so, havinge taken or leves of the Consoll, he apoynted one to carrie our garlick to the townes end before us. Goinge Downe the ladder from the scaffould, upon bothe sides of

---

[1] Raspis = raspberry.

the ladder did stand the chefeste wemen in the towne, in degrees one above Another, to se us at our goinge awaye; they stoode in suche order as we myghte se theire facis and bristes nakede, yeat weare they verrie richly appareled, with cheanes aboute theyre neckes, and juels in them and in there eares, theire heades verrie comly dresed with rebbininge of diverse collores; but that which made us moste admiere them was their beautie and cleare complecktion. I thinke that no parte of the worlde can compare with the wemen in That contrie for beautie; but afterwards we understood that yf we had gone to the Cittie, which was but sixe myles further, se should have bene muche better entertained, for in that Cittie was an Inglishe Consoll, whose name was Mr. Willyam Aldridge, a fine jentlman, but our Mr. would not put in thare, for feare of beinge put to som charge; for he was a verrie myserable and sparinge man, all for his owne profitt, and not regardinge to satisfie other mens Desieres, or to give his passingers anye Contente.

Beinge Come aborde our ship with our bage of garelicke, it was not so selenderly regarded but that we myghte have had chapmen (buyers) for it, and our monye againe with profitt.

The same Daye Anker was wayed, and we under sail, but we profetted litle, for before the morninge we came to an Anker againe somethinge neare to the same place.

The nexte daye, beinge the 16 daye, we wayed Anker againe, and weare becalmed before the greate toone of Scio, verrie neare unto it, but our Mr. would not suffer any man to goo ashore.

The 19th of July we came to the Iland Tenedoes, the which is ryghte over agenste the southe Ende of the platt or ruins of the great Cittie of Troye, the wynde beinge Direcklly againste us, and also a great Currante which comes from the rever of Hellisponte. We came to an

Anker by the Shore, neare to that southe gatte of Troye ; a greate parte of the gate is yeat standinge, with som hudge peecis of those myghtie wales that hathe bene.

The xxth Daye we wayed Anker againe, but could do no goode, for the wynde and currante was againste us, and we came to an anker againe neare to the same place.

The 21 Day, Died a boye Caled John Felton, who was borne at Yarmouthe.

Also, the same day, I and som more of our company wente a shore, and sawe som monimentes in Troy, peecis of wales, sutchins,[1] and marble pillares.

We beinge come aborde againe, ii of the greate Turkes gallis cam by us, some rowinge and som saylinge; bucause they should not com a borde us, our Mr. caused Anker to be wayed, and towardes nyghte, the wynde faylinge, we came to an anker againe.

The 22th Day, tow friggotes which came down the ryver Hellisponte, seinge our ship, and knowing her to be a ship from Inglande by her flage in the mayn top, tow Inglishe men that weare in one of the friggotes desiered of ther Captaine that they myghte haile our shipe. The captaine was verrie willinge so to dow, The which our captaine, or Mr., persavinge, and knowing the frigotes to be Turkes, and because theye should not come a borde us, he caused Anker to be wayed with all speede ; for the Turk's condition is suche that, yf they come a borde, the captaines would have had a presente, or have beged somthinge.

So by that time that theye weare com unto us, we weare under saille. Than the tow Inglishe men caled unto us, and, after som salutations, theye tould our Mr. thate thare was cominge at hande The Amberall of the greate Turkes navie, and, in his Company, 15 gallis more ; and also showed how we myghte knowe the Amberall from

---

[1] Escutcheons.

the reste, for his gallie had tow lanthorns on his poupe, and the reste but one a peece. And so these friggotes departede.

No souner weare the frigotes gone but we discried the gallies verrie neare unto us, for theye cam downe the rever Hellisponte, at a corner by the wales of Troye. The sighte of these gallis, to our thinkinge, was a marvalus show, they weare so curiusly paynted with fayre collors and good varnishe. The slaves that weare in them rowinge satt all nakede. As they weare rowinge towardes Tenedoes, the wynde cam fayer for them, and than they cut ther sayels, and the slaves weare covered with a peece of canves that over sprede them all. When the gallis weare under saile they showed muche better than theye did before. The sailes weare made of cotten woll, and one clothe verrie whyte, and another verrie blewe, and the masts of the sam colores.

As theye weare sailinge by us, our Mr. caused the gonors to give them thre peecis, the which was but meserably done; yeate, beinge so neare the wales of Troy, the eckco was suche that everie peece semed to be five by the reporte.

Than the Amberall sente a gallie unto us to demande his presente, and also to aske whye we did salute him no better. The gallie beinge com unto us with his messege ourMr. answered that the Amberal's presente was caked[1] under the hatchis, nether did he know what it was untill he came to our imbassador at Constantinople; and for that thare was no better salutation, or more shott given to the Amberall, the reason was That he did [not] knowe that the Amberall was thare. Yf he hade he would have given him all the ordinance in our shipp.

---

[1] Caked=calked. "The windows close shut and calked." (Ben Jonson, *Silent Woman*, i, 1.)

ENTERING THE DARDANELLES. 49

This excuse beinge made, the captaine of that gallie, who did not com a borde us, but sente a litle boate to our ship sid, for the gallie durste not com neare us, but the men in this boate sad that their captaine myghte not returne to his amberall excepte he carried him som smale presente.

Than our Mr., makinge deligente seartche in our ship, he found tow holland chestis, the which he sente to the amberall. Than the captaine of that gallie demanded a presente for him selfe. Our Mr. answered that he had nothinge. Than he desiered to have som tobacko[1] and tobackco-pipes, the which in the end he had. And so he sailed to Tenedose, wheare the Amberall and the reste of the gallis weare come to an Anker. At his departur, our Mr. gave him one peece with the shott.

Aboute tow houres after this gallie was gone, the wynde beinge verrie smale, and touke us shorte righte befor Cape Jenisarie, by som people caled the Cape of Janisaries.[2] Thare I wente a shore wythe som of our martchantes, wheare we founde a litle scateringe villidge, inhabited with Greekes. Thare we boughte som breade and hens.

Also thare we saw more at large the rewins of the wales and housis in Troye, and from thence I broughte a peece of a whyte marble piller, the which I broke with my owne handes, havinge a good hamer, which my mate Harvie did carrie a shore for the same purpose; and I broughte this

---

[1] Tobacco-smoking was just then in its infancy; it was introduced into England by Sir John Hawkins in 1565, and grew rapidly in the next decades. A curious old book of travels in Wales, says, "William Myddleton, elder brother of Sir Hugh Myddleton, projector of the New River, is remarkable for having been one of the first three who smoked tobacco in England, when crowds gathered round to witness the phenomenon." Shakespeare never once alludes to tobacco.

[2] Cape Janissary is on the Asiatic side of the entrance to the Dardanelles.

E

peece of marble to London. This Cape Jenisarie is aboute ten myle from Tenedose.

Now, beinge Come aborde our ship, we sett saile the same Daye, and entered into the rever Hellisponte seven leagues, and thare came to an Anker neare unto the tow Castels caled Sestose and Abidose. Sestose is in Thracia, and Abidose in Litle Asia. These tow Castels are verrie strongly kepte for the defence of entringe the Straites of Hellisponte aforesaid, which is the waye that all shipinge muste pass by that goethe to Constantinople.

The 24 a Captaine of one of the Castels came aborde our shipp, and broughte with him a presente.

Diverse other Turkishe captains came a borde us in the time that we stayed thare, and also the Consoll of Gallippelo.[1] Beinge thare by chance he came a borde us. This Consoll is a frier, and verrie fine Jentlman.

AUGUSTE.

In the time that we stayed heare for a wynde, we wente many times a shore, but what hapened, and what we saw at this time, I pass over.

But our Imbasador who was than at Constantinople, hearinge that our shipp had layne longe thare for a wynde, he sente downe a Chirmagee[2] to fetche up sartaine letters, and also for us that weare for the present; in the Chirmagee came Mr. Thomas Glover,[3] Mr. Baylye of Saulsburie, and a Jenisarie. From Constantinople to that place is neare aboute tow hundrethe and fiftie myle.

The nexte morninge, being the fifte of Aguste, not only we that weare for the presente, butt also Mr. Maye, our

---

[1] Gallipoli.
[2] Chirmagee=a boat rowed by *chiurme*, or slaves.
[3] Thomas Glover subsequently went out, in 1602, as Ambassador to the Porte, with power to appoint Consuls, and regulate the trade.

preatcher, and other Jentlmen that wente to sarve the Imbassader, would needes leave the shipe and goo with us, for it was thoughte by our fizitions that one of our sailores was infeckted with the plague.

The Chirmagee would not carrie us all, but Mr. Glover did hier tow boates more. We weare, in all, 16, with Mr. Glover and Mr. Baylye.

The sixte Daye we arived at Gallipilo, and cominge to the Ittallian Consol's house, who is a frier, he recaved us verrie kindly, but our staye was so shorte that we had no time to se the Cittie. Haveing fayer wynde, we made haste to sea againe. Aboute the mydle of the nyghte followinge, haveinge no wynde at all, and our men wearie with rowinge, we wente a shore, wheare we founde 3 or 4 wynde myls and the wales of an ould Castele. Though it was verrie Darke, yeat some of our men rowed up and downe till theye founde a litle cottage, wheare they gott some fiere. Others broke downe an ould hedge; and so we made a greate fier under the Castle wale. At Gallipilo, the daye before, at our goinge to sea, we boughte halfe a mutton, and heare we boyled the one halfe, and rosted the other. Thoughe it was but in a homly fashon, yeat we eat it bothe merrily and sweetly. Our fier was so large that we hade hyghte (heat) enoughe.

Before the morninge we wente to sea againe. When it was Daye, the wynde rose so greate that we weare forced to goo a shore, and to hale our boates on lande at a greate Towne Called Relezea.[1] Thare we founde wyne and breade greate plentie, but some of our Company did wake into the feeldes, and entered into a vinyarde to gather grapes; but beinge pursued by the Greekes that owed the vinyard, they weare not only in Dainger of recavinge som hurte, but also of lousing theire garmentes.

---

[1] *Relezea* corresponds in position to modern *Ereklidia*, which is mentioned by Wheeler as *Heraclissa*.

Cuthberte Bull had loste his Cloake, and one that wente to be the Imbassaderes Couke was pinyonede, his girdle and knyfes taken awaye ; but one Mr. Gonzale, a verrie stoute man, redemed those thinges againe, and made the Greeks rune awaye, for he beate them wythe their owne weapons, but not in theire owne grounde. Than the pore Greeks made a greate complainte unto the governor of the towne, whoe was than in our company, and had broughte us a sheepe for a presente. He quickly made us all frendes, and Mr. Glover was verrie willinge to make the Greekes restetution for the hurte was Done them. This governor, or Captaine of this towne, is a verrie stoute and stronge man of his person, but actevitie he hade none, for som in our company did prove him many wayes: he could nether run, leape, wrastell, pitche the barr, the stone upon the hande, trowe the sledge,[1] nether any defence with sorde or cudgell ; but yf he did catche a man in his armes fadem wyse,[2] he would so crushe him, that he would make his harte ake, and reddie to stop his brethe. He beinge askede the reason whye he could do none of these exercisis, he Answered that Turkes would never pracktise the same that Christians did. At this toune we stayed alnyghte. The nexte morninge, our captaine, Mr. Glover, gave unto this governor or captaine, 2 or 3 peecis of goold caled chickenes,[3] for his love and good company, for he was verrie willinge to make us merry and lothe that we should departe.

---

[1] Sledge=sledge-hammer. "The blacksmith's sledge, and the scythe of the mower." (Longfellow, *Evangeline*, i, 2.)

[2] *Fadem*, old form of word "fathom". A.-S. *fœdm*=the space reached by the arms extended, a grasp:—
    "I fadmede al at ones
    Denemark with mine longe bones."
                      (Havelock, i, 294.)

[3] Sequins.

The same daye, beinge the eighte daye, we touke our jurnaye by lande, towinge our bootes by the shore ten myles.

In the after nowne we came to a towne called Hora,[1] for our boates was not able to goo any further, the wynde was so hie and the sea so roughe; thare we stayed alnyghte. At this towne, but espetialy at the laste before, is great store of corne and vinyardes, verrie good; also greate store of silke wormes, wyne a pottell[2] for one penye; but the inhabytans of all these townes ar verrie pore, the Turks dothe kepe them so under, levinge upon the frutes of these pore. peoples labures. All this contrie which we traveled through from over againste Troye, or the place wheare we lefte our shipp, is Thratia, whearin Constantinople doth stande.

The nexte daye, beinge the nynthe daye, we lefte our boates at Horra, and wente 3 myles farther to a towne caled Cannosea,[3] but farther we could not goo anythinge neare to the sea, for it is so hillie and full of woodes, a verrie wyldernes; so thare we stayed that daye and alnyghte ever loukinge for our boates, but they could not com. Our captaine, Mr. Glover, when we had well vewed the towne and se that the condetion of the people was not to our lykinge, he made choyce of a house for us to lodge in, that was next unto the sea. The towne stode upon a hill, and this house upon the verrie brinke or end of the hill, beinge the heighte of St. Paules Churche a bove the sea; and we weare to go up a ladder into a gallarie, that was made at the end of the house, loukinge towardes the sea, and thare was a litle dowre to go into the roume wheare we shoulde lodge upon the bare bordes.

---

[1] Greek village called Chora; modern pronunciation, "Hora".
[2] A pottle was a quart jug. " Potations pottle deep." (*Othello*, ii, 3.)
[3] Ganos.

For, in all this time that we traveled, we never put of our clothis, nether did we finde any beed to rest in. In this roume thare was not so muche as a stoule or forme to sitt upon, nor anythinge in the house but one shelfe, whereon stood tow pitcheres and tow earthen plateres; note one wyndoe to give lyghte, but one litle hole throughe a stone wale.

We beinge at this towne before nowne, to pass awaye the time after we had made a shorte diner, we walked downe to the wood sid, which is close to the sea; a wildernes or desarte wood, which is put to no use, as we did thinke, by the sighte of it. Thare we saw diverse sortes of varmen, which we have not the like in Inglande.

Growinge towardes nyghte, and rememberinge whate hard lodginge we should have in our new In, findinge a thicke softe weed, that growed by the wood sid, everrie one of us that was thare gathered a bundle of it to laye under our heades, when we should sleepe.

Nyghte beinge come, and our supper ended, everie man chalked out his ristinge place upon the bare bordes; our jenisarie placed him selfe upon a borde that laye louse upon the joistes. Everie man had his Sorde reddie Drawne lyinge by his side; tow of our company had musketes. When we had layne about halfe an houre, we that had our weeden pillowes weare sodonly wonderfully tormented with a varmen that was in our pillowes, the which did bite farr worss than fleaes, so that we weare glad to throw awaye our pillowes, and swepe the house cleane; but we could not clense our selves so sowne. Thus as we laye wakinge in a Darke uncomfortable house, Mr. Glover tould us what strainge varmen and beastes he had sene in that contrie, for he had lived longe thare. He spoake verrie muche of Aderes, snaykes, and sarpentes, the defferance and the bignes of som which he had sene.

Passinge awaye the time with such lyke talke, the moste

parte of us fell a sleepe, and som that could not sleepe laye still and sayd nothinge for disquietinge of the reste, all beinge whyshte. Mr. Baylye had occasion to goe to the dore to make water, the dore was verrie litle, and opened very straitly into the gallarie, the wynde blowed marvalus strongly, and made a greate noyse, for the house lay verrie open to the sea and wether. Mr. Baylle, when he lay downe to sleepe, had untied his garters a litle, so that when he came into the gallarie, the wynde blew his garter, that was louse and trayled after him, rounde aboute the other legge; it was a greate silke garter, and by the force of the wynde it fettered his legges bothe faste together. Our talk a litle before, of Aders, snakes, and sarpentes, was yeat in his rememberance, and the place was neare wheare muche varmen was. He thoughte they had swarmed aboute him, but aboute his legges he Thought he was sur of a sarpente, so that soddonly he cried oute with all the voyce he hade: A sarpente! a sarpente! a sarpente! and was so frighted that he could not finde the doore to gitt in, but made a great buslinge and noyse in the gallarie. On the other side, we that weare in the house, did thinke that he had saide: Assalted! assalted! for before nyghte we doubted that some tritcherie would hapen unto us in that towne, so that we thoughte the house had bene besett with people to cutt our Throtes. Thare was 15 of us in the house, and it was bute a litle house; everie man touke his sorde in hande, one reddie to spoyle another, not any one knowinge the Cause. One that could not finde his sorde, goot to the Chimnay, and offeringe to climbe up, Downe fell a parte of the chimnaye tope upon his heade, and hurte him a litle; another, that was sodonly awakede, strouke aboute him with his sorde, and beate downe the shelfe and broke the pitcheres and plateres which stood thar on; the roume being verrie darke, for it was a boute mydnyghte. Otheres did thinke that they weare pullinge downe the house over our heades. Our janisarie, who should have bene our garde, and have protecked us from all Daingeres, he lykwyse doubtinge the people of the towne, and hearinge suche a noyse sodonly, he touke up the louse borde wheare on he laye, and sliped Downe into the valte. As we weare thus all amayzed, at the laste Mr. Bayllye founde the waye in at the doore. When Mr. Glover saw him com in, he sayd unto him: How now, man, what is the matter, who do you se? Mr. Baylle was even bretheless with feare, cryinge out, and with struglinge to gitt in at the doore, so thet he could not answer him at the firste; at last he sayd : A sarpente! a sarpente! had trubled him. When Mr. Glover harde him say so, than feare was gone, and he wente to the Dore, and thare he founde Mr. Bayllis' garter reddie to be carried away with the wynde. After we a litle wondered at our greate amayzmente for so smale a cause, Mr. Glover caled everie man by his name, to se yf any man weare slayne or wounded; for thare was sixtene of us in all, our weaperns all drawne, and the roume was but litle. Everie man beinge caled, we weare all alive, and but smale hurtes done. At laste we founde our janisarie wanting; who myghte well be ashamed to make it knowne wheare he was; but Mr. Glover callinge him verrie earnestly, he answered in the valte. He could not git out any way, but Mr. Gonzale Touke up the borde that laye wheare he wente downe, and lyinge a longe upon the floure, he could but hardly reatche him, to take him by the hande; without muche adew theye puled him up. When he leaped into the valte, beinge verrie sore frighted, he caste of his uper garmente, and lefte it behind him in the valte, but no man could perswade him to goo downe againe and fetche it, for the place was lothesom, and it should seme that he was thare frighted with somthinge, in that kinde Mr. Baylye was; so his garmente remayned there till the morninge, that he who oued the house did fetche it.

The nexte morninge, Mr. Sharpe, Mr. Lamberte, and tow jentlmen more, hiered mules, and touke theire jurnaye by lande to Stambole, or Constantinople, the which was 3 dayes jurnaye.

The same Daye, when these 4 jentlmen weare gone, we returnede to Hora againe, wheare we lefte our boates, and stayed thare alnyghte.

In the morninge we departede, and in the afternowne we wente ashore at a towne caled Heragleza,[1] other wyse Rellinge. Betwyxte this towne and the sea, upon a hill Dothe stande tow and twentie fayer wynde milns; everie milne hathe six sayles. They stande upon a straighte lyne, and of an equalle distance, so as theye made a verrie fayer shaw when we weare upon the seae. We weare at this towne verrie Curtiusly entertained, wheare we made merrie till mydnyghte, than Entringe our boates. In the morninge, beinge the 14th Day, we came to Selabrea,[2] a faire and large towne. We wente thare a shore for wyne and water, but we stayed not so longe as to se all the towne. Heare I se greate abundance of moske mylyons,[3] that weare as big as our sidrums or pumpions,[4] sould for the vallue of one penye or 3 halfe penis a peece.

The 15th day, beinge Wednesday, we arived at Constantinople.

The 16th our shipp Came neare to the Seven Towers, which is the firste porte that we com unto of the surralia (seraglio) which doth joyne close to the Cittie. From that poynte or corner of the surralia unto the Cittie it is almoste

---

[1] Heraclia.
[2] Selibria, anc. Selymbria.
[3] Musk melons.
[4] Citrons or pumpkins. Pumpion is old form of word pumpkin, showing its derivation from French *pompon*, Lat. *pepo*. "As flat and insipid as pompions." (Goodman, *Winter's Evening's Conference*, pt. 1.)

tow myles; thare our shipp cam to an anker, and the nexte daye she begane to be new payntede.

The 17th we wente aborde our ship for the presente, and carried it to our imbassaders house in the Cittie of Gallata, in the vines[1] of Peara[2]; and because there was no roome heie enoughe to sett it up in his house, he caused a roome to be made with all speed withoute the house in the courte, to sett it up in, that it myghte there be made perfitt before it should be carried to the surralia.

The twentethe daye, beinge Mondaye, we begane to louke into our worke; but when we opened our chistes we founde that all glewinge worke was clene Decayed, by reason that it hade layne above sixe monthes in the hould of our ship, whicte was but newly bulte, so that the extremetie of the heete in the hould of the shipe, with the workinge of the sea and the hootnes of the cuntrie, was the cause that all glewinge fayled; lyke wyse divers of my mettle pipes weare brused and broken.

When our Imbassader, Mr. Wyllyam Aldridge, and other jentlmen, se in what case it was in, theye weare all amayzed, and sayde that it was not worthe ii$d$. My answeare unto our Imbassader and to Mr. Aldridge, at this time I will omitt; but when Mr. Alderidge harde what I sayede, he tould me that yf I did make it perfitt he would give me, of his owne purss, 15li., so aboute my worke I wente.

The 23, the kinge of Ffess[3] cam to se my worke, and he satt by me halfe a daye.

The 27, our ship cam nearer unto the surralia. The same daye the kinge of Fess came againe to se our worke.

The 28, the Heckter, our ship, made hire salutation to

---

[1] Vineyards.   [2] Pera.
[3] The old line of the Kings of Fez was driven out by the Emperor of Morocco in 1548, and the country annexed. Presumably the exiled family took refuge in Constantinople.

the Great Turke, thare called the Grande Sinyor, on the northe side of the Surralya, the Grande Sinyor beinge in his Cuske (kiosk), upon the wale which is close to the sea.

This salutation was verrie strange and wonderfull in the sighte of the Great Turke and all other Turkes. She was, as I have saide before, new paynted (upon everie topp an anshante,[1] viz., mayne top, fore top, myssen top, sprid saile top, and at everie yardes arme a silke penante). All her braurie[2] I cannot now relate; her faightes[3] was oute, and in everie top as many men, with their musketes, as coulde stande conveniently to descharge them.

Anker was wayed, the Daye verrie calme and fayere. Althinges beinge reddie, our gonores gave fiere, and discharged eighte score great shotte, and betwyxte everie greate shott a vallie of smale shott; it was done with verrie good decorume and true time, and it myghte well desarve commendations.

But one thinge I noteed, which perswaded my simple consaite that this great triumpte and charge was verrie evile bestowed, beinge done unto an infidell. Thare was one man sicke in the ship, who was the ship carpinder, and wyth the reporte of the firste greate peece that was discharged he died.

Lyke wyse at the verrie end of this sarvis an other man, who was one of the stouteste saileres in the shipp, and all this whyle had plyed a great peece in the beake heade of the shipe, as he was raminge in his cartridge of pouder, som fier being lefte in the bretche of the peece, the pouder

---

[1] Anshante = ancient, a standard; corruption of "ensign". "Ten times more dishonourably ragged than an old-faced ancient." (1 *Hen. IV*, iv, 2.)

[2] Braurie = bravery. "With scarfs and fans and double change of bravery." (*Taming of Shrew*, iv, 3.)

[3] *Vide* p. 7, note 2.

touke fire and blew that man quite awaye in the smoke; aboute 3 dayes after all his lower parte, from his waste downward, was founde tow myle from that place, and his heade in an other place. When all was done the Grande Sinyore sent tow men abord our shippe to se how many greate peecis thare was, for he thoughte there hade bene four score, and there was but 27.

The 30th daye my worke was finished, and made perfitt at the imbassaderes house.

SEPTEMBER.

The seconde day, the Grand Sinyor desieringe to take a better vewe of our shipp, he came in his goulden kieke (caïque) upon the watter, and wente round a boute the shipp; but he came so sodonly that his beinge there was not knowne till 2 or 3 houres after.

One houre after him came the Sultana his mother, in the lyke maner.

The thirde Day, our imbassader Delivered a presente to the Vizeare Basha at his house.

The 4 day the Grande Sinyores secritarie, caled the Cappagaw,[1] came to se our instrament.

The 7th day the Gebustaniebashaw[2] came to se; lykwyse also the Heade Patriarke was expeckted, but he came not, because som Turkes dined with my lord that daye.

The 8 day, beinge Satterday, we began to take Downe our instramente, for that day the Grand Sinyor went from the surralia som six myles by water to an other surralia wheare the sultana his mother dothe live; for one monthe in the yeare it is tolorable for him to goo to that place, ether in Auguste or in September; at any other time he

---

[1] Capougee, lit. gatekeeper.
[2] Bostan Pasha = Chief of the Gardens.

may not goo so farr from his owne Surralia, excepte he be garded with a hunreth thousande men.

The 11th Daye, beinge Tusdaye, we Carried our instramente over the water to the Grand Sinyors Courte, Called the surralya, and thare in his moste statlyeste house I began to sett it up. This watere which we crosed from Galletta to Surralia is a streame that comethe from the Blacke Sea, and is called Hellisponte, which partethe Asia and Thratia, and as it comethe Downe by Galletta, a creke of that rever[1] goethe up into the contrie aboute sixe myles, which partethe the tow Cittis of Constantinople and Galletta; they maye go betwyxte them by lande, but it is 12 myle, and to cross the water it is but one myle. At everie gate of the surralia thare alwayes sitethe a stoute Turke, abute the calinge or degre of a justis of the peace, who is caled a chia; not withstandinge, the gates ar faste shut, for thare pasethe none in or oute at ther owne pleasures.

Beinge entered within the firste gate, thare was placed righte againste the gate five greate peecis of brass, with Christians armes upon them. . . . Than we passed throughe verrie Delitfull walkes and garthins; the walkes ar, as it weare, hedged in with statly siprus tres, planted with an equale Distance one from thother, betwyxte them and behinde them, smaler tres that bearethe excelente frute; I thinke thare is none wanting that is good. The garthenes I will omite to wryte of at this time. The waye from the firste gate to the seconde wale is som thinge risinge up a hill, betwyxte wales aboute a quarter of a myle and better. The gats of the second wale was also shutt, but when we came to the gate, my Intarpreter caled to those that kepte it within. Thoughe they had Knowledge of our cominge, yeat would they not open the gates untill we had caled and tould them our busines. These gates ar made all of massie

---

[1] The Golden Horn.

iron ; tow men, whom they do cale jemeglans,[1] did open them.

Wythein the firste wales ar no housis but one, and that is the bustanjebasha his house, who is captaine of a thousande jemeglanes, which doo nothinge but kepe the garthens in good order ; and I am perswaded that thare is none so well kepte in the worlde. Within the seconde wales tharis no gardens, but statly buildinges ; many courtes paved with marble and suche lyke stone. Everie ode[2] or by corner hath som exelente frute tre or tres growing in them ; allso thar is greate abundance of sweete grapes, and of diveres sortes ; thar a man may gather grapes everie Daye in the yeare. In November, as I satt at diner, I se them gather grapes upon the vines, and theye broughte them to me to eate. For the space of a monthe I Dined everie day in the Surralia, and we had everie day grapes after our meate ; but moste sartain it is that grapes do grow thare contenually.

Cominge into the house whear I was appoynted to sett up the presente or instramente ; it semed to be rether a churche than a dwellinge house ; to say the truthe, it was no dwellinge house, but a house of pleasur, and lyke wyse a house of slaughter ; for in that house was bulte one litle house, verrie curius bothe within and witheout ; for carvinge, gildinge, good Collors and vernishe, I have not sene the lyke.[3] In this litle house, that emperor that rained when I

---

[1] *Jemeglans* = adjemoglans = sons of strangers (*adjemi*). The adjemoglans were either captives in war, or sons of Christian parents taken when young, and designed for the more servile offices of the seraglio which a Turk would not do. The Bostangee-basha, or head-gardener, rose from their ranks and often obtained great power.

[2] *Oda:* Turkish for a compartment.

[3] Mohamed III put nineteen of his brothers to death on his accession ; he was the last of the heirs allowed liberty. Henceforward, they were kept in the *Kaweh*, or cage, in the seraglio, from which they came out to rule or die. Presumably it is the *Kaweh* which Dallam describes.

was thare, had nyntene brotheres put to deathe in it, and it was bulte for no other use but for the stranglinge of everie emperors bretherin.

This great house it selfe hathe in it tow rankes of marble pillors; the pettestales (pedestals) of them ar made of brass, and double gilte. The wales on 3 sides of the house ar waled but halfe waye to the eaves; the other halfe is open; but yf any storme or great wynde should hapen, they can sodonly Let fale suche hanginges made of cotten wolle for that purpose as will kepe out all kindes of wethere, and sudenly they can open them againe. The fourthe side of the house, which is close and joynethe unto another house, the wale is made of purfeare (porphyry), or suche kinde of stone as when a man walketh by it he maye se him selfe tharin. Upon the grounde, not only in this house, but all other that I se in the Surraliae, we treade upon ritch silke garpites, one of them as muche as four or sixe men can carrie. Thare weare in this house nether stouls, tables, or formes, only one coutche of estate. Thare is one side of it a fishe ponde, that is full of fishe that be of divers collores.

The same Daye, our Imbassader sente Mr. Paule Pinder, who was then his secritarie, with a presente to the Sultana, she being at hir garthen. The presente was a Coatche of six hundrethe poundes vallue.[1] At that time the Sultana did Take greate lykinge to Mr. Pinder, and after wardes she sente for him to have his private companye, but there meetinge was croste.

The 15th, I finished my worke in the Surraliao, and I wente

---

[1] The Sultana Valide, mother of Mohamed III, was the celebrated Sultana Safiye, favourite wife of Amurath III. She was of Venetian origin, being captured when young. She ruled Turkey during the lifetime of both her husband and son; hence the expediency of sending her so handsome a present. Mr. Paul Pinder, afterwards Ambassador, amassed great riches in the East, and built a most beautiful house in Bishopsgate Street.

once everie daye to se it, and dinede Thare almoste everie Daye for the space of a monthe ; which no Christian ever did in there memorie that wente awaye a Christian.

The 18 daye (stayinge somthinge longe before I wente), the Coppagawe (Capougee) who is the Grand Sinyor's secritarie, sente for me that one of his frendes myghte heare the instramente. Before I wente awaye, the tow jemaglanes, who is keepers of that house, touke me in theire armes and Kised me, and used many perswations to have me staye with the Grand Sinyor, and sarve him.

The 21, at nyghte, it was a wonder to se what abundance of lampes thare was burninge rounde aboute all the Toweres of the Churchis, bothe in Constantinople and Galleta.

When we demanded the cause, they tould us that as that nyghte Mahamet, theire Messies, was borne.[1]

The 24, at nyghte our ambassodor Caled me into his Chamber and gave me a greate Charge to goo the next morninge betimes to the surralia and make the instrumente as perfitt as possibly I could, for that daye, before noune, the Grand Sinyor would se it, and he was to Deliver his imbassage to the Grand Sinyor ; after he hade given me that charge he toulde me that he had but done his dutie in tellinge me of my dutie, and cothe he : Because yow shall not take this unkindly, I will tell you all and what you shall truste unto. . .

The Imbassadores spetche unto me in Love after he had given me my charge :—

Yow ar come hether wythe a presente from our gratious Quene, not to an ordinarie prince or kinge, but to a myghtie monarke of the worlde, but better had it bene for yow yf it had bene sente to any Christian prince, for then should yow have bene sure to have receaved

---

[1] The Feast of Bairam.

for yor paines a greate rewarde; but yow muste consider what he is unto whom yow have broughte this ritche presente, a monarke but an infidell, and the grande Enymye to all Christians. Whate we or any other Christians can bringe unto him he dothe thinke that we dow it in dutie or in feare of him, or in hoppe of som greate favoure we expeckte at his handes. It was never knowne that upon the receaving of any presente he gave any rewarde unto any Christian, and tharfore yow muste louke for nothinge at his handes. Yow would thinke that for yor longe and wearriesom voyege, with dainger of lyfe, that yow weare worthie to have a litle sighte of him; but that yow muste not loake for nether; for yow se wheat greate preparinge we made and have bene aboute ever sense your cominge, for the credite of our contrie, and for a Deliveringe of this presente and my imbassadge, the which, by Godes helpe, to-morrow muste be performede. We cale it kisinge of the Grand Sinyor's hande; bute when I com to his gates I shalbe taken of my horse and seartcht, and lede betwyxte tow men holdinge my handes downe close to my sides, and so lede into the presence of the Grand Sinyor, and I muste kiss his kne or his hanginge sleve. Havinge deliverede my letteres unto the Coppagawe, I shalbe presently ledd awaye, goinge backwardes as longe as I can se him, and in payne of my heade I muste not turne my backe upon him, and therefore yow muste not louke to have a sighte of him. I thoughte good to tell yow this, because yow shall not heareafter blame me, or say that I myghte haue tould yow so muche; lett not your worke be anythinge the more carlesly louked unto, and at your cominge home our martchantes shall give yow thankes, yf it give the Grand Sinyor contente this one daye. I car not yf it be non after the nexte, yf it doo not please him at the firste sighte, and performe not those thinges which it is Toulde him that it

F

can Dow, he will cause it to be puled downe that he may trample it under his feete. And than shall we have no sute grantede, but all our charge will be loste.

After I had given my Lorde thankes for this frindly spetche, thoughe smale comforte in it, I tould him that thus muche I understoode by our martchantes before my cominge oute of London, and that he needed not to Doubte that thare should be any faulte ether in me or my worke, for he hade sene the triall of my care and skill in makinge that perfickte and good which was thoughte to be uncurable, and in somthinges better than it was when Her Maiestie sawe it in the banketinge house at Whyte Hale.

The nexte morninge, being the 25, I wente to the Surralia, and with me my mate Harvie, who was the ingener, Mr. Rowland Buckett the paynter, and Myghell Watson the joyner.

Aboute an houre or tow after my lorde was reddie, and sett forwarde towardes the surralya, he did ride lyke unto a kinge, onlye that he wanted a crowne.[1] Thare roode with him 22 jentlmen and martchantes, all in clothe of goulde; ye jentlemen weare these: Mr. Humfrye Cunisbye, Mr. Baylie of Salsburie, Mr. Paule Pinder,[2] Mr. Wyllyam Alderidg, Mr. Jonas Aldridge, and Mr. Thomas Glover.[3] The other six weare martchantes; these did ride in vestes of clothe of goulde, made after the cuntric fation; thare wente on foute 28 more in blew gounes made after the Turkie fation, and everie man a silke grogren[4] cape, after

---

[1] Sir Henry Lello was Ambassador to the Porte at that time. For an account of him, and his correspondence with Lord Salisbury, *vide* Introduction.

[2] Mr. Paul Pinder was subsequently appointed Ambassador at Constantinople.

[3] Afterwards Sir Thomas Glover, Ambassador to the Porte.

[4] Grosgrain, from French *grosgrain*, *i.e.*, thick, coarse.

the Ittallian fation. My Livery was a faire clooke of a Franche greene, etc.

Now when I had sett all my worke in good order, the jemyglanes which kepte that house espied the Grand Sinyor cominge upon the water in his goulden Chieke (caïque), or boate, for he cam that morning six myles by water; whear I stoode I saw when he sett foote on the shore.

Than the jemyglanes tould me that I muste avoyd the house, for the Grand Sinyor would be thare presently. It was almoste halfe a myle betwyxte the water and that house; but the Grand Sinyor, haveinge a desier to se his presente, came thether wythe marvalus greate speed. I and my company that was with me, beinge put forthe, and the Dore locked after us, I hard another Dore open, and upon a sodon a wonderfull noyes of people; for a litle space it should seme that at the Grand Sinyore's coming into the house the dore which I hard opene did sett at libertie four hundrethe persons which weare locked up all the time of the Grand Sinyore's absence, and juste at his cominge in theye weare sett at libertie, and at the firste sighte of the presente, with greate admyration did make a wonderinge noyes.

The Grand Sinyor, beinge seated in his Chaire of estate, commanded silence. All being quiett, and no noyes at all, the presente began to salute the Grand Sinyor; for when I lefte it I did alow a quarter of an houre for his cominge thether. Firste the clocke strouke 22; than The chime of 16 bels went of, and played a songe of 4 partes. That beinge done, tow personagis which stood upon to corners of the seconde storie, houldinge tow silver trumpetes in there handes, did lifte them to theire heades, and sounded a tantarra.[1] Than the muzicke went of, and the orgon

---

[1] Spanish *tantarara*, the redoubled beating of a drum.

played a song of 5 partes twyse over. In the tope of the orgon, being 16 foute hie, did stande a holly bushe full of blacke birds and thrushis, which at the end of the musick did singe and shake theire wynges. Divers other motions thare was which the Grand Sinyor wondered at. Than the Grand Sinyor asked the Coppagawe[1] yf it would ever doo the lyke againe. He answered that it would doo the lyke againe at the next houre. Cothe he: I will se that. In the meane time, the Coppagaw, being a wyse man, and doubted whether I hade so appoynted it or no, for he knew that it would goo of it selfe but 4 times in 24 houres, so he cam unto me, for I did stand under the house sid, wheare I myghte heare the orgon goo, and he asked me yf it would goo againe at the end of the nexte houre; but I tould him that it would not, for I did thinke the Grand Sinyor would not have stayed so longe by it; but yf it would please him, that when the clocke had strouk he would tuche a litle pin with his finger, which before I had shewed him, it would goo at any time. Than he sayde that he would be as good as his worde to the Grand Sinyor. When the clocke began to strick againe, the Coppagaw went and stood by it; and when the clocke had strouke 23, he tuched that pinn, and it did the lyke as it did before. Than the Grand Sinyor sayed it was good. He satt verrie neare vnto it, ryghte before the Keaes (keys), wheare a man should playe on it by hande. He asked whye those keaes did move when the orgon wente and nothinge did tuche them. He Tould him that by those thinges it myghte be played on at any time. Than the Grande Sinyor asked him yf he did know any man that could playe on it. He sayd no, but he that came with it coulde, and he is heare without the dore. Fetche him hether, cothe the Grand Sinyor, and lett me se how he

---

[1] Gatekeeper.

dothe it. Than the Coppagaw opemed that Dore which
I wente out at, for I stoode neare unto it. He came
and touke me by the hande, smylinge upon me; but
I bid my drugaman aske him what I should dow, or
whither I shoulde goo. He answered that it was the
Grand Sinyore's pleasur that I should lett him se me playe
on the orgon. So I wente with him. When I came
within the Dore, That which I did se was verrie wonderfull
unto me. I cam in direcktly upon the Grand Sinyore's
ryghte hande, som 16 of my passis (paces) from him, but
he would not turne his head to louke upon me. He satt
in greate state, yeat the sighte of him was nothinge in
Comparrison of the traine that stood behinde him, the
sighte whearof did make me almoste to thinke that I was
in another worlde. The Grand Sinyor satt still, behouldinge
the presente which was befor him, and I stood daslinge my
eyes with loukinge upon his people that stood behinde
him, the which was four hundrethe persons in number.
Tow hundrethe of them weare his princepall padgis, the
yongest of them 16 yeares of age, som 20, and som 30.
They weare apparled in ritche clothe of goulde made in
gowns to the mydlegge; upon theire heades litle caps of
clothe of goulde, and som clothe of Tissue[1]; great peecis of
silke abowte theire wastes instead of girdls; upon their
leges Cordivan buskins,[2] reede. Theire heades wear all
shaven, savinge that behinde Their ears did hange a locke
of hare like a squirel's taile; theire beardes shaven, all
savinge theire uper lips. Those 200 weare all verrie
proper men, and Christians borne.

The thirde hundrethe weare Dum men, that could nether
heare nor speake, and theye weare likwyse in gouns of

---

[1] Tissue=interwoven or variegated. "The chariot was covered with cloth of gold *tissued* upon blue." (Bacon.)

[2] Made of Spanish leather. "I will send you the Cordovan pockets and gloves." (Howell, *Familiar Letters*, 1650.)

riche Clothe of gould and Cordivan buskins; bute theire Caps weare of violett velvett, the croune of them made like a lether bottell, the brims devided into five picked (peaked) corneres. Som of them had haukes in theire fistes.

The fourthe hundrethe weare all dwarffs, bige-bodied men, but verrie low of stature. Everie Dwarfe did weare a simmeterrie (scimitar) by his side, and they weare also apareled in gowns of Clothe of gould.

I did moste of all wonder at those dumb men, for they lett me understande by theire perfitt sins (signs) all thinges that they had sene the presente dow by its motions.[1]

When I had stode almost one quarter of an houre behouldinge this wonder full sighte, I harde the Grande Sinyore speake unto the Coppagaw, who stood near unto him. Than the Coppagaw cam unto me, and touke my cloake from aboute me, and laye it Doune upon the Carpites, and bid me go and playe on the organ; but I refused to do so, because the Grand Sinyor satt so neare the place wheare I should playe that I could not com at it, but I muste needes turne my backe Towardes him and touche his Kne with my britchis, which no man, in paine of deathe, myghte dow, savinge only the Coppagaw. So he smyled, and lett me stande a litle. Than the Grand Sinyor spoake againe, and the Coppagaw, with a merrie countenance, bid me go with a good curridge, and thruste me on. When I cam verrie neare the Grand Sinyor, I bowed

---

[1] Sir Paul Ricaut, in his book on Turkish policy, thus describes the dumb :—" They are called *Bizebani* or mutes, which are taught mute language made up of several signs, in which, by custom, they can discourse and fully express themselves. Eight or nine are called favourite mutes, who serve for buffoons to sport with, whom he sometimes kicks, sometimes throws in the cisterns of water, sometimes makes fight together . . . the mute language is much in vogue at Court, amongst others, as it is rude even to whisper in the Grand Signior's presence . . . the dwarfs are called *Giuge*, and especially valued if they are also eunuchs and deaf."

my heade as low as my kne, not movinge my cape, and turned my backe righte towardes him, and touched his kne with my britchis.

He satt in a verrie ritche Chaire of estate, upon his thumbe a ringe with a diamon in it halfe an inche square, a faire simeterie by his side, a bow, and a quiver of Arros.

He satt so righte behinde me that he could not se what I did; tharfore he stood up, and his Coppagaw removed his Chaire to one side, wher he myghte se my handes; but, in his risinge from his chaire, he gave me a thruste forwardes, which he could not otherwyse dow, he satt so neare me; but I thought he had bene drawinge his sorde to cut of my heade.

I stood thar playinge suche thinge as I coulde untill the cloke stroucke, and than I boued my heade as low as I coulde, and wente from him with my backe towardes him. As I was taking of my cloake, the Coppagaw came unto me and bid me stand still and lett my cloake lye; when I had stood a litle whyle, the Coppagaw bid me goo and cover the Keaes of the organ; then I wente Close to the Grand Sinyor againe, and bowed myselfe, and then I wente backewardes to my Cloake. When the Company saw me do so theye semed to be glad, and laughed. Than I saw the Grand Sinyor put his hande behind him full of goulde, which the Coppagaw Receved, and broughte unto me fortie and five peecis of gould called chickers,[4] and than was I put out againe wheare I came in, beinge not a little joyfull of my good suckses.

Beinge gotten oute of the surralia, I made all the spede I could to that gate where the imbassador wente in, for he and all his Company stode all these tow houres expecktinge the Grand Sinyors cominge to another place wheare he should deliver his imbassege and Letteres.

---

[1] Sequins.

When I came to that greate gate I sawe our Imbassador takeinge horse to begone. As I was making haste towardes him, he saw me, and came to me, Askinge me yf the Grand Sinyor had sene the presente. I tould him yeas, and that I had sene the Grand Sinyor, and that I had gould out of his pockett; whearat he semed to be verrie glade.

As he was speakinge unto me thar cam towe brave Turkes ridinge to my lord, bidinge him take his place and staye a litle; than my lord bid me take my place awhyle, for he desiered to heare more of that good neues.

So, when everie man had taken his place, thare was a greate gate opened on one side of the courte, and sodenly thar came oute at that gate five hundreth men on horsbacke, whose habbittes wear strainge to us, and their horsis wear verrie good.

Lykwyse thare came 500 jenisaris on foute, everie man havinge in his hande a great cane like unto a beadles staffe, and theye wear also in a strange habitt. This thousande men did but only cross the Courte for a show; they beinge gone, thar came sixe brave Turkes, well mounted, to our imbassador, and conducted him to the water side.

When my Lord was com to his owne house, he, with the 12 jentlmen, entred into his Chamber, and than he sente for me to tell him in what maner the Grand Sinyor had sene the presente, and how I came to se him. When I hade tould them the discource of it, they weare all verrie glad that he did so well like the presente; but my lorde sat still a good whyle, and said nothinge untill one asked him what he did stodie, on seinge althinges proved so well. My lord Answeared him, that he was sorye for onethinge, the which was that he never had any thoughte of my cominge into the Grand Sinyors presence, nether that any other would make it doubtful unto him, for if he had but mystrusted it never so litle, he would have bestowed 30 or 40*li.* in apparell for me.

The laste of September I was sente for againe to the surralia to sett som thinges in good order againe, which they had altered, and those tow jemoglans which kepte that house made me verrie kindly welcom, and asked me that I would be contented to stay with them always, and I should not wante anythinge, but have all the contentt that I could desier. I answered them that I had a wyfe and Childrin in Inglande, who did expecte my returne. Than they asked me how long I had been married, and how many children I hade. Thoughe in deede I had nether wyfe nor childrin, yeat to excuse my selfe I made them that Answeare.

Than they toulde me that yf I would staye the Grand Sinyor would give tow wyfes, ether tow of his Concubines or els tow virgins of the beste I Could Chuse my selfe, in Cittie or contrie.

The same nyghte, as my Lorde was at supper, I tould him what talke we had in the surralya, and whate they did offer me to staye thare, and he bid me that by no meanes I should flatly denie them anythinge, but be as merrie with them as I could, and tell them that yf it did please my Lorde that I should stay, I should be the better contented to staye ; by that meanes they will not go about to staye you by force, and yow may finde a time the better to goo awaye when you please.

OCTOBER.

The seconde of October my Lord Imbassader held a feaste abord our ship, and invited the baylie of Venis and sartaine Turks.[1]

---

[1] The Baily of Venice at Constantinople at that time was one of the Capello family, celebrated for their admirals and statesmen. He retained the office from 1596 to 1604.

The 12, beinge Fridaye, I was sente for to the Courte, and also the Sondaye and Monday folloinge, to no other end but to show me the Grand Sinyors privie Chamberes, his gould and silver, his chairs of estate; and he that showed me them would have me to sitt downe in one of them, and than to draw that sord out of the sheathe with the which the Grand Sinyor doth croune his kinge.

When he had showed me many other thinges which I wondered at, than crossinge throughe a litle squar courte paved with marble, he poynted me to goo to a graite in a wale, but made me a sine that he myghte not goo thether him selfe. When I came to the grait the wale was verrie thicke, and graited on bothe the sides with iron verrie strongly; but through that graite I did se thirtie of the Grand Sinyor's Concobines that weare playinge with a bale in another courte. At the firste sighte of them I thoughte they had bene yonge men, but when I saw the hare of their heades hange doone on their backes, platted together with a tasle of smale pearle hanginge in the lower end of it, and by other plaine tokens, I did know them to be women, and verrie prettie ones in deede.

Theie wore upon theire heades nothinge bute a litle capp of clothe of goulde, which did but cover the crowne of her heade; no bandes a boute their neckes, nor anythinge but faire cheans of pearle and a juell hanginge on their breste, and juels in their ears; their coats weare like a souldier's mandilyon,[1] som of reed sattan and som of blew, and som of other collors, and grded like a lace of contraire collor; they wore britchis of scamatie,[2] a fine clothe made of coton woll, as whyte as snow and as fine as lane[3]; for I could desarne the skin of their thies throughe it. These britchis

---

[1] Mandilion=a soldier's cloak. "A mandilion that did with button meet." (Chapman: Hom., *Il.*, x.)

[2] *Scamatie*, deriv. Italian *scamatare*, to beat off the dust of wool.

[3] Muslin or lawn.

cam doone to their mydlege; som of them did weare fine cordevan buskins, and som had their leges naked, with a goulde ringe on the smale of her legg; on her foute a velvett panttoble[1] 4 or 5 inches hie. I stood so longe loukinge upon them that he which had showed me all this kindnes began to be verrie angrie with me. He made a wrye mouthe, and stamped with his foute to make me give over looking; the which I was verrie lothe to dow, for that sighte did please me wondrous well.

Than I wente awaye with this Jemoglane to the place wheare we lefte my drugaman or intarpreter, and I tould my intarpreter that I had sene 30 of the Grand Sinyores Concobines; but my intarpreter advised me that by no meanes I should speake of it, whearby any Turke myghte hear of it; for if it weare knowne to som Turks, it would presente deathe to him that showed me them. He durste not louke upon them him selfe. Although I louked so longe upon them, theie saw not me, nether all that whyle louked towards that place. Yf they had sene me, they would all have come presently thether to louke upon me, and have wondred as moche at me, or how I cam thether, as I did to se them.

The nexte daye our shipp caled the Heckter, beinge reddie to departe, I wente to carrie my beed and my Chiste aborde the shipp. Whyleste I was aborde the shipp, thar came a jemoglane or a messenger from the surralia to my lord imbassador, with an express comand that the shipp should not departe, but muste stay the Grand Sinyores pleasur. When my lord hard this messidge, with suche a comande, he begane to wonder what the Cause should be. He thoughte that thare hade bene som forfitt made, or that som of the chips company had done

---

[1] The high shoe is still worn by Turkish women. (*Vide* note, p. 2.)

horte or given som greate offence unto som greate person; but, what so ever it was, he knew that the Grand Sinyores comande must be obayed; tharefore, when he had stodied longe what the cause myghte be, and beinge verrie desirus to know the truthe, he wente to the messenger and desiered him to tell him the cause whye the Grand Sinyor had sente this comande, or whearfore it should be.

The messenger tould him that he did not know the cause whye, nether whearfore, but he did hearde the chia say that yf the workman that sett up the presente in the surralia would not be perswaded to stay be hind the shipe, the ship muste staye untill he had removed the presente unto another place.

When my lord had got thus muche out of him, he began to be somwhat merrie, for he was muche greved before, thinkinge it had bene a greater matter; for the martchantes was bound in 5 hundrethe pounde unto the owneres of the shipe that she should departe that day, which was the Thursday folloing, yf wynd and wether sarved; also for the time that she stayed there her Chargis was everie day 20*li*.

Than my Lorde inquiered for me and sente one to the ship whear I was, who tould me that I muste com presently to my Lorde; so when I came to my lorde I found with him another messinger, who broughte the sartaintie of the matter that it was for no other cause but for my stainge to remove the organ; but when my lord tould me that I muste be contented to staye and Lette the ship goo, than was I in a wonderfull perplixatie, and in my furie I tould my lorde that that was now com to pass which I ever feared, and that was that he in the end would betray me, and turne me over into the Turkes hands, whear I should Live a slavish Life, and never companie againe with Christians, with many other suche-like words.

My Lord verrie patiently gave me leve to speake my

mynde. Than he lay his hand on my shoulder and tould that as he was a Christian him selfe, and hooped tharby to be saved, it was no plote of his, nether did he know of any suche matter as this till the messinger came. In the ende cothe he: Be yow contented to staye, and let the ship goo; and it shall coste me 5 hundrethe pound rether than yow shalbe Compeled to staye a day Longer than yow are willinge your selfe after yow have removed the presente; and yow shall stay heare as longe as yow will, and goo assoune as yow will, or when yow will make choice of your company; and yow shall wante nothinge, silver or gould, to carry yow by seae or Lande, and goo muche safer and more for your pleasur ten times than yow could to go with the shipe, for the ship goethe to Scanderoune, in the botem of the straites, which is oute of her way homwardes, and thare will staye a monthe at leaste to take in her loadinge; and the place is so corrupte and unhe(lth)full that many of her men will thare grow sick and die, and yow shall by this means be oute of that dainger.

My Lorde did speake this so frindly and nobly unto me, that upon a sodon he had altered my mynde, and I tould him that I would yeld my selfe into Godes hand and his.

Than said my Lorde: I thanke yow, I will send to the shipe for suche thinges as yow desier to have lefte behinde, for yow muste goo presently to the surralia to se the place wheare yow muste sett up the presente, or els they thinke that yow mean not to com at all; so away wente I with my drugaman or interpreter my ould way to the surralia gates, the which they willingly opened, and bid me welcom when I came to that house wheare the presente did stande. Those jemoglanes, my ould acquaintance which kept that house, and had bene appointed by the Grand Sinyor to perswade me to staye thare allwayes, as indeed theie had done diveres times and diveres wayes, now they thoughte that I would staye in deed, theye imbraced me verrie kindly, and kiste me many times. What my drugaman said to them I know not, but I thinke he tould them that I would not staye, tharfore, when I was gone oute of the house doune som 4 or 5 steps into a courte, as I was puting on my pantabls, one of these jemoglanes cam behinde me and touke me in his armes and Carried me up againe into the house, and sett me doune at that dore wheare all the Grand Sinyore's brothers weare strangled that daye he was made Emprore. My intrpreter folloed apase. When he that carried me had sette me doune, I bid my drugaman aske him why he did so, and he, seinge me louk merrely, he him selfe laughed hartaly, and saide that he did so but to se how I would tak it yf they should staye me by force. Than I bid my drugaman tell him that they should not need to go aboute to staye me by force, for I did staye willingly to doo the Grand Sinyor all the sarvis that I could.

Than these 2 jemoglanes wente with me to show me the house wheare unto the presente should be removed.

The waye was verrie pleasante throughte the garthens, whear did grow store of siprus trees and many orther good frute trees in verrie comly and desent order. Beinge paste the grdens, we entred upon a faire grene, wheare we founde som galland Turks ridinge horses on the easte sid of that grene or plain upon the wale of the surralia. Close to the sea sid Dothe stande a prittie fine litle buldinge which theye cale a Cuske (kiosk), made for a bancketinge house; but espetially, as I persaved, it is a place wheare the Grand Sinyor dothe use to meet his Congquebines twyse in the weeke. It is finly covered with Leade, and bulded squear on the topp; in the midle a litle square tour like a peramadease (pyramid?) on a greate heighte, and on the top of that a litle turrett well gildede, and on the side nexte to the sea a faire large gallarie wheare men may stande and se bothe up and doune the rever of Hellisponte, and lik wyse over it into Asia.

On the other 3 sids towards the grene ar verrie larg pentazis (pent-houses), supported with fine marble pillers, the flore spred with fair carpites, the roufe under the pentas verrie Curiusly wroughte withe gould and collors; but cominge into it it is a litle wonder, I cannot duly discrib it; but the roufe is a round hollo, verrie curiosly

* * * * *

[*A page is lost here.*]

pipes and Laid them in order on the carpites. By chance I caled to my drugaman and asked him the cause of theire runinge awaye; than he saide the Grand Sinyor and his Conquebines weare cominge, we muste be gone in paine of deathe; but they run all away and lefte me behinde, and before I gott oute of the house they weare run over the grene quit out at the gate, and I runn as faste as my leggss would carrie me aftere, and 4 neageres or blackamoors cam runinge towardes me with their semetaries drawne; yf they could have catchte me theye would have hewed me all in peecis with there semeteris. When I cam to the wickett or gate, thare stood a great number of jemoglanes, praying that I myghte escape the handes of those runninge wolves; when I was got out of the gate they weare verrie joyfull that I had so well escaped their handes. I stayed not thare, but touke boate and went presently to my Lord and tould him how I had run for my life. Asoune as my drugaman came home, my lord made him beleve that he would hange him for leaving me in that dainger; but at laste granted him his Life, but forbid him to com to his any more. He was a Turke, but a Cornishe man borne. Now, as I was runinge for my life, I did se a litle of a brave show, which was the Grand Sinyor him selfe on horsbacke, many of his conquebines, som ridinge and som on foute, and brave fellowes in their kinde, that weare gelded men, and keepers of the conquebines; neagers that weare as blacke as geate (jet), but verrie brave; by their sides great semeteris; the scabertes semed to be all goulde, etc.

The 21, my Lord would not suffer me to goo to worke, because it was our Sabothe daye.

And that did louse me somthinge, for that daye the Grand Sinyor had appointed to com and sitt by me to se how I put my worke together, and was come upon the grene, which when the jemoglanes persaved, they run to mete him, and tould him that I came not to worke that daye. Than he returned againe, and thoughte that I had kepte my selfe awaye of purpse, and tharefore he would not com any more.

The 24 my worke was finished.

The 25 I wente to that place againe with the Coppagaw, to show him somethinges in the presente, and to se that I had lefte nothinge amise.

And than those jemoglanes was verrie earneste with me in perswation to stay and live thare.

The Laste of October my Lord imbassader wente to the vizear's house with all his train of Inglish men; for that daye the vizear[1] had appointed to end a contrivarcie which was betwixte him and the Franche imbassader[2]; but the Franche imbassader seinge us go by his house with a

---

[1] The vizier. Ibrahim was Grand Vizier just then, a creature of Mohamed III and the Validè Sultan's. He was the third Grand Vizier appointed in the year 1598, and was himself appointed for the third time. He had pillaged Egypt, assassinated the Druses, and during his period of office as Grand Vizier, which continued till his death in 1601, he perpetrated every horror possible. He married a daughter of the Sultan's, and kept in the favour of the Sultan's mother by giving her magnificent presents. (Von Hammer.)

[2] The French Ambassador at that time was François Savary de Brèves; he was appointed in 1589, and remained till 1606.

greater company than he could make, he would not com after us, the which was litle for his credditt. The 2 imbassaders made sute bothe for one thinge, and the vizear recaved great bribes of the Franche imbassader.

NOVEMBER.

The 12th of November I wente to Andranople gate, that is the farthest gate of Constantinople, towardes Andranople. Upon a goodly plaine withoute that gate, I se a carravan of the Taleste (tallest) Camels that ever I had sene in all my time. Than we returned into the Cittie to see Diverse monymentes, the which I would not for anything but that I had sene them. I have not time now to wryte them, but of force muste leave them un named untill a time of better Leasur.

This daye, in the morninge, I put on a pare of new shoues, and wore them quite oute before nyghte; but this daye I touke a great could with a surfett, by means whearof I was sore trubled with a burninge fever, and in great dainger of my Life. When I was somthinge recovered, by the helpe of God and a good fisition, it hapemed that thar was good Company reddie to com for Inglande, suche as in 2 or 3 years I could not have had the lik, if I had stayed behinde them, and they weare all desierus to have my company. My Lord was verrie unwillinge that I should goo at that time, because I was verrie wayke, not able to goo on foute one myle in a daye. But I desiered my lord to give me leve, for I had rether die by the way in doinge my good will to goo hom than staye to die thare, wheare I was perswaded I could not live if I did staye behinde them.

G

OF OUR PASIGE BY SEE TO VOLA (VOLO) IN ROMALEA.

My lord Ambassador would have me to carrie may beed with me, and gave order for the carreinge of it on ship borde, and also that when we came to travell by lande that I should have one horse to carrie me, and another to carrie my beed and my Clothes.

The 28 of November, beinge Weddensdaye, at 4 acloke in the after nowne, we departed from the cittie of Constantinople and Gallata in a Turkishe ship caled Carmesale,[1] in the which we had a discontented voyege, the Mr. and sailer wear so barbarus.

The nexte daye we came to the tow Castles caled Sestoes and Abidose, wheare som of our company wente ashore and touke in as good wyne as the worlde yeldethe, but it was but for their owne provition.

DECEMBER.

The firste of December we departed from thence, and after 7 myles we came to the ruins of Troy, and sailed behinde Tennidose, leavinge it on our Lefte hande.

The wynde beinge tow Large for our waike (weak) shipp, we came to an anker at the iland Lemnos the same daye.

At this place we weare in greate dainger of beinge caste awaye.

The sixte day we sett saile againe, havinge a faire wynde, but towardes nyghte we weare becalmed.

The 7th daye, the wynde beinge contrarie, we came to an anker by the shore of Romalea, the maine lande of Grece.

---

[1] *Carmesale*, probably from Karamosel, a seaport on the Gulf of Ismidt.

JOURNEY ACROSS GREECE. 83

The 8 day, the wynde cominge faire, we sett saile, and entred the rever.

The nexte morninge, beinge Sunday, we arived at Vola, in Romalea, the maine of Greece, not farr from Thessalonica.

The 10th we touke horsis, and began our jurnaye by land over the Confines of Thessale.

The 12th daye, at nyghte, we came to a towne caled Zetoune.[1] Beinge come to this towne, our horsis and mayls (mules) returned to Vola ; and heare we rested tow dayes. I may say rested, for I am sure we had no reste in the nyghte, our lodginge was so bade, be side the greate feare we wear in of haveinge our throtes cutt. The beste comoditie we had was that we had good store of good wyne and good cheape (sheep).

Heare we hired freshe horsis and mayles (mules). We weare but 8 men, yeat we had everie daye 12 horsis. . . . . Four of them weare to carrie our clothes, my beed, and wyne and vitell for 3 dayes. For some nyghtes we weare like to ly without dors, and at som touns we could not gitt any vitels. Whyle we weare in this toune we weare warned to keep close, for thar weare som of the Grand Sinyor's souldiers that weare cominge from the wars.

The 14th we departed from Zetoun, and haveing rid 6 or 7 myles, we began to climbe the hills of Parnassus, wheare we had all maner of ill wether, as thundringe, lightninge, rayne, and snow, and our waye was so bad as I thinke never did Christians travell the like. The mountains weare huge and steepe, stony, and the wayes verrie narrow, so that if a horse should have stumbled or slided, bothe horse and man had bene in greate dainger of theire lives.

Also we weare doged, or followed, by 4 stout villans that

---

[1] Zeitoun or Lamia, on the Gulf of Lamia.

weare Turkes. They would have perswaded our drugaman, which was our gid (guide), to have given his consente unto the Cuttinge of our throtes in the nyghte, and he did verrie wysely Conseale it from us, and delayed the time with them, not daringe to denye ther sute; and so theye followed us 4 dayes over Parnassus; but our drugaman everie nyghte give us charge to keepe good watche, espetialy this laste nyghte, for theye did purpose to goo no farther after us, and our Turke, whome I cale our drugaman, had premeded (permitted) them that that nyghte it should be don. Now, after he had given us warninge to kepe good watche, he wente unto them and made them drinke so muche wyne, or put somthinge in there wyne, that theye weare not only drunke but also sicke, that they weare not able to attempte anythinge againste us to hurt us, for the which we had verrie greate cause to give hartie thanks unto Almyghtie God, who was our chefeste savgaurd.

This nighte we Laye in a lytle village under a wonderfull heie rocke. Thoughe that countrie be contenually could, yeate the wemen thare never weare anythinge on their feete; they ar verrie well favored, but their feete be blacke and broade.

This man that was sente with us to be our drugaman, or intarpreater, was an Inglishe man, borne in Chorlaye in Lancashier; his name Finche. He was also in religon a perfit Turke, but he was our trustie frende.

The nexte daye, beinge the 17th, we came to Lippanta,[1] wheare our Turke revealed all this unto us, and these men we had sene, but never more than one at once, and he never stayed longe in our companye, for he came but to speake with our Turke aboute their vilanus plott.

This day we had bothe wynter and somer; in the

---

[1] Gulf of Corinth, or Lepanto; modern town called *Epakto*, ancient *Naupactus*.

morning we did tread upon froste and snowe; before nowne we came to the bottem of the mountaine, wheare did run a rever, so bige and stifly, beinge fulle of stons, so that we durste not adventur to rid over it; but our Turke, ridinge up and doune by the rever sid, espied tow stoute fellowes, the which wear naked and more than halfe savidge or wyld; he caled them unto him, and they unwilingly came. Than when he had talked with them, he comanded one of them to take his horse by the bridle and leade him throughe the rever, and so he did, havinge a greate stafe in his hand; than the other savige man touke Mr. Paul Pinder's horse by the heade and led him over, and than Sir Humfray Conisby his horse, and so one after a other. This rever was thicke and moddie, and was no other than mearly snow water, that dothe desend from those hils wheare it dothe contenualy snow.

Longe before nyghte we came to Lippanta, whiche is a greate haven toune. The people in it ar Turkes, Greekes, and Jues (Jews); but the greateste parte be Jues, the second Turkes. This Lippanta is a good haven toone, lyethe close to the sea, in the risinge of a hill, and upon that hill is a castell, the which hathe 2 counter wales, etc.

In diverse partes of the tounc are verrie fine Springs of exelente watter, and som of them do drive myls, the which myls be verrie straingly made, for only one water whele, withoute any cogwhele or anythinge els, dothe turne the stone, and will grinde 30 bushils a daye and upwards.

To make the like I am able to giv direckion.

Aboute this toune theye make greate store of verrie pleasante wynes, bothe whyte and reed.

Also heare dothe grow good store of Currante, greate plentie of orringis and lemons, palm sidrons, palm garnetes (pomegranates), dates and almons, and verrie good ayle (oil).

We lodged heare 3 nyghtes in the house of a Jew, who is by Inglishe men caled the honeste Jew, for he is verrie lovinge unto Inglishe men.

The 20th daye we touke a boote and croste the Gulfe of Lippanta, and the same nyghte came to Petras (Patras), in Morea. All our way thether we weare in good hoope to have hade greate entertainmente thare by Mr. Jonas Aldredge, an Inglish man who was Consoll thare; but he was gone 40 myles from home to hange a Jew. By misinge of him we weare constrained to lodge at a Romain's[1] house in suche maner as we (did) all our jurney; for thouge we had house roum enoughe, yeat we laye in our clothes upon the grounde, savinge at the Jewe's house in Lippanta thare was tow bed steades, Inglishe fation; but those would not sarve us all.

At this place Mr. Cunisbe was like to have cutt of a Jew's heade, who railed againste our Saviour; but Mr. Paull Pinder and the reste of our Company, with muche at dow, prevented it.

This Petrace (Patras) is in Morea, ether adjoyninge or a parte of Greece. Hear is a good porte for ships; but the towne is neare halfe a myle from the sea, in the risinge of a hill. A litle a bove the towne is a castle, but the towne and Castele ar but of smale strength.

Hear is indiferente store of Currante and ayle, and greate store of corne, for theye doo sell som to other contris that wante; also good store of goates and shepe and other catle. Because som of our companye was sicke, we restede heare 3 dayes.

The 24, being Christmas Eeve, we proseded in our jurnaye throughe Morrea. A bout nowne we came to a rever that we muste pass throughe; and, determaninge thare to baite, for we ever had vitals reddie dreste for

---

[1] The house of a Greek, "Romaic" as they call modern Greek.

3 dayes, we pitched and placed ourselves under the alder trees, to kepe us from the son; for thoughe it was Christmas eve, yeat we thoughte it to be as hoate wether as we have it in Inglande at Whitsontide, and swallowes came fliinge a bout us. Our dinner ended, we croste the rever, and entred into a foreste-like Cuntrie, wheare we saw nether towne nor villidge, but somtime a shipheardes Hoote (hut). At nyghte we founde 3 litle pore cottidges. In this wylde cuntrie, wheare we rested the moste part of the nyght; and whyle 4 of us slepte, the other 4 did watche, for we touke the place to be daingerus to sleepe it. I was one of the 4 that did watche in the fore parte of the nyghte. Betwixte 11 and 12 of the clocke we saw a bale of fierr, as bigge as a greate foot bale,[1] risinge out of the easte, and did rise of a greate heighte, and did give a greate lighte; than, faulinge towardes the weste, the lighte and fier bothe was less and less. Mr. Conisbe was verrie sorie that he had not sene that fier bale.

At 4 a clocke in the morninge, beinge Christmas daye, we Sett forwardes. This day we could not number the heardes of swine which we saw and paste throughe, and also heardes of shepe and goates, and we weare verrie muche trubled wethe shepheardes' doggs, the which weare like to pluck us of our horsis.

This cuntrie is a parte of the plains of Arcadia. Aboute (an) howre we cam to a villidge, wheare we did thinke to have boughte som vittels, but we could gitt nothinge but 8 egges.

When we weare a myle oute of this towne upon the plains, the day before was verrie fair, but now thar fell a

---

[1] The game of football is much older in England than cricket; the first mention of it is in the reign of Edward III, and it became so rough a game in the time of James I, that, in his *Basilikon Doron* he describes it "as meeter for laming, than making able the users there-of."

sodon shower of raine, the which came downe as if it had bene powered downe with bouls, and no winde; but our horsis stood stone still, and would not stur one foote. The shower lasted not a bove halfe a quarter of an hour, and for a great parte of that time for a myle round aboute us we could se no ground for water. Upon a sodon it seaste, and the water was gone, all savinge som which laye in hollow placis.

Pasinge throughe this plaine, upon our righte hande we myghte se the seae, and upon the sandes an infinite company of wyld swans.[1] Upon our lefte hande we sawe highe mountains.

At nyghte we came to a Castell, caled Castell Turneaes,[2] the which dothe stand upon a verrie hie hill, posseste with a garreson of Turkes, and is 3 myles from the seae. It is a Castele that may be kepte with a verrie few men. The waye to it is so lade[3] that ordenance cannot be broughte anythinge near it.

On St. Stevn's Day we did thinke to have croste a parte of the sea to the iland Zante, but the wynde was so hie that we could not.

On St. John's Day, the wynde beinge somwhat abatted, we carried our supportes[4] and other Lugedge to the seasid, wheare we weare in hoope to find som boats. Cominge thether, we founde a great markett of swyne and other cattell, and so thar is everie day, beinge faire weather. The iland Zante hathe all theire provition of vittell from thence. From this place it is but 12 or 18 myles by sea, yeate we had muche adow to hier a hogge boate to carrie us to Zante. For our passage and carriege of our stufe we payed seven Chickens (sequins), or 7 pecis of gould which weare nyne shillinges a peece.

---

[1] Probably cranes.
[2] Castel Tornese.
[3] Ugly, Fr. *laide*.
[4] Supportes, *i.e.*, provisions.

Heare, at the sea sid, we parted from our drugaman, or the Turke that was our gidd from Constantinople. Thoughe he was a Turke, his righte name was Finche, borne at Chorlaye in Longcashier.

OUR ENTERTAINMENT AT ZANTE.

Beinge come to Zante, we could not be permited to goe a shore, because the governers of the toune did understand that we came from Constantinople, or oute of Turkie. It (is) ther Custom to deale so with all straingers that come out of Turkie, if they have not a letter of health from some Venitian or Ittalian.

So by the judgimente of the Provodore and the tow Sinyors of Healthe, we wear comited to the lazaretto, which is a prison for all suche travelers, and thare to remaine for 10 dayes; and if, at the ende of 10 dais, any man be founde sicke when the Sinyors of Healthe com to examon and se them, than they muste remaine thare for 10 daies more.

JENNARIE.

By suche meanes as our martchantes who ar facktors thare did use, we had poticke (pratique) the 6 of Jenuarie, but at our firste cominge we weare in doubte to have laine thare longer in this prison, but we hade a greate favor showede us, for we weare not put into the ordenarie preson, but into a new house wheare never any bodie had dwelte, and it was cloce to the seae. Also the water men which brought us from Cstell Turneas[1] was commited with us, because they broughte us in theire boote; and we weare constrained to finde them vittals for 7 dayes; for than the Sinyors of Healthe came unto us to se if any man weare

---

[1] Castel Tornese.

sicke. Than Mr. Paule Pinder desiered that they would releace the water men, and ease us of that charge. So theye weare contented that the water men should have proticke, or libertie, if theye would leape out at a window into the sea, and washe them selues over heade with theyer clothis on; the which theye weare verrie lothe to dow, but Mr. Connisbye drew his simmeterie, and swore a greate othe that if they would not leape out quickly he would cut of theier legges, and made them perforce leap oute; and so we weare rid of them.

Many thinges which hapened in the time of our impresoment, for wante of time I doo omit.

Februarie.

We stayed in the iland of Zante fortie and 6 dayes, ever expectinge som ship to com in thare that would Carrie us to Venis, or els for Inglande, but the firste that came war the Heckter, in the which I wente out of Inglande; and we did thinke that she by that time had bene in Inglande. When I saw her I was somwhat sorie, for I had a great desier to have gone to Venis; but yeat I was glad againe, because I knew that in her was a sur passidge, and emongste men that did know me.

The 26 of Februarie, in the morninge, we departed from Zante. The nexte day we had ill wether and the wynd contrarie, so that we returned again, and went in at Safflanee,[1] in Morea. In our company was the Edward Boneventur[2] and the Swallow. In that harbur we founde

---

[1] Bay of Argostoli in Cephalonia.

[2] The *Edward Bonaventure* and the *Susan* are the two ships which Richard Hakluyt, in his Collection of Voyages, vol. ii, 285, tells us had a fight with 11 gallies and 2 frigates of the king of Spain, within the Straits of Gibraltar, and came off victorious.

In Harleian MS. 1579, f. 150, we find "a note of all the shipps that's bound for Turkey out of England and the burden of them and the

the great Susan[1] of London, a ship of 3 hundrethe tun ; and thare was the Riall Defence of Brstoll. The laste of this monthe cam in thare the martchante Boniventur.

MARCHE 1599.

The firste of Marche came in a litle shipe caled the Diamon.

In this contrie is verrie good muscadine,[2] and thar is also som Currante. This harbur is verrie good ; what wether so ever blow, a ship is without dainger thare. On the weste sid dothe stand a pretie toune caled Luksere[3] ; on the easte, a Castell. When we wente to sea from hence we weare in Company eighte ships ; beinge 4 or 5 leages at sea, the wynde came contrarie, and like to be foule wether, so that we returned againe to the same harber ; in the morninge the wynde came fair againe, and we sett saile againe.

The sixte daye we paste the Gulfe of Venis, the which daye the wynde came all southe weste a smale gale, so that we could not keepe our course ; but as we weare

---

Captaynes names". The *Hector* is given in this list as of 300 tons, and under the command of Captain Harris. The *Bonaventure* was also 300 tons, Captain Childie. Dallam here distinguishes between the merchant ship *Bonaventure* and the Queen's ship *Edward Bonaventure :* this latter ship and the *Swallow* were both probably those engaged in the destruction of the Spanish Armada, when the *Bonaventure* was commanded by Captain Regmon and the *Swallow* by Captain Hawkins. The *Bonaventure* appears in the list of many of the expeditions of the time under Frobisher and Sir Francis Drake. (*Archæologia*, vol. xxxiv.)

[1] Perhaps the ship *Susan* which in 1581 carried our first Ambassador to the Porte, Mr. Harbone, to Constantinople.

[2] Ital. *moscato*, a name given in those days to several sweet Italian and French wines.
"Quaff'd off the muscadel."
(*Taming of the Shrew*, iii, 2.)

[3] Lixure, in Bay of Argostoli in Cephalonia.

turninge in the nighte, the wynde came faire at southe and by easte, and contenued the nexte daye.

The 9th daye we descried Mount Etnaye, but thare it is caled Muntabell,[1] the burninge mountaine in Cisillia. In the Afternoone we came under the shore of the same lande; at the firste we did thinke to com to an anker because the wynd was bad, yeate torninge up and downe by the shore, we saw the watche toweres make lightes at the topp of theire tours, to shew unto other watche toures how many ships they saw that weare not theire frendes; for thare be of those touers round aboute the iland, so that yf one Touer do show so many lightes one after another as they se ships, it will goo round aboute the iland in a verrie shorte time. Yf we had com to an anker we feared them note, but theye weare a frayed of us; yeat doubtinge the wynde would be worse, or else no wynd at all, we kept at sea. The next day we weare so neare the shore that we saw a greate company of souldiers, bothe horse and foote, gathered together.

For all that, towardes eyghte we came to an anker neare the shore. When the wynde came faire, everie ship sett saile before our Anker was upe or wayed. The other 7 ships beinge under saile, they gave chase to a Spainishe shipe which was goinge to Malta with wheate, and when she saw so many Inglishe ships under saile she thoughte it better for her to goo backe againe to Sesillia than to keepe her cource. Our shipe beinge the hindmoste of all the 8, yeate we out wente them all, and touke that prise There was but 10 men in her; it was but a smale barke; she was loden with wheate. When our sailers had pillidged her our Mr. gave the ship and wheate to Captain Coke, a man of ware; we had out of her verrie fine whyte

---

[1] *Montebello.* Cf. the Greek love of euphemism, which gave the name of *Kalliste*, or the most beautiful, to the volcano of Santorin.

breade and good Chese. In the nyghte folloinge thare rise a myghtie storme, the wynde at weste, at which time we weare 30 leages from Capp Passaro,[1] wheare we weare laste at Anker. This storme contenued 48 houres, that we weare not able to beare any saile; in this storm the prise which we hade taken was Caste awaye.

The 13th day, beinge Weddensday, we weare in sighte of Cape Passaro againe, beinge driven backe againe thre score Leagues, and thar came to an 'Anker againe, wheare we founde a greate Flemishe shipe. That nyghte the watche touers made lightes as they did before. The nexte morninge we wayed Anker again, but we weare driven further backwardes. The second nyghte after we recovered that place againe; this truble we touke to be a punishmente for takinge of that prise. The nexte day, beinge Sundaye, and the 16th daye of Marche, it was verrie calme and extreame hoote wether; at 8 a clocke at nyghte we sett saile, for the wynde came faire at easte, but a verrie smale gale; the next day we weare becalmed betwixte Malta and Cesillia.

The 19th we mett with an Inglishe ship caled the John and Francis, neare the coste of Cesillia, loaden with Turkes and Jues bounde for Alicksandrea.

The 21, beinge Good Fridaye, the wynde came faire, and broughte us to Panthaleara (Pantelaria).

One Easter day the wynd was direcktly againste us, and drive us backe.

The 25, beinge Tusdaye, we mett with the Rebeka of London and the Gren Dragon of Bristoll.

The 29, the wynde beinge faire, we paste by Cape Bone; 10 leagues from that we paste by a litle Ilande caled Simbre,[2] a verrie hie mountaine also the same daye by Porta Farren,[3] the goinge into Tunis.

---

[1] Cape Passaro is southern Cape of Sicily. [2] Zembra.
[2] Porto Farina, the western point of the Bay of Tunis.

The firste daye of Aprill we Croste the Gulfe of Lions. Our vitals beinge verrie badd, I was invited to diner with our marchantes in the great Cabbin, and beinge at diner, we harde the crye of a mearmaide, like as yf one had hailed our shipe ; but our bootswane forbid any man to make answeare or to louke oute.

The second daye the wynde came faire; the thirde day the wynde being bade, we came to an anker at Firma[1] Teara, wheare our botes wente a shore for freshe water and stores, not inhabeted, but with bannished men thare. Neare unto a watche tower we founde a man lyinge deade withoute a heade, for it had bene cut of by som Turks as we supposed. This Iland is verrie neare a place or towne in Spaine caled Iverse.[2] Our ship did rid but a litle from the toune and Castle, which Castell is verrie stronge. The 6 daye, beinge Sondaye, in the morninge, as we weare wayinge anker, Thare came a boate from that toune, and broughte our marchantes for a presente tow gootes, oringis, Lemons, leekes, and Chibbals,[3] and grene beans, indeco, lettes, and other earbs. The 7th daye we sailed by Caldaroune[4] and by Alligante, which is an hondrethe Leagues within the straites mouthe ; thare we mett with tow Flemishe sale that came from Talloune.[5] The 8 daye we weare becalmed before Alligante. The 9 daye we paste by Cape Pale,[6] in the nyghte folloinge by Cape

---

[1] Formentera, one of the Balearic Islands.
[2] Iviza.
[3] Chibbal ; Fr. *ciboule;* Ital. *cipolla,* a small onion or chive.
" Ye eating rascals,
" Do execution upon these, and *chibbals.*"
(Beaumont and Fletcher, *Bonduca.*)
[4] Las Calderonas, a small village on the borders of Alicante and Murcia.
[5] Walloon.   Teuton name for Celts of Flanders and Isle of Walcheren.   [6] Cape Palos.

Degate[1]; in the morninge we weare becalmed before Alama,[2] a fair toune in Spaine, as it is said, not moche inferrier to London. We weare in a maner becalmed all that daye and the nyghte followinge.

This day we saw greate store of the spane (spawn) of whales, whearof they make spermacetie; it did swym upon the water as the whale lefte it: upon the water it showed reed; but when we touke upe som of it in a buckete, it was whyte, and like grease.

Also this daye, beinge a verrie smale gale of wynde, a great fishe caled a storke (shark?), of a marvalus length, did follow our ship, sid by sid, with his eyes a bove water waytinge for a praye; for if a man had come withe in his lengthe of the water, he would hardly have escaped him.

Our Mr. goner made reddie his harpinge iron, and, when the sutle fishe se him reddie to pitche it at him, he staied and fell behinde the ship, and came up on the other side, and sarved him so 2 or 3 times; but at laste he hitt him a litle behinde the heade with a full blowe, but his skine was so harde that the iron turned duble and would not enter anythinge at all, only we myghte se a litle whyte spott wheare it lighte. Nether did the fishe make any show of felinge it, but turned him a boute, and wente awaye direcktly from the ship.

The 11th daye, the wynde beinge muche againste us, as we weare turninge to gitt somthinge of the wynde, we came neare unto the Castell Defeare[3] in Spaine, and verrie neare unto the shore, we loukinge still when the Castell would shoute at us, but they would not. Than, beinge com less than a league from the shore, we had no wynde at all, and so it contenued all the nexte daye. By this meanes our fleete weare scattered one a league from

---

[1] Cape de Gata.   [2] Alhama.   [3] Castel de Ferro.

another, so that yf the Spainishe gallis had come forthe they myghte have taken us one after another.

That daye it was strainge to se how the porposis did rune in greate fleetes or scoles (shoals), in what maner it is credable to reporte, and the noyes that they made.

The 13th we mett with a ship of Yarmouthe. The 15th we came neare to Gibletore,[1] wheare we mett with 3 Inglishe men (or ships) and one Flemin, which made our fleete 14 saile; but the wynde was so contrarie that we coulde not com neare the narrow gutt of the straite's mouthe, but laye becalmed unto Budgrow,[2] also to Marvels,[3] and Grande Malligan.

The 16th we weare becalmede. The nexte morninge we saw 2 greate whalis, which wear so huge that we thoughte them to be tow gallis or frigates: ite was an extreame hoote day.

The 17th, at 10 a clocke, the wynde came faire at northe-easte, so that aboute a 11 of the clocke at nyght we entred into the narrow gutt, which is 4 leagues in lengthe. At the son risinge we paste bye Cape Sprott,[4] which is 10 leages withoute the straite's mouthe, at which time we had in our sighte 21 saile of ships.

The same daye, towardes nyghte, one shipe in our Companye, caled the Rebecka, the which at that time was the moste speedie of saile, touke her leve of us, with an intente to bringe the firste newes into Ingland of our safe cominge homwardes.

The nexte morninge, beinge the 19th, we descried Mount Chegos,[5] a hie lande in Spaine, 7 leagues from the Southe Cape.

The 20th, in the morninge, beinge Sundaye, verrie arlye,

---

[1] Gibraltar. [2] Burgo.
[3] Marbella. [4] Cape Spartel.
[5] Probably Los Guigos, behind Algeciras.

one in our mayntope saw a saille Cominge towardes us
direckly; and when we myghte well desarne the hull of
her, we did know her to be the Rebecka, the same shipe
that touke her leve of us tow dayes before to carrie newes
of our safe cominge homwards. The Cause of the returne
of that ship was for that tow galliouns of Spaine did give
Chace unto her, yeate nothinge so good of saile as she;
but the Mr. of the Rebecka thoughte them to be Carreks[1]
Cominge from the Indies loden with greate welthe, whearin
he was muche desaved, for theye weare tow men-of-warr
that did ly in wayte for our ship, as afterwardes theie
confesed. When they weare come neare unto us, we did
also thinke them to be but than cominge from the Indies.
One of them was a shipe of one thousande tow hundrethe
tone, the other 8 hundrethe. Our Mr. was verrie unwillinge to feighte with them, but our saylors was verrie
desierus; so we presently wente to prayers, and than our
gonors made reddie their ordinance, feightes[2] oute, and
everie man his place appointed, and all thinges in reddines,
we havinge the wynde of the Spanishe ships. Our ship,
caled the Heckter, laye sid by sid to the greate gallioune,
and an other Inglishe shipp Called the Greate Susan laye
close by the other, ever expectinge who would give the
firste shoute. All the other ships that weare before in our
Companye weare gone a league and more of from us,
without dainger of any shott. Thare was great odes
betwixte our shipp, that ship was caled the Great Suzana

[*Here some pages are missing.*][3]

unto him, and desiered him to give me and my mate

---

[1] Large ships of burden, Spanish *caraca*.
"They were made like *carracks*, only strength and stowage."
(Beaumont and Fletcher, *Coxc.*, Act ii.)
[2] *Vide* note 1, p. 8.
[3] These pages, doubtless, relate the battle, which, as the sequel shows, was a victory for the English.

Harve leve to go a shore thare, and we would take poste horse, and make what speed we Could to London ; so at laste he granted me and 3 more leve to goo, upon Condition that we would take the Spainishe Captaine with us, and bringe him safe unto the marchantes, the which we promesed to doo.

Than we wente a shore at Dover, and our trompetes soundinge all the waye before us into the towne, wheare we made our selves as merrie as Could, beinge verrie glad that we weare once againe upon Inglishe ground. After diner, thar Came into the toune a Franche imbasseter, beinge accompened with divers knightes and jentlmen of Kente; so, at tow of the Clocke, we touke poste horse to Canterburrie, and from thenc to Rochester that nyghte, and the nexte day to London.

PART II.

DR. COVEL'S DIARY.

DR. COVEL'S DIARY.

CAP. 2.—OUR LEAVING THE DOWNS, AND PASSAGE THROUGH THE CHANNEL TO SEA.

EPT. 21. In the morning we had a fresh gale at N.N.E., and it so continued between N. and E. a fair wind for us. About half-an-hour after eleven we set sail out of the Downes, being seven general ships, for the Levant; Captain Partridge in the Turkey Merchant, for Scanderoon.
Capt. Joh. Hill, in the London Merchant,} for Smyrna and
Capt. Pain, in the Speedwell,   } Constantinople.
Capt. Dier Roles, in the Mary and Martha,}
Capt. Kerington, in the Levant Merchant, } for Smyrna.
Capt. Stocy, in the Pearl,   }

Capt. Bromwell, in the Tho. and Frances,} for Smyrna and Scanderoon.

Our convoy were, Capt. Robinson, in the Greenwich,[1] as Admiral (who was to leave us at the next end of Candia, and go on to Scanderoon with the Turkey Merchant), and

---

[1] Most of these ships are alluded to in the State Papers, when they came in to be cleaned, when they brought in a prize, etc., etc. Sir Thomas Allen was once in command of the *Greenwich*.

Capt. Wild, in the Assurance, as Vice-Admiral, who was to go with all the rest of us as far as Smyrna, with *Virginia men*, and some *coasters* and *streightsmen*.[1] We made up in all about 100 sail going out of the Channel. I took my passage upon the London Merchant, with that very able and long-experienced Seaman, a most carefull and understanding commander, Capt. John Hill, whose honest, sober, and discreet management of all his affaires I can never sufficiently commend, as I must never forget his singular respect and kindnesse to myself.

CAP. 3.—OUR PASSAGE FROM THE LAND'S END TO THE STREIGHTSMOUTH.

Saturday, Sept. 24. About $\frac{1}{2}$ an hour past two, afternoon, we weigh'd anchor, and stood of with an easy sail. Next morning, by eight o'clock, we were clear of *the Land's End*, leaving it N. 6 W. about nine leagues, and we told 75 sail in company.

Sept. 26. The wind came up at South. It blew hard, and brought much rain. We made several tacks, and our *Freshmen* passengers were all in a miserable, squeamish, and puking condition. I had held up perfectly well till that morning, when I began (as well as the rest) to find some odde wamblings in my stomack. Wherefore, counting it very healthfull, at first coming to sea, to evacuate what humours might overflow, I went and sat down in the Captaine's Round-house[2] on purpose to provide that designe; for the higher any one sit within the ship, the motion of it affects him the more, and cause his giddinesse and *mawkishnesse* to be the greater. After I had sat there

---

[1] Those which went into the Mediterranean.
[2] The Round House was an erection abaft the mainmast for the accommodation of the ship's officers.

till I was sufficiently squeamish, I went down to the Cook and got at least thre pints of warme small beer into my belly, and then returned up to the Round-house again, where the reeling of the Ship had its desired effect. I then went down and took a second dose of warme beer, and so came up to the Round-house again; and after somewhat a longer pause then before, I fell to my former exercise. This I repeated several times, till at last, when I cam down to the *wast*[1] of the ship, and took a turn or two there, I found my stomack begin to settle. I immediately drank a spoonful of *Purle*[2] *royall* (as they call it), that is, *sack and wormwood*, and a little while after I took as much more. Thus for a while supping not above one spoonfull at a time (sometimes of old Hock, sometimes of sack, ʼwith wormwood), I afterwards continued walking gently and santering up and down the Ship, till by noon I could have eaten and drunk as well as any one. But I dined onely with a little fresh broth, and as much *Cremor tartari* in it as made it palatable; and with a cautious and moderate diet, I was very well in lesse than 24 houres, and I thank God I never was in the least sea-sick after in any weather whatever.

Sept. 29. The Admiral called all the Turkish commanders on board. He told them that the Dutch and we had chased six Algier men of War on shoar at *Cape Spartel* (which is the most northern *Cape* of Africk, just at the *Streight's* mouth) not far from *Tangier*, and that we had sunk, and fired, and destroy'd them all, and released

---

[1] "The waist of a ship is a hollow space of about five feet in depth, contained between the elevations of the quarter-deck and the forecastle, and having an upper-deck for its base or platform. (Falconer, *Shipwreck*, ii.)

[2] *Purl* was the name originally given to beer with an infusion of wormwood. A *Purlman* was one who sold it to sailors in the Thames. (Mayhew, *London Labour and London Poor*, vol. ii, p. 108.)

many English and Dutch prisoners. He had received the news by some Dutch Merchant ship, which that day past by us; for all ships, if friends, when they meet upon the sea, *share* up to one another, and sometimes lay by their sails, or send of their boats, mutually to hear and relate what newes they have.

Saturday, October 1*st.* The Admiral and Vice-Admiral, and several Commanders, came on board us, and dined with us; and on the 3rd we all dined on board *the Turkey Merchant.* When we thus treat one another, if the weather be fair and will permit it, we seldome fail of some merry fellows in every *ship's crew,* who will entertain us with several diversions, as divers sorts of odde Sports and Gambols; sometimes with their homely drolls and *Farses,* which in their corrupt language they nickname Interlutes; sometimes they dance about the mainmast instead of a may-pole, and they have variety of *forecastle songs,* ridiculous enough.

Oct. 5. The wind blew hard all night, and with the labouring of the Ship the table and chaires in the great Cabin brok loose from the cords with which they were *lash't,* and hurt our surgeon and some of the gentlemen that were up there.

Oct. 7. At 6 o'clock at night we saw to S.E. 25 sail going southward, and we saw them again, next morning, about 6 o'clock. We took them for *Newfoundland* men going for Lisbon and the Streights.

Oct. 8. About 10 o'clock *the Burlinges* appear'd S. from us (which are rocks lying of from the nethermost Cape of the last stretch before you go into *Lisbon*). We were in 39° 55′ of latitude, and observ'd a current on those coasts setting Southwards. That night we lay by. Next morning we reckon'd 26 sail between us and the Rock of Lisbon. They were Flemings, and we supposed them to be the same which we had seen the day before standing to the Southwards.

Oct. 9. Sunday, about 2 afternoon, some Hollanders came into our Company. It blew a violent *gust of* wind; we lay by with our head to the westward all night till next morning.

Oct. 11. At 4 afternoon the ships from *Cadiz* or *Cales* went in. We saw there in the Harbour a great ship at Anchor, with the English Flag at the main top mast head, which we concluded to be Sir Thos. Allen.[1]

Oct. 12. At noon we were in 18 fathom water northwards of from *Tangier.* The Admiral's boat went ashoar to carry letters and newes, but stay'd not long, so that in 18 dayes we went from Plymouth Sound to the Streight's mouth.

CAPT. 4.—FROM THE STREIGHT'S MOUTH TO TUNIS.

* * * * *

The seamen have a custome to demand passage-money of every one that never past the streights before. Those that refuse to pay, they seise them and duck them down from *main yard* end into the Sea. There were several that chose rather to be plunged than to part with their money; for many that could swim would in calm weather, for a smal reward, leap from *the main yard* and into the Sea, but they alwayes took care to fall streight up (end wayes) upon their feet, with their legs close, into the Sea; for to fall otherwise so high on the water (especially upon the belly) would bruise or spoil a man.

---

[1] Sir Thomas Allen is frequently alluded to by Pepys as a brave soldier and sailor in the wars against the Dutch. He was an admiral of high repute during Charles II's reign. In 1664 he was appointed to command the Mediterranean squadron, and captured the Dutch "Smyrna fleet".

Our seamen told us that they had the very same custome whenever they past between the *Burlenges* and the main land of *Portugal,* in their voyages to *Lisbon ;* and a French sailor who was on board us told us of a mad ceremonious fashion they had of dousing every freshwaterman (with a pail of sea-water), which they nicknamed his Baptism, if he never before had past between *Les Scenes* and the firme land at Bretaigne.

Having run a convenient while on the Barbary coast, we shar'd of toward *Gibraltar,* and Oct. 12, at 4 o'clock, we were within lesse than a league of it, having it N. b. W. We saw two Flag Ships in the Bay. The mountain that overlooks the Town of old was called *Calpe.* It seem'd, indeed, very high—much higher than *Abila,* especially when we were near it.[1] The side to the south shows reddish, and hollow'd in, as if it had been battered down or mouldred away. The top is little and flat, and this, perhaps, might make some of the Antients to compare it to half of a broken pitcher inverted, or turn'd with the bottom upwards. It shew'd very steep towards the E., but in all its shapes as we past bye I could by no means fancy either it or Abila in the least.

At six o'clock we met with two of our men of war going out of the Streights. About 12 o'clock that night, or something after, *The Pearl* fell foul upon our Ship, and rent of *the Gallery* on *the Larboard* side. Some of the passengers (who lay in the G. Cabin) were up, and one of them had just been in that very gallery, but feeling it somewhat cold, he did not stay, but stept into the G. cabin, and in that very moment this damage happened. The crash of the gallery alarmed us all, but we soon recovered ourselves when we understood the whole matter. However, we had all, indeed (especially that Gentleman) a

---

[1] Calpe and Abyla, anciently known as the Pillars of Hercules.

great deliverance, for had the wind or waves become so high as to have rowl'd *the Pearl* upon us with greater violence, we might have (one or both) gone to the bottome. S. D. G.

Oct. 13. About 11 o'clock the whole fleet was becalm'd on a sodain under *C. Malaga;* yet, by 6 that evening, we had a stiff gale for half-an-hour. At 8 we came to anchor before *Malaga,* in 14 fathom water. Next morning, about ten, we went on shore and hosted with Signor Carlos, an Irishman.

The first thing we went to see was the *Major Domo,* or great Church. It is, to the best of my remembrance, in a manner, round, *Scalop't,* as it were, on the sides into 6 or 7 hollow moldings, like vast great *niches;* and in every one was an Altar for private Masse.[1] The Cupola is hang'd upon rows of pillars, set in a round likwise, so as we may walk conveniently between them and the Entrance into those round Isles or *niches.* We were there in the time of high masse, yet, so long as we were bare-headed, and behaved ourselves gravely and civilly, we might walk up and down and se every thing without the least molestation. One of our company (a young man who had had the misfortune of too precise an Education), seing we design'd to go into the *Domo,* came to me and my brethren (the other two Chaplaines going for Smyrna and Aleppo), and askt us whether we were not afraid, and touch't in conscience, to go into an *Idol Temple,* as he cal'd it. I told him I was of St. Paul's mind, *To me an Idol is nothing.* I could myself freely go into it, if it was an *Idol Temple,* for God, the searcher of hearts, knowes that I do not do it to joyn in their way of worship, but onely to se it and be the better able to discourse of it as an eye witnesse, and confute what was really unlawfull in it. But I bad him have a

---

[1] There are fifteen side-chapels in Malaga Cathedral.

care; if he had any scruple, I advised him to go home, which he did. I mention this passage here, because this young man that was so extremely scrupulous, fell into great debaucheries afterwards at Smyrna, and at last turn'd Turk. Let the greatest Saint *that thinketh he standeth, take heed lest he fall.*

We thence went to see Sta. Victoria, which is a convent of *Augustines.* In their Church are (ἀναθήματα) *offerings* hang'd up without number, in memory of deliverances and miracles wrought by that Saint, which they there call *virgo miraculosissima.* Amongst the rest is a small boat of reeds, cover'd over with a kind *of Tarpaulin,* about 4 or 5 yards long, in which 7 Christians (after their prayers, I suppose, to this Saint) escaped from captivity at Algiers to this port. There hangs up the effigies of a child that was raised from the dead, and a serpent of great length (I guest it 4 or 5 yards), which had been destroy'd by Christians in Africa, and sent hither. There is within (as in most convents) a fair square court, cloyster'd above and beneath; in the upper cloyster are the Brethren's cells, in the lower the walls are hang'd with pictures, most of them representing miracles wrought by their saints. One was how a dish of fry'd fish, by a crosse of the Saint's finger (I think it was the founder of their Order), revived, and leapt down out of the dish as quick as ever they were. Another was how he supported a stone of 100 tons weight (that was falling upon him and his attendants) only with his stick, or, rather, with a bullrush in his hand. My brother Huntingdon[1] and I convers't with the good Fathers that went about with us in the Latine, and as any very remarkable thing occurr'd we interpreted the story in English to our company. Now it happen'd that one *Paulo,* a Greek (who had been in England some time to learn our

---

[1] *I.e.,* brother clergyman.

language, in order to be a *Turgeman*[1] to our nation at Smyrna), being by, and hearing us recount these miracles, very indiscreetly broke out into a loud laughter. The Fathers were very highly and very justly incensed at it, and we had much adoe to pacify them, and excuse the folly of the fact. It hath been a warning to me to make better choyce of my company in such places ever since, least I might suffer for the men's rudeness and childish indiscretion.

Therefore that evening, with more wary friends, we went and saw (*San Domingo*) the Convent of the Dominicians. It was a very fine and sweet place, built much after the fashion of the former, but much more beautifull and stately. In the middle of the court was a little garden, enclosed with a hedge of oranges and lemons, like our codling[2] hedges; in the quarters stood small orange and lemon trees, and pots of several very pleasant greens. Santering up and down, we walk't into the Upper Cloyster; and seeing a door and entry open into a fair room, where somebody was talking, one of our company, who spoke Spanish, ventur'd boldly in, but sodainly made a profer to retire, as being mistaken. It happen'd to be a very Reverend Father's lodging, who presently stept out to us and accepted our apologyes as being strangers, and not knowing our way out. He earnestly invited us in and gave us a noble treat of sweetmeats and fruits, and several sorts of wine. He afterwards caryed us down into a large garden, and bad us gather what oranges and lemons, and what fruits and flowers we pleased, and at last brought us out to the gate, where, with all decent respect, and many thanks for his extraordinary courtesy and civility, we took

---

[1] Dragoman.
[2] Codling = a crab- or hedge-apple. "A codling when 'tis almost an apple." (*Twelfth Night*, i, 5.)

our leave. He had in his chamber very many excellent pictures; one was of Christ taken from the Crosse, which he valued at 3,000 dollars; besides the admirable painting, I took especiall notice of the unusuall manner of the head, the face being roundish, the hair being flaxen, or inclined to yellow, and the beard short and curl'd round about the chin.

Next morning, Oct. 15, an ingenious Gaille man[1] (one Mr. Jolly) and I, by chance were standing by one of the gates of the City towards the Sea, and talking of the strength of the Town. I happen'd to say that gate seem'd so decay'd and crazy, as surely it could not well be moved without falling to pieces. There stood a man just by us in mean habit (but dressed in all things like a Spaniard) who, in as good English as we could speak, said, *Yes, Sir, I assure you it is shut every night and opened every morning, as you may guesse by the Hinges;* which were then almost worn away. We were not a little surprised, and we made this reflection in ourselves upon it, that Strangers ought to be very carefull what they talk in their own language in other Countryes before them whome they know not, for they may be better understood then they think for, and easily entrapt or involved in difficultyes beyond what they intended or imagin'd. However, it happen'd otherwise with us now, for, talking farther with him, he proved an high man who was maryed and lived in Town; he was extreamly civil to us, and offer'd to show us what we had not yet seen of the City. We accepted the favour, and with him we went to several Nunneryes, where, instead of dull, mopish, vapour'd women, or grave precise matrons, as we expected, we found as pleasant, bright, and airy ladyes as ever I met with all elsewhere in all my life. Their particular chat is not worth the recounting,

---

[1] Galley-man.

but it was extreamely gentile, merry, and diverting. We past for Captaines (I suppose our Interpreter had named us so), and they beg'd of us every where for some cheese, or butter, or Holland, or thin stuffs. We always stick to one answer, assuring them that we had no provisions to spare, for we put into that port on purpose to buy some; we were laden only with Tin and Lead for Turkey, and some cloth which was not our own. They offer'd us many fine works and several sorts of sweetmeats to sale; we bought some which were very admirably well done. My Lord Baltimore[1] had then a daughter in one of these Nunneryes which we saw (I think it was at *San Bernado*); she was but a girl, and placed there onely for education, and undoubtedly (setting religion aside) it is a way of breeding infinitely beyond all our English Schools. A very lovely sister there beg'd a silver pick-tooth and case of me, and return'd me for it a pretty little picture of the V. M., curiously wrought, all with coloured straw. Platonic love is here very much esteem'd and practised, and really I have that charity and Justice to believe it may be done with perfect innocence. In one place we found a jolly Friar talking at the grate with the Sisters, who, with great civility, retired so soon as we came in. Once, as we were sitting by them, in came a surly, stately Don, very richly attired; and after a profound reverence towards the Ladys, and a kind of a scornfull nod to us, he lean'd his head to the wall by the side of the grate, and with his armes and leggs acrosse, and his eyes fixt upon one of them (which was very ingenious, but not handsome), he stood thare in such a fixed posture as, had it not been sometimes for a sneaking silly sigh (true or feign'd, I know not), you

---

[1] A daughter of Cecil, second Lord Baltimore, who founded the colony of Maryland, which his father, the first Lord Baltimore, had projected.

would have thought he rather saw Medusa's head then his dear Dulcinea's face. He spoil'd all our mirth; all was hush'd, and after a decent pause we left him to his *Devotions*. He askt our Interpreter whether we were Catholics; he answered Yes, and all past very well.

One of our English Merchants there (of good repute, though I shall not vouch the truth of his story), hearing me recount this adventure, told us that about 7 or 8 years before, soon after his first coming to Malaga, he had got acquainted with a young Sister, and often waited upon her, as well to divert himself as to perfect his Spanish Tounge; for there at the grate you have all the newes that is stirring, and the best and most refined language. He by degrees was wheedled into such fondnesse, as the presents which he had at several times made her came in a short time to about 40 lb. He found (being but a young beginner) that his trade would not bear so expensive a diversion, where upon his visits were more seldome, and his presents very few and meane, and at last he came no more at her at all, nor answer'd one line, though he received many most passionate ones from her, and there had past many such (as the manner is) betwixt them before. Not long after, he was one evening set upon by a Rogue (which she had hired), and was desperately wounded, and narrowly escaped with his life. The *Rufian* soon after confest it, being himself mortally wounded and taken in such another enterprise. And here I cannot omit another story of our worthy Captain. About 8 or 10 yeares since, he had great concernes with a wealthy Spaniard, a merchant of this City, and very much kindesse past between them, insomuch as they call'd brothers, and Captain Hill lay on shoar at his house and was freely treated there, sometimes for many dayes together. It happen'd that another Spaniard (a neighbour who often came thither, and was of both their familiar acquaintance), being a great *Bigot*, and very zealous for the Roman way of worship, often made attempts upon our Captain to make him a Prosolyte; and there being once some great Festivall and a solemne procession to be made, he desired our Friend to be there, adding that he doubted not in the least that he would then yield and be convinced of all his errors. The Captain, having appointed either some business or some other recreation, civilly excused himself, and thank't him for his kindnesse and good wishes. It so fell out in the procession that, as they were carrying the Image of the V. M. on men's shoulders in Triumph (as their manner is on such occasions), either by the stumbling of the bearers or some other miscarriage, over she tumbled, and fell down directly on her face upon the stones. At night all three met to sup at the merchant's house, and immediately this zealot accosted the captain: "O, Sir, had you been here to-day at the procession to have seen the many miracles which were wrought, I am sure you could no longer have resisted the truth; such a blind man received his sight, and such a deaf woman recover'd her hearing, and a poor neighbour of ours, that hath gon with crutches to my knowledge these many yeares, threw them away, and leap't and walk't as well as I can do." Our Captaine, who had heard of the Ladye's misfortune, reply'd: "Surely, Sir, it is a wonder indeed that the B. V. cured the Deaf and the Lame and the Blind; I heard she fell down and broke her own Nose. I pray, can you tell whether she cured that or no?" The Bigot, at this gibe, fell into such a rage, as nothing at first would serve turne but the poor Heretique must go into the Inquisition; and neither former friendship nor Interest nor persuasion could prevayl of a good while to pacyfy him. The good Merchant himself (the common friend), being not a little offended, though it was spoken onely in merriment, and under (*the Rose*, as we say) the freedome and protection of his own house. So nice a thing it is in some countrys to jest or meddle with the publick Religion.

There is a Nunnery here (as I remember, it is call'd San Joseph) where young infants are received and brought up : Poor people that are not well able to provide for their children, or others who have Bastards, secretly bring them in the night, and, pulling a bell to give notice, they lay them in a moving kind of *hollow Roller* placed in the wall on purpose, and so turn them in, themselves who bring them being unseen and undiscovered. If the child be baptised, the name is noted or written upon the breast, and oftentimes mention is made of some peculiar mark made by nature or Art somewhere on the body, by which they may be known again ; and there is also a register kept in the convent of all that are so brought in. In my opinion it is a very great peice of charity to allow such places, though at first thought they may indeed seem a kind of encouragement for lew'd persons more securely to commit wickednesse ; yet, undoubtedly, they save the lives of many poor innocent Babes. I have met with those who have ventur'd to say, that if a poor Votaresse there, or any where else in Town, should by chance steal a taste of forbidden pleasure, the Fruits of her frailty and the honour of the Society are this way secured ; but I always look't upon this as a satyrical conjecture rather then a known truth.

The Spaniard's common diet in Malaga, such as it is, is extraordinarily cheap. We took my landlord's dinner the first day, which was a large *ensalada* or sallet, a pottage of onyons, gourds, and herbs ; a little fry'd fish, dryed and cold, with oyl ; *mala infana* (which they call here *Melongenas*), a sort of gourd, pear-fashioned, some as big as my fist (I think Gerard calls them in English *mad-apples*[1]), split

---

[1] Mad-apples, or Jews'-apples, are fruit of *Solanum Melangena*.

and fil'd with a little pepper, oil, and salt, and then broil'd or stew'd: these, thus drest, they count rich food, and they slice them also into their pottage. Of these and such stuff eight of us eat what we could, and paid but a *Real* (about 6*d*.) for all, besides bread and wine; but at night, for 4 fowles and a neck of mutton stew'd, six of us paid a dollar and half apiece, besides wine, which is near 50 Shillings of our money; and next day, at dinner, for one joynt of mutton and a little forequarter of Lamb and two foules, 12 of us paid a dollar a piece, besides wine, which is about 3 lb. English.

We staid one night with mine Host on shoar, and we had a proud fellow which entertain'd us a while with a song or two to a *Guitarra*. He first lay'd by his old threadbare cloak with great deliberation and wonderfull gravity; then, with his dagger behind and his hat cock't, his eyes staring, his browes bent, and his *Mostachos* new brush't, he yell'd and acted with that strange state and fiercenesse, as if he had been swaggering at some desperate criminals and threatening to hang them; but, with a *Real* or two we came off well enough. After supper and a little chat we thought of our lodgings. All that lay on twills and bedsteads were sorely bitten with little bugs, which left hard knobs and pimples wherever they seised. I, with one or two more, had the fortune to putt our twills for coolnesse into the middle of the floor, which (as all above stairs as well as those below are) was laid with brick, and we escaped all these pestilent companions. These insects, so well known in all hot countryes (but to us never seen before), are here called *chismes* and *chinches*, and in Italian *cimici*, from the Latin *cimex*, in French *punaises;* they are shaped much like a spider, but far lesse, with six legges and a bottled[1] breech, the back being often reddish. They

---

[1] "Bottled" here means bulging like a bottle. Cf. blue-bottle.

are truly cal'd by *Pliny*[1] most nasty animals, for besides their venomous bite they have (especially if they are bruised) a most intolerable filthy smel. One of our comrades, catching one in the night as it was preying upon him, and thinking it had been a flea (after a slovingly custome which he had got), bit *it with his teeth, thinking so to kill it ;* but the abominable stink set him on vomiting in such a manner as he verily thought he had been poyson'd ; which make me amazed how they came to be prescribed inwardly by the antients as a medicine against feavers,[2] unlesse it was that (after the Italian proverbe, *Un Diavolo scaccia il altro*) *one devil drives out another ;* but, perhaps, being drunk in wine, they may go down whole, and not prove so nauseous. We started a controversy, whether these *chinches* and fleas, and gnats (and flyes) have any smeling or no, and we concluded clearly in the affirmative, not only because these never stir out of their holes and lurking-places till the steam and perspiration of your bodyes invite them, but because all strong smels drive them away, as the savour of wormwood, Lavender, Rue, Hemp, Hops, Russia Leather, and the like, and the smoke of these and such other strong smelling herbs doth the same. And we were told here that many use the *Squilla* or *Sea Onyon*, cut into pieces, and thrust into the joynts and crevices of their bedsteads, or strew'd on their mats ; as likewise they presse out the juyce of them, and use it in like manner. It is manifest that the fierce *effluviums* of these things very grievously affect these vermin, and seeing they all have eyes, why may they not as well have organs of smelling, or something *Analogous* to it ?

Malaga is prettily well fortifyed for fear of surprise from

---

[1] L. 29, c. 4, *animalia fœdissima*.
[2] Dioscor., l. 2, c. 33, *contra febres et Aspidum morsus*.

the Moors ; it hath two Castles—one upon the side of a hill, and the other at the bottom of it on the East side of the Town ; and there is a communication between them both, made by two walls reaching from one to the other ; but there appears a higher place, which, if it was possest and planted with canon, could command them both. There s also an Arsenal, but what store of armes and warlike provisions were in either this or them I know not, for we were told we should not be permitted to se them, and therefore never attempted it. It is a part where most vessels going to or coming from the *Levant* put in. There is a great trade driven there ; it is famous for Almonds, Raisins, Oile, great olives, and rich Sack. The grapes which make the Raisin are very fat and fleshy, affording nothing near so much juyce as those that make the Sack, and therefore they are the sooner dry'd by the Sun. We tasted their old wines in many places, and to my palate they seem'd all much more fulsome and sweet than our old *Malagas* in England, which have had the advantage of the Sea to refine and harden them. We brought good store of the best we could find on board, with plenty of all sorts of fruits and fresh provisions.

That night, Saturday, Oct. 15, about 11 o'clock, we weigh'd Anchor, and Capt. Pool, in another man of warre, came out of port with us. I think he was in the *Guernsey* frigot. Next day the Admiral, Vice-Admiral, and several Commanders came on board and din'd with us.

Oct. 27 we dined on board *the Martin*, and our Admiral gave us new orders in case we should be engaged to fight with any Enemies, and that evening we discouered thre ships with white ensigns, which proved French, of *Monsieur Martells* Squadron, lying about *Tunis* and *Tripoly*. The French Admiral himself was in one.

Oct. 29, Saturday, we lay on the South end of Sardinia,

with Epulo[1] N.E. b. N., 10 or 12 miles distant from us. The Admiral that Evening call'd a Council of all our Commanders, and told them he had orders from the Duke of York to go to *Tunis* and stay some time there ; That he had a letter for the King of *Tunis* from our King about continuing our league and peace with him, For at that time we had peace with *Tunis*, but war with *Argieres ;* the *French* on the contrary had peace with *Argieres* and war with *Tunis*, and we had a current report that Sir Tho. Allen and *Monsieur Martel,* the French Admiral, had agreed to let English ships of Merchandize go freely into *Tunis*, and French Merchant Ships into *Argieres*, provided they caryed no provisions, or ammunition, or stores for war. We had met thre French men of war, and we understood two more lay near *Tunis* to block up that Port. From all this arose a grand dispute amongst the commanders, whether it was safe for us to go into *Tunis* or not. Whether we should hazard such a prize as all our Merchant ships were. It was urged that there might be more French ships there than we knew of, and it was uncertain what they might do with us. That the *Tunesas* might break with us upon such an opportunity as this, and seize our ships and Merchandize. Some dowbted that the Admiral had no such order, and it was thought when we dined on board *the Martin* (who was bound for *Tunis*) that the Captain of her contracted with our Admiral to se him safe in, and so all was mere pretence and fiction. Some question'd whether the Admiral could command us to attend him ; others, whether by their *Charter party* with the Turkey company they were not obliged to ply their voyage and accompany the convoy no farther than it consisted with their safety. It was asked who could justify the agreement between Sir *Tho. Allen* and *Monsieur Martel ?*

---

[1] Capo di Pula.

and many such *quæres* and difficulties were banded to and fro; but at last the Admiral positively resolved to stand by his order, and our Capt. and all the Commanders of our Turkey ships agreed to go in with him except Capt. Partridge, who was as stifly set against it; and, returning on board his own ship, he divulged the whole businesse amongst his passengers, adding all the aggravations of our danger, and suggesting all the arguments of Fear he could to them. Presently came many on board us sorely frighted, and zealously opposed our going in, insomuch as the two new Treasurers of the Turkey Company (then going out, one to *Smyrna*, and the other to *Aleppo*) threatened to enter into a protestation with Capt. Partridge against the Admiral's proceedings, and courted us to joyn with them. We civilly denyed it, telling them that we trusted in the known prudence and careful conduct of our own Captain, and should cheerfully go along with him wherever he caryed us. However, all this while these disputes were kept, as much as possible, from the common seamen, for fear there should have arose a Faction among them likewise; yet secretly all commanders were thinking of some preparation against the worst, and that night we shaped our course for *Tunis*, steering S.E. ½ S. Next morning, Oct. 30, about nine o'clock, we spied the two *Frenchmen* of war, just upon the Coast of *Africk*, as we thought, setting out of *Porto Farina*; they stood towards us a little, then went westerly, and never came near us by 7 or 8 leagues. We bore away directly for *Tunis*, and upon this all the rest of our ships in company went along with us; and that afternoon at 2 o'clock we got under *Cape Carthage*, where all the Commanders went on board the Admiral, and soon were agreed and well pleased; and at 3 we came all to anchor before *Tunis* castle, in 4 and 5 fathom water, the Cape lying N.N.E., the Castle W. b. S.

CAPT. 5.—OUR STAY AT TUNIS AND CARTHAGE.

That night we went on shoar for water, but were not then permitted to have any; yet we might freely ramble upon the shoare. The Castle seems very strong to the Sea. We were not suffer'd to view the other side to the Land. By the Castle they have several pools or ponds of standing water, one of which (as we were told) can, at pleasure, have communication with the sea. These are full of fish. We bought good store of Mullet, and there we had one true *Bream*, large and very fat. We had them very cheap, as we thought, but our Interpreter counted them dear. There were several sorts of fruit brought to us— excellent melons, Pomegranates, Limes, and *salating* herbes, with which we stock't ourselves, and so came again on board. Next morning (Oct. 31) we went on shoar at the watering-place, where were come down many country people with Eggs, Hens, Sheep, Goats, Bullocks, milk, Pompions, Fish, Pigeons, citrons, Dates, Oranges, Lemons, and Limes (which are a sort of *hedge* or *crab* Lemmons), with whose juice our Seamen make their punch. There was also store of bread to be bought. They make some of it of pure good wheat, most of it of *millet*, some of what we call Turkish wheat (maize), much of barley flour, and *lighten* it with leaven of salt and sower'd honey and oil, which give it a brackish taste, yet it is not unpleasant whilst it is new. They bake it flat, with a rising in the middle like a coppled[1] cake. Every ship stored themselves from hence with what they wanted of sea provisions. Our Capt. caried a net on shoar, which by all our Seamen was called a *Sain* (I suppose from σαγλιόν, *Sagena*, Math. xiii, 47). It was a sort of drag net. Having obtained leave, we turned it twice or

---

[1] Coppled = with a peak or cop, sugar-loaf form.

thrice in the sea, but we catch't few fish, and those very small ones. They wer *Mullet, Barboni*, and our common *plaice*, and a little sort of what we call *Maids*. I hang'd a little *Barboni* up in my cabin, and it gave forth a little thin light, like that of rotten wood, for many nights together; and by degrees, as it grew dryer, it at last vanish't. I did not then take notice of the change of colour in them (whilst they are dying) which *Pliny*[1] mentions, and for admiring of which *Seneca*[2] rebukes and flouts at some Romish gluttons.

Some of our Captaines and Passengers with me hired a couple of their Janisaryes, or rather souldjers, to be our Guides, and away we went together to see the Ruines of *Carthage*, which reach quite from the watering-place near the Castle up beyond *Cape Carthage*, agreable to what we read in Polybius,[3] near upon ten miles as we guest, but the guides said it was fifteen, which may seem probable enough, for *Strabo*[4] makes the old City only to have been in compasse thre hundred and sixty *stadia*, which is five and fourty miles, at eight *stadia* to a mile; yet Livy[5] makes it not much above half as much. And the ground lay in hills and dales, so as we could by no means make any tolerable judgement. Of from the shore, for a mile together, the Land was then sown with Barley, but all that ground is so full of small rubbish as a man can hardly set his foot upon cleer Earth; *Jam seges est ubi magna stetit Cathago*. We went first by the sea side, where they make Salt by letting in the Sea Water in Summer into broad shallow flats, and, after the Sun hath exhaled the moisture, the Salt remains in great panes behind. We saw great quantities of it here and there heapt up, which they told us was for the *Grand Signor*. Whether they have the art to refine it, or whether they send this coarse (*bay*) salt (as we

---

[1] L. 9, c. 17. [2] *In Quæst*, l. 3, c. 18.
[3] L. 1, p. 730. [4] L. 17, p. 512-40. [5] *Epil.*, c. 51.

call it) to him, I did not think to enquire. However, I
find in *Pliny*[1] that, of old, the Africans made great quantities of salt upon this coast, about *Utica*, now call'd *Biserta*,
which is not above thirty miles from hence to the west,
just on the other side the River *Bograda*. These men may
as well now be said to make *Hills of salt* as those were
then, and I believe it is altogether as *dry and hard* as that
was. Perhaps some of that which we cal'd common salt at
Constantinople came from hence. We were informed by
our Guides, who spoke broken *Italian* and *lingua Franca*
(which is bastard Spanish, mixt with words of most trading nations), that from *Cape Carthage* to the Castle was
once *Terra firma*, full of rubbish as the rest now is, but by
an Earthquake it sunk down. It is very likely, or perhaps
the foundations of the city were laid in the Sea, for we
saw from the shore many broken pieces of walls and
ruines of buildings under water; and our Seamen, in
Haling the *sain*, found the bottome very foul ground a
good way from the Shore into the Sea. Along by the
sea side remain at land many, many Vaults, some cover'd
in part, some all over, some quite open. In summer,
people come down from several places, and keep shop
here. The hardnesse of the mortar in these and other
remains is very remarkable; a stone will very hardly break
it, yet it is not fine, but the sand, or red earth, intermixt, is
very grosse, and full of small pebbles. One Vault, a little
distant from the shore, seem'd to go far under the ground.
We could see in about a furlong, but did not go in far because we wanted lights. It was crosse-arched to a row of
pillars in the middle. I fancy'd it might have been part
of the stables underground for Elephants, which Strabo[2]
saies went in the neck, or *Isthmus*, from Sea to Sea, sixty
stadia, or about seven miles. We found, now, great quan-

---

[1] Lib. 31, c. 7. [2] L. 17.

tities of bones of Foules and other little creatures in it, and it smelt strong, so as we believed it now to be a receptacle or den for foxes or wolves, or such beasts of prey.

We went thence up from the sea towards the middle of the Ruines. All the way there remaines pieces of walls and buildings, but not one pillar or stone of any note. There lye heaps of rubbish so thick that it is impossible to plough in that part, unlesse they removed it, which would be at most as tedious a piece of work as to rebuild it. There was amongst the rubbish much Alabaster, Marble of all sorts (white, Black, Red, streaked red and white, white and black, and the like), a sort of red stone, porish, but much harder then brick. We observed not one Flint, no sort of Free-stone, very little brick, onely in one side going up to *Cape Carthage* all was brick, and nothing else, but not one whole one nor half one was to be found. The earth at a distance shews red with the crumbled and scatter'd pieces. There was also much white brick, extream hard. In one place we found small pieces of Porphyry, and some thin flat bits (like broken pavements) of blackish marble spotted with green, like a sort of what we call *serpentine stone*. I am more particular in this point, that we may from hence have some guesse at the Beauty and Majesty of this City when it was standing in its Glory, for if our houses in London shew so well, being all built with plain brick, what would they have done had they been all of various Marble?

*   *   *   *   *

At last we came up to a place which our Guides and our Seaman call'd *Queen Dido's Tomb*. We all concluded at first that these were the Elephant Stables so much talkt of by old Authors, but at last I chang'd my opinion, and do now verily think that they were onely cisternes for keeping of water, as Tunis[1] is also now supply'd by such cisternes. We were told that farther up towards *Cape Carthage* there are more considerable mines, and finer things to be seen; but there was a *Mosque* there, and several houses about it, where we were informed many *Dervises* or holy men lived, and that it was dangerous going amongst them. Leo Africanus makes them very great, but we were not near enough to judge anything of their Grandeur. However, I and another happened to straggle a little that way from our company, and one of our guides threw down his mantle and his staf, and would not stir till we came back; for he said his head would go for it if we should commit any error, or come by any harme through his neglect, so he hallow'd us backward, and we obey'd. It seems sometimes there are streight Arabs (*i.e.*, Arabs from the Straits) lye lurking about, not far off from the shore, who, if they can conveniently snap any stranger, they will spirit him away and sell him for a Slave; so that upon all accounts I think it was very well that our curiosity carried us no farther that way.

* * * * *

When we were come on board, we design'd next morning to go and see *Tunis*, but this unhappy accident disappointed us. Most of our *malcontents*, before mentioned, went thither in the morning when we went to Carthage. We had no Factory there, but onely an English Consul to do all our business, whose name then was Mr. Earlesman. They waited upon him and embroyl'd him with their story. Our Admiral had wrote to him the night before to invite him to dinner that day, but the letter chanced to pass through some of their hands, and came not to him till past ten o'clock, being then delivered by one of them.

---

[1] Leo Afri., l. 5, p. m. 562.

The Consul (whether upon this account, or whether he staid to entertain them, I know not) staid at home, and returned no answer to the Admiral, who staid dinner for him, and at last was disappointed in his design'd treat. About eight at night the Consul came to him to excuse himself, but the whole matter was so ill-resented by the Admiral, as he resolved to weigh Anchor that night. The Consul urged that the *Martin* (the ship which the Admiral was so earnest to bring in there) was almost unladen (for all our ships' crews helpt him with their long bootes), and would infallibly be ready to go with us by twelve the next day, being bound for Zant. But the Admirall thought himself too much neglected; first, because the Consul came not of his own accord to wait upon him; next, because he came not when kindly sent for; so, in a heat and a hurry, we were all forced to weigh Anchor that night about elven o'clock. Several, perhaps, that staid at Tunis all night, were left behind. *Paulo*, the Greek, with whom we were embroyl'd at Malaga, was one, and one of the Admiral's passengers was another, being an Armenian Bishop, who had studyed sometime in Italy, and now went home as a Roman *Emissary* or *Seminary*. All our Ship's company were, by good fortune, on board, and we came away together.

CAPT. 6TH.—OUR PASSAGE FROM TUNIS TO CERVI.

We had newes at *Tunis* that twelve Algerine men of war were gon to the Eastward; some designing for the *Archipelago*, others for *Rhodes*, *Cyprus*, and those parts towards the end of the Mediterranean. This made our whole fleet keep company together, and for this reason the Consul was more earnest that the Admiral should take the *Martin* away with him, but it was left behind. Notwithstanding this ruffle between the Admiral and Consul, when the Consul went of (which was about nine or ten at night) he was complimented with nine guns, being in that station the King's representative.

Nov. 7th. At two o'clock the Admiral call'd all the commanders on board to a consult, and the next day we dined all on board the Assurance.

Nov. 8th. Tuesday, when we were past *Zant* (having *C. Matapan* to the E. about eight leagues, and *Sapienza* about ten to the N.), about five after noon we saw a *spout* to the Northward. We had most dismal turbulent weather for thre whole dayes and nights, and a constant rain, with most dreadful thunder and Lightning almost all the time. The dry weather which we had till now had so *parch'd* the wast[1] of the ship and the upper timburs, and made all above so leaking, as I could not keep my cabin dry; one night I was soundly wet as I lay on my bed. I was informed that it was very usuall to have such tempestuous weather hereabouts at this time of the year; and our captain told us that in *Zant* earthquakes are very frequent, that he hath known twelve in a week. That the people in summer almost all leave their houses and live abroad till winter. That on the west side, far from the Sea, is a mountain that spues forth a sort of *petroleum,* or Bituminous Lime, as black as soot, and it will grow hard and look like it, which was not unknown to Pliny.[2] This issues out on the *East side* of the mountain, and flames alwayes arose plentifully when the *west* wind blowes, and hath then a stronger smell then at other times.

Wednesday, Nov. 9th. The Sailors that had been on the watch told me that in the night, after the storme was over, they had seen two little *Lights,* one at the foremast top, the other hanging upon one of the *main stayes.* They call'd them *Corposans;* I suppose from *Corpo Santo,* as the

---

[1] *Vide* note, p. 103. [2] L. 35, c. 15.

THE FIRE OF ST. ELMO. 127

Italians name them, believing them to be the Ghosts of some saints who come to relieve them. But our men would hardly be persuaded but that they were not some *Hobgoblins* or *Fairies*, or the inchanted Bodyes of witches, and we had many a fine story told to that purpose. The Heathens of old when they saw but one named it *Helena*,[1] when two, both, that is, *Castor* and *Pollux;* why they were then made the Seamen's Tutelar Gods or saints you may see at large in *Natalis Comes*,[2] and determine whether the antient or modern superstition is more justyfiable. Our seamen assur'd us that in many voyages to the *Indyes* and elsewhere they have seen sometimes six or seven together (sometimes many more parted or splintr'd into small globulor sparks, like pills), and *hanging as it were* on the *yards* and sails, or upon the masts, but most commonly aloft, which makes me adde this one reason to what *Carles*[3] hath given us why so many sometimes appear together in our dayes, whereas not above thre at most (and that most rarely) are mentioned as ever seen together by the antients, viz.: as our Ships are bigger, and of more ballast and burthen, so their masts and yards and riggings are caryed much higher, and by consequence more of that unctious gleam, which after the dissolution of the clouds and ceasing of the Tempest remains dispersed in the Air, and affords *matter* for these *Meteors*, is rather aloft than nearer to the Hull of the ship, and so is more plentifully met with all by the upper rigging and tackles, and cleaves to them. And asking farther about this point, they told me these *lights* are oftner seen and more together upon a tall ship then upon a *pinnace* or small vessel.[4] I was not a little dis-

---

[1] Lucian, *In Novigio*, p. 933.   [2] L. 8, c. 9, p. m. 860.
[3] *Meteor.*, c. 7, 4.
[4] These lights are known now by the Greeks as τελώνια, and by the Italians as "fire of St. Elmo".

pleased with our seamen who were on the watch that night, because they did not call me; whereupon the next night (Nov. 9) they did call me, for after very much Thunder and Lightning and tempestuous weather, about four o'clock appear'd two more, one towards the *main top*, which disappeared before I got out, the other was at the very top of the fore-mast. They told me it was beginning to fade. It seem'd a dim light, as of a flame, shining through a steam or smoak,[1] about the bignesse and shape of an ordinary egge, the top a little wavered, and growing fainter and lesser it soon went out. When I came back into the great *Cabin*, there appear'd a Circle about the candle which stood on the Table; I would call it rather a *Halo*, because it was very little coloured. The farther we were from it the plainer it appear'd and bigger (almost as broad as both my hands); as we came nearer to it it lessen'd proportionably, and just at it we could not perceive it, all which depended on the various refractions through the moist and mixt vapours which then fill'd the Air. One of our *Mates* told me that once, as he sailed formerly in these *streights*, there appear'd a very bright Helena at the very *spindle* of the *main top mast*, and one of their men went up and moved his hand round about, and neither saw nor felt anything, when they below saw it all the time. We sent up one to ours, but before he got at it it went out; perhaps his approaching might move and part the Air, and contribute something to its so soon vanishing. But if what our Mate told us be true, it requires more consideration than I thought fit to afford it at that time, unlesse I had seen the like.

Nov. 10. *Cape St. John* (or the west end of Candia) lay in sight of us S.E., and the Admiral came about ten o'clock on board us to take his leave. After two houres stay he

---

[1] *Tal.*, c. 1, fig. 4.

went of, and we gave him seven guns, the three last with shot, as a token of more respect. His Ship answer'd again with great civility. *Capt. Partridge*, with the *Turkey Merchant* (whether he had not yet fully digested his discontent about our going into *Tunis*, or whether it was the natural rugged temper of the man, I know not), sailed away before the Admiral, for *Scanderoon*, without taking any civil leave, or firing one gun. We remained now but seven in company: six Turkey Merchant Men and Capt. *Wild* in *the Assurance*, our Convoy and Admiral. After *Capt. Robinson* and *Capt. Partridge* were gon, *Capt. Wild* came to dine with us, and as we were set newes was brought in by one of our *powder monkey's* from the Top Mast head that there were five great ships *a Head*, coming *stem for stem* towards us. We all concluded that they were some of the Algerines before mention'd, therefore Capt. Wild immediately returned to his Ship, and gave the signal to the whole fleet to make ready to engage them. At the *top mast* head, with a glasse, I made seven of them, there being two small vessells besides the first five. It was pleasure to se the great alacrity and readinesse, I may say the eagernesse, of our Seamen in preparing for the dispute. All their Hamocks were down in a trice; their chests and lumber turn'd out into the boates, or stived[1] by the *main chains* or elsewhere, out of the way. We had a clear ship in a very little while, and all our men posted in their several quarters, and rounds of powder and ball provided by every gun. Our Captain told me, if I pleased I might go down into the *hold*, and be safe there with the Chirurgeon. I told him if he would give me leave I would rather stand by him all the while, for I should as heartily and (he need not doubt) as earnestly pray for our good successe there as any where else. He thankt me, and told me it would not a

---

[1] Stived = packed away, stuffed.

little encourage his men to se me above board. With that all our Passengers took heart and came and stood with me upon *the quarter deck*, where were armes and ammunition provided for us all. We were to be the second Ship in the line, and after we had all made a little back till we were all ready, we bore up bravely to them. But when we came at them they proved five French men of warre, with one *Satée*[1] and another small vessell with a *meson*[2] and *stay sail*,[3] which I suppose were as *Tenders*.[4] They belong'd to the same Squadron with those which we saw by *Tunis* under *Monsr. Martell*. One of their Lieutenants went on board our Admirall, and told him that they came from *Toulon*, and had been looking out for *Tripoleses* and *Tuneses*, who it seems had been there abouts six or seven days before. Being asked, he said the *Algerines* were about *Rhodes* and *Cyprus*. And thus our *scare fight* past over, without any blowes. My Curiosity was fully gratyfied with this Prelude of a battle, for I believe I could give a shrewd guesse at all the rest, and that I then thought enough. Though indeed I did not see the least sign of fear or want of courage in any one, yet I suppose all of us were well satisfyed and pleased to sleep that night in a whole skin.

For thre or four dayes the wind was full in our eye; we tacked and tumbled backwards and forwards between *Cerigo* and the W. end of *Candia*; then we got between *C. Matapan* and *Cervi*; and having been thus beaten up and down, and made no progresse, and little hopes being left of a fair wind, by consent we came all to Anchor on

---

[1] In Taylor's works, 1630, we have a description of a *satée:* "A satie, which is a ship much like unto an argosey, of a very great burthen and bignesse."

[2] *Meson*, an old form of the word "mizzen".

[3] Stay-sail=a triangular sail hoisted on a stay.

[4] "Tender" is a word used for a stay or a spar, or any kind of beam.

the S.W. side of *Cervi*,[1] in nineteen fathom water, about five o'clock, Nov. 14, afternoon. That evening I went with the Captain in his pinnace sounding the several depths in the bay, and then went on board onr Admiral, where all the Captaines resolved to go on shore next morning for what provisions we could find, especially of wood (whereof there is plenty), and fresh water if we could find any. Next morning our Capt. and I and two of our Gentlemen passengers went on shore in the *yale*[2] betimes, before any of the other Commanders appear'd. We landed at a spot where it was plain ground and an open place, and therefore free from *Ambuscades*. Immediately came down an old Greek from the top of the mountain in a poor patch't habit, in a thick coarse jacket, a woollen shirt, with no stockings nor shoes, but onely some pieces of a raw hide of an oxe or bull wer laced[3] on to the soales of his feet with the hair side inwards, which I suppose never go of till time and rottennesse separate them. With these his feet are so plyable that he can easily go up or down a rock which our shoes will not suffer us to do, at least with that dexterity. Old Hesiod was born not very far from hence, and I thought we had had one of his old acquaintance risen from the dead and come to us, his *coat* and *socks* and *shirt* being exactly in his Boetian fashion. He had a skul cap on, border'd with a Lambskin, which he pull'd off, and came boldly to us. We had a native Greek in our boates crew, and he was our Interpreter, for I spoke as good school Greek to him as I could in our pronunciation, but my language seem'd as perfect gibberish to him as his did to me. We askt for Flesh: Sheep, bullocks, goates, and the

---

[1] *Cervi* is an Italian translation of the Greek form ἐλαφόνησον, or stag island, in the Bay of Kolokythia.

[2] Yale = yawl or jolly-boat.

[3] These raw-hide shoes are still worn by Greek peasants, and called τσαρούκια.

like. He told us they were all driven of the Island the day before, for they took us for *Africans* and Enemyes, seing us lying so long upon their coast. We askt for water. He told us there was none but what was preserved from the rain in hollow basins in the Rocks, which he directed us to; and I afterwards tasted of it, and found it good. There are no people who continually live there, but they come from the continent to till the ground, which lyes on the edges of the mountain round by the Sea, and had good corn then growing on it; they likewise bring sheep and other cattel sometimes from the main land to feed here. We asked him if he could procure any cattel or other necessaryes to be brought over for our money. He said he would go and informe his friends, and see what he could do; he doubted not but we might have something; in the meantime he shew us where we might try for water. He answer'd all along with such a show of innocent simplicity as we were much pleased with him; and I gave him a Tunbridge knife which I had in my pocket, and everyone likewise gave him something, which he received with a wonderfull submissive reverence, and promising us a very grateful returne of our kindnesse, away he went, running directly up the mountain. By this time all the other Commanders (except Capt. Wild) and a great many of their men were come on shore. Most of them brought fire Armes with them, and in all we might then make about a hundred Firelocks. All the Captaines strictly commanded their men not to stir far from the shore; and our Captain, to make us more wary, told us that in the year (as I remember) 1664 our general ships passing by here for Turkey came to an Anchor, and many went on shore on the mainland there, whereof thre worthy merchants and six or seven others were snapt by the natives, who lay in wait for them, and it cost them 1,600 dollars for their redemption. The Turkes call that part of *Peloponnesus* (as well as all Thrace) *Romania ;* and from that word (by an *Aphaeresis*) these wicked people are called *Maniotes* (as the inhabitants of *Smyrna, Scio, Cyprus, Candia,* are called *Smyrniotes, Sciotes, Cypriotes, Candiotes,* and the like elsewhere). These who live upon the Rocks and mountaines by the Sea are a sort of lawlesse people, and the Turkes themselves cannot govern them or reduce them into any good order. These miscreant wretches lye constantly watching upon the Rocks and Mountaines, not so much to secure themselves from the injuryes of Pirates as themselves to Thieve and rob whome they can catch, and all the Christian Passengers which they can seise on the shore they sell to the Turkes to serve in their Galleys or otherwise as slaves ; and I have been assured that if they can conveniently *spirit* away Turkes themselves they will serve even them in like manner, and sell them for slaves to any Christian who will be their chapman.[1] There was a fawning cunning *varlet* came to those Gentlemen then, and pretended to procure them all manner of provisions which they could desire, but betray'd them then, as this vile wretch did us now. I could not but call to mind old *Sinon* in Virgil,[2] for our *Cheat* seem'd to pretend to the very same motto: *Poor, but very honest.* Believe me, Greeks are Greeks still ; for falsenesse and treachery they still deserve *Iphigenia's* character of them in Euripides,[3] *Trust them and hang them,* or rather hang them first for sureness. We kept in little bodys near the shore, where there were small thickits of Juniper and mirtles with their berrys then ripe, and we had excellent sport in killing *Fieldfares* and *Thrushes,* and such other birds, which were there at feed in great abundance. Some went towards the Sandhills, where was

---

[1] *I.e.*, buyer.
[2] *Æn.*, 2, l. 79.
[3] *Iphigen. in Taur.*, Act v, p. 1205.

store of game in little plashes made by the sea-water, which was cast in there by winds and stormes. After we had sported our selves a while with shooting in these thickets and Plashes,[1] two or thre of our Commanders invited me to a Collation, and as we were set in the shade under some pieces of rocks, we saw several of our men (notwithstanding all the Captaine's commands, and our Captaine's History) struggling up the Mountain. One was habited something like our Captain, and, at a distance, appear'd indeed to be him; whereupon some Gentlemen coming by us would by all meanes have tempted my Curiosity to have follow'd them, but our Captaine's lecture at our coming on shore had stir'd up such wary apprehensions and jealous reflections in my mind, as I could not possibly be persuaded that it was he; and the Captaines there with me were in a very great rage to see such inconsiderate people running into that danger. No sooner had these gentlemen left us but we hear'd thre or four guns go of upon the Mountain; and, looking up, we saw some of the Straglers posting down in wonderful haste; and presently appear'd several Men brandishing their *cutlasses* or *Cimitars*, and making them glitter against the Sun. We immediately rose, and went to the body of our Company to hear what was the matter. It happen'd that five or six gentlemen had got some seamen with them, and away they had ventur'd up the mountain. The Gentlemen (I know not whether it was by good Fortune or Policy) were hindermost, and just as their Vanguard was got on the brow of the other side the Mountain, up rose about a dozen Rogues, who had layn sculking there in the thickets, and ran upon them. They being scatter'd abroad, and not near one another by fourty or fifty yards or more, at this

---

[1] Plash=puddle. " Makes meadows, standing pleashes." (Browne, *Buttamina's Pastorals*, i, 1.)

surprise fired upon the Rogues without doing any execution (perhaps most of them were charg'd only with small shot). So soon as their fire was over, the Rogues came more boldly on, though armed onely with half Pikes and *Cutlasses*. Our Seamen, who had not in the least considered to make good their retreat, threw down their Armes, and betook themselves to their heels. But our gentlemen had the start of them, and so, God be thanked, these all escaped, though very narrowly, all coming down without their Armes, most without their Hats, some with but a piece of a Shoe, their feet and leggs being battered and torne, and their bodyes bruised with rushing through the Shrubs and jumping down prœcipices, for they came right forward, thinking the shortest way was best. Four of the poor Seamen were taken—two of the *Mary and Martha's* men, one of the *Levant Merchant*, and a fourth of the *Tho. and Francis*, whome they first had slightly wounded in the face, then they seised him and tyed his hands behind him, and left him with thre Rogues to guard him. These drove him before them, and because he often linger'd and offer'd to stop, they pricked him forward in the back, and wounded him in several places with their half pikes. The poor man was a very stout fellow and a good wrastler, and feeling the thing which bound his hands something loose, slipt his right hand out, and, with great courage and presence of mind, turn'd upon the Rogues, who were uselesse, and thought they had him safe. With this advantage, he ran the first quite over, and struck up the heels of the second; the third (who was a little behind the other) made a blow at him with his *Cimitar*, which he saved from his head with his lefte arme, and lay'd hold of the weapon with his right hand. The Rogue, drawing it a little back, cut the poor fellow's hand badly. Yet this saved him from a second stroke, for he being something under the Rogue, he struck him up *hand and foot*, and before the other two could come at him, away he came. The great concerne which he had for his dear life and dearer liberty added something more then natural vigour to his leggs, and as much lightnesse to his heels. At last he got to us, and told us all that had past. There were, in another place, two of our seamen (one the native Greek) who made a very soldjere-like retreat. As they straggled from us, they kept together, and, out of a thicket, up start five or six *Maniotes*, and made towards them. They, standing together, presented their Muskets (resolving not to fire but to good purpose, and therefore not till they were very near). Down the Rogues dropt again. The Seamen retreated; they again follow'd. The Seamen presented again, and they again squatted down. Our Greek at last spoke to them, and told them to *keep of* in their own language; at which they stopt, and so these two retired leasurely and safely to us. After some debate what we ought to do, we all in a body were marching up the mountain to rescue our men; but *Captain Wild*, being all this while on board, and observing all which had happened, thought we were not strong enough; and, therefore, firing a great shot over us, call'd us back; and sometime after came all his soldiers on shore well armed; and then Mr. Day (his Lieutenant), a brave stout man, marshall'd us all, and put us in order: and away he led us up the mountain. But when we arrived, we saw we were come too late; for all the Rogues had crost the water in their bootes, and were just landing on the Main, and with our glasses we could discover our poor Captives amongst them, bound. The Lieutenant was earnest for bringing our boates about and going to them, for they appear'd in all much short of a hundred men. Our Captaines, though all brave men, were utterly against that, for being, by their Charter-party, bound to ply their Voyage, they could not tell how they could answer such an adventure, for we knew not what event our landing on the main land in a Hostile manner might produce, so some of them came back presently; but the Lieutenant and the rest rambled all over the Island, where they saw not one man left, nor found so much as one house. Here and there were Coves, in which they found some tatter'd cloths, and a few poor utensils; as likewise a sack of meal, and good store of onions and such-like very mean booty. I hardly believe that this *Maniotes* do ever bring any cattle hither (though our honest *Sinon* told us they did), or, at least, they feed them on the other side the Mountain, and not in view, for fear of *African* or other Pirates, who would sweep them of. They onely come here to till the ground and reape the corne, and now and then to make such *Ambuscades* as these; and very slender provisions will serve them upon these occasions. Some of our men, as they march't, found some Hats, swords, pistols, and such like (it seems uselesse) baggage, which our first *Myrmidons* had discreetly scattered in their retreat. At last all came down, and we went on board, much lamenting our sad misfortunes, and all concluded that if we had proceeded on at our first march, and not staid for Captain *Wild's* souldiers, we had certainly rescued our men, and perhaps sufficiently chastised those Sons of Belial. After some little conference with all the Captaines, we joyntly agreed to contribute to their ransome, and everyone setting down their good will, we had that night subscribed about 1,500 dollars, the poorest seaman giving one. Next morning the Admiral sent out his boat, and we went in ours with white flags of Truce round the Island, but not one man appeared to treat with us, or to take the least notice of us. Wherefore the money was collected and deposited in the Consul's hands at *Smyrna*, and, about two yeares after, the poor slaves were found in the galleys and redeemed, though they proved most ungrateful wretches, for I heard that when they got into England they offered to sue their Captains for their wages, which they pretended was due to them for all that time.

CAP. 7.—OUR PASSAGE TO SMYRNA.

Nov. 17. At noon we weigh'd Anchor, and with the wind at S.S.E. and S.E. we turn'd out between *Cerigo* and *C. St. Angelo.* Next day being entered the *Arches*,[1] we staid for the *Levant Merchant*, and dined there.

Nov. 19, *Saturday.* We had very much rain all the day, and all the following night. The wind to E. to S.E., we got nothing of our way, but with much ado we kept *our own*. This ill weather continued for the most part till Nov. 21 about noon. That Evening we saw 4 sail in *Argentiera*[2] bay, one with a flag at the *Topmast head.* We could not tell who they were; if friends, we had no reason to fear them; if foes, they certainly feared us. We past between *Milo* and *Antimilo;* between *Serfon* and *Sifanto*[3]; between *Tino* and *Micono;* between *Scio* and *Ipsera*.[4] And Nov. 23, in the morning, we got past *C. Calaberro* (or, as our seamen call it, *C. Tobbernose*), from the true Turkish word *Caraburnes*[5] (*black nose* or black *snout*), *where mill stones were cut out,* so call'd, I suppose, from the black rock out of which they were taken. And if there be yet such *a black* quarry there, I should conclude that the Turkes also nam'd it *black Nose* from thence. We went on with a fair gale at W.N.W., but the Admiral and *the Speedwell* running more in to the shore, was becalm'd and left *a stern.* At 2 afternoon we came up to *the Castle,* where lay without the port of *Smyrna* two

---

[1] The Archipelago.
[2] *Argentiere* is the Italian name for Kimolos, a great halting-place for ships in those days.
[3] Seriphos and Siphnos.   [4] Psara.
[5] *Kara-bournon* = Turkish, black point or nose.

AT SMYRNA. 139

Holland men of war. We saluted the Admiral with thre guns, and he return'd us thre. Our English Merchants came on board us, and at five o'clock we came to Anchor at *Smyrna,* and saluted the Port with seven guns. I went on shore, and lay at Mr. James Adderley and Mr. Nath. Thurston and Mr. Jon. Prideaux their house, where I was most courteously and nobly entertained. The *Assurance* staid without the Castle, and the *Speedwell* came not in till the next day. None of our men of war must go into any of the Turkish Ports so far as to be commanded by any of their Castles. It seems that the Turks formerly have been very insolent, and have laid an *Imbargo* or Arest upon some of our men of war which were in Port, and, as I have been told, have made use of them in the last *Candia* Warre ; to prevent which inconvenience for the future, our men of war always lye without the Castles. And several French men of war in my time came up to Constantinople, and lay at Anchor there sometime, and great embroil was like to have happened thereupon about a Knight of Malta who escaped, of which more elsewhere.

CAPT. 8.—WHAT HAPPENED WHILST OUR SHIPS STAID AT SMYRNA, AND OUR JOURNEY TO EPHESUS.

Rambling about the Town, one of our passengers, who had lived at Smyrna before, caryed me to a rich Turkes house, who was one of his old acquaintance. I think they call'd him *Eusine Chabbey*, a very courteous man, and friendly to all our Nation. They told me that he once invited them all at the *cutting* or circumcision of one of his sons, and treated them very generously. We found him at Supper, and he very earnestly prest us to sit down, which we did, *Taylor like*, crosse leg'd, for we saw neither chair nor stool, nor anything else but the floor cover'd with carpets. We tasted of his cheer, which was good, plain, wholesome food. All things being so quite different from our own way of living did very much surprise me with wonder and delight. But of Turkish entertainments and other customes I shall give a large account more conveniently elsewhere.

Novemb. 26. Our Consul, the worthy Sir Paul Ricaut,[1] treated us at his country house, which was six or seven miles out of Town, in a village called *Sedjagui;* I was told the right Turkish name name is *Seghiahkioi*, as much as *Strangeham*. It seems the word *Kioi* in Turkish signifies a *Hamlet* or Village, and therefore it is made the termination of country villages very frequently, as our *ham* is in English names, and it is pronounced something near the work *qui*, so in *Bailgradqui, Hosqui, Ortaqui,* and infinite more everywhere. Several of our nation have likewise houses of retirement there, as also the Dutch Consul, *Jaques von Dam*, and others of that nation then had. It is a very pleasant and convenient place for divertisement, especially in summer. I took much notice of an old *Coffe* man there, who was an *Afionjè* or Ophiunjè), *a great eater of Opium*. He seem'd much above 60 yeares old, and told us that in a morning till he had taken a little dose, as much as a half nut or more, he had no strength to get up, or to raise or turne himself in his bed ; but after it, he had vigour, briskness enough to do anything. He was very lean, the flesh, or rather the skin of his cheeks, hanging like Spanish leather ; and he had very oft (almost every minute) a strange kind of *spasme* in the muscles of his breast, or a jerking motion like those who have a strong Hickock.

Nov. 30. Some of this generous Factory designing to

---

[1] Sir P. Ricaut was twelve years Consul at Smyrna, and wrote a work on *Turkish Policy*.

accompany several gentlemen, their friends (which now came from England), to Ephesus, were pleased to admit me into their *caravan*, and my very kind friends where I lodged accoutred me and furnisht me out with their own Janisary and everything necessary for that Journey. We were, in all, about two or three and twenty, all very well provided with horses and armes. That night we lay at a country town, call'd by our Europeans *Jamovasy*, but I am told its true Turkish name was *Jaman bakgia*, or *bachi*, that is, *terrible garden;* it is about four miles beyond ·*Sedjaqui*. It is a pretty large town with several *Moscheas* in it, which are all shaded with tall Cypruses and some pines, whose verdure at some distance seems very stately and very pleasant. From thence we went through a plain for six or eight miles somewhat wet or moorish (which, I suppose, might happen from the rains falling on either side from the mountains, and staying there, where it was but narrow). It was spread with *Agnus castus* in great plenty, which I have often observed to love such a moist soil ; there was nothing then on the boughs but their seed, which was very good, and of a stronger smell then that with us. Next we came to firme sandy ground, fill'd with Oakes (without any underwood), like some of our parks. They were all short, snoggy trees, much loaded with boughs; I saw not one good piece of Timber amongst them. Then we ascended a rocky mountain, not continued smooth at top, but broken into many and deep dales, for the most part cover'd with several sorts of middle-sized trees, with shrubs amongst them ; the way both going up and going down was *filled with loose stones*, *being very difficult*, yet our horses had been used to such places, and caryed us very safely on. This road is very dangerous by reason of Thieves, who lurk in the thickets and dens that are upon it. Many people lay buryed here and there who had been murdered and slain, and many bones of men lay scattered above ground. We often saw several people at a distance peeping at us, and one came and joyn'd himself with us for a mile or two, and then stole away from us; we thought it was for no good end, but we were too numerous and strong for them to venture on us. This mountain is now called *Aliman*, and all our former Travaylers take it for the Antient *Mimas*, and my good friend Dr. Pickering[1] would needs have the very word *Aliman* jumbled from *Almiman*.

[Dr. Covel here gives a long and technical account of all he saw at Ephesus—of little value now, since the light of recent excavations.]

* * * * *

CAPT. 10.—OUR DEPARTURE FROM SMYRNA.

At last, *Dec.* 22, *Thursday*, about eleven in the morning, we weigh'd Anchor with a fair gale at S.E.

Saturday, Dec. 24. In the morning I had a little Aguish distemper: I fancy'd that I had gotten cold with overheating myself in wading and labouring upon the sand-bank the last day we were there a shooting. The wind blew very hard most part of the day at N.N.E., and we had a very boysterous Sea. We split our Fore sail, and it almost blew away: we had stood in close under *Lesbos* all night, and that day, about four o'clock in the afternoon, we came to Anchor before *Tenedos*, in ten fathome water. Soon after, we sent our purser a shoar to wait on the *Aga*, who, by him, invited us to come and take what Provisions we wanted. He sent us some fish; amongst the rest *Sea Breme* (as our Capt. call'd them), with a large, very sharp

---

[1] Dr. Pickering and Dr. Covel are mentioned by Spon and Wheeler as being at Smyrna. "And so in the good company of Doctor Pickering, physician to the factory at Smyrna, Dr. Covel, who was so kind as to bring us some part of the way, and divers merchants, we parted hence."

prickly fin all along the back, and some fish which feel'd rough, like perches, with two prickly fins on their back, and on either side they had just eleven streaks or laces fore and aft (to use the seaman's phrase), parallel to one another from the back downwards, of a bright *gold colour*.

The *Agá* beg'd some glasse bottles of our Capt., which were sent to him next day by our Purser, who went a shore and bought all the provisions which we wanted, and with them good store of white Muscadine, a rich, sweet, heavy wine. I was so ill as I durst not venture out, but shall hereafter give you an account of what I observed when I came there a second time.

Dec. 27, Tuesday. About five in the morning we weighed Anchor, and by eleven o'clock following we were at the mouth of the *Hellespont*.

A little beyond the innermost castles of old *Sistos* and *Abydos*, on the Southern Shore, lyes a little sand bank, which reaches on round about a sharp point of land directly opposite to *Magla* (antiently *Madgla*). Our second Mate, being on the watch, kept the south side of the Stream (which continually set out here to the West), for the advantage of the Eddy and the easier passage on that west side of the point; but, bearing in too near the South Shore, about two o'clock, ran our ship on ground. We had but one easy gale, just enough to stem the current, and the sand and mud at the bottom were soft, so we were in no great danger, and, carrying out an Anchor a sterne (as is usuall in such cases) with the Winlace, we soon wrought the ship of again, and so plying our voyage, by five o'clock we safely doubled the point, and got sea room enough.

Dec. 28, Wednesday. About ten in the morning we came to an Anchor before *Galliopoli* (the Greeks still call it by the old name *Callipolis*) in 20 fathom water. We stay'd not above two houres, and then weigh'd again for *Constan-*

tinople, where, on Saturday, Dec. 31, at thre in the afternoon, we came to Anchor at the custome house on *Galata* side, having saluted the Seraglio as we past by with 11 guns.

I went immediately up to my Ld. Ambassador, *Sr. Dan. Harvey*, and deliver'd those letters of consequence which I thought not fit to venture with others by the common *messo* from Smyrna; and, the next day being New Yeares Day, I entred upon my employment.

When I went to get my books and other things on shore, the Customes ript open my Trunkes and boxes, and searched and rifled every thing. However, at last I mist nothing but *Niceron's Thaumaturgus opticus*, which I shrewdly suspect was filch't from me by one who was indeed call'd a Christian, but had not, it seems, the honesty of a common Turk.

[In Dr. Covel's MS. there here follows a long and detailed account of Constantinople, which differs little from those given by other travellers of the period, and has therefore been omitted.]

Extracts from the General Diary extending over the whole of Dr. Covel's Residence in Turkey.

Aug. 15*th*, 1671. 'Tis observ'd by the Greeks as the feast of Assumpt. B.V.M. with great solemnity. They all repair to Church, Men and Women apart. Masse is mumbled over. The priest does not consecrate a wafer or a whole loaf, but cuts a long square cut about $\frac{3}{4}$ of an inch broad; with his nail he makes a crosse on it. After the prayer of consecration he elevates it, and they adore; then there is the discourse from the Patriarch. After masse the Priest comes out with holy Water in a pot, a crosse, and an aspergillum of hyssop, or lime, or rosemary, or what he can get green (that at the holy fountain was Basil), and Holy

CONSECRATION OF THE PATRIARCH. 145

bread on a dish. By use in the Greek Church none are to eat or drink till they cut it. Everyone comes up towards that place in order: first the Men, then Women. He gives them a piece of bread, ζυμὸς, leaven'd (it is as that for the Eucharist), and he holds the Cross for the kisses; he washes them on the face; they lay down their aspers,[1] and depart. Those that have paines in their head or are ill come to the Priest, and lean down their head (Men and Women), on which he layes his book, and reads some piece of the Gospell; they present aspers for that. All being done, there is brought to the Church doore a charger of boyld wheat, cover'd over with crosses made of blancht almonds and raisins; everyone that will takes one of it, but is obliged to say a Pater Noster and Ave for the souls of the dead there buried. Masse is said in the same manner.

Nov. 8th, 1674. I was at the consecration of the new patriarch Dionysius, Archbishop of Larissa (or Metropolite).[2] Parthenius had brought out Methodius, and disoblig'd the greatest part of the Greek Metropolitans; they joyned against him, bring him out, and get him banish't and sent to the Pasha of Cyprus. Mathias, with all the Metropolites and thre ex-patriarchs, were in the sacristia; it being ended, out comes the ex-patriarchs with their pastoral staffs in their hands. They are prettily coloured, like your gaudy tobacco-pipes with globular joynts, the crosse or handle at top, two serpents' heads, yellow like gold. First was Παίσιος, second Διονύσιος, third our

---

[1] *Aspers:* a coin, worth a halfpenny at that time, according to Sir Paul Ricaut.

[2] The Patriarchate at Constantinople was then in a deplorable state. The price of the dignity was, Von Hammer tells us, then 20,000 crowns. Dionysius and Parthenius were constantly quarrelling for the office. Dionysius was deposed because he quarrelled with Panagiotes, the great dragoman's wife (*vide* Introduction), but returned to office on his death. Parthenius did well for the Greek cause in abolishing the temporary unions of Greek women with Turks.

L

Μεθόδιος; and took their seats on the left of the quire (as you enter) just over against the Patriarch's seat, which is like a chair with 4 steps up to it, a tilt like a flat pulpit over it, supported with a back behind, and two little posts before. They sat in their order, Παίσιος uppermost, next the Sacristia, and then followed all the Metropolites, and took their places on the patriarchs' side from his seat towards the door in order. Then in a Pulpit high on the wall of the ex-patriarch's side an officer of the Church (I suppose their λογοθέτης)[1] read a long declaration against Parthenius to justify their proceedings, wherein he made him the veryest Rogue in the world, calling him διάβολος κακοῦργος, τῶν δαιμόνων δοῦλος, etc., and at the end he pronounced him ἀφωριομένος, ἀνάθεμα τρισκαταραμένος, at which the ex-patriarchs and all the Metropolites, wagging their heads, cryed out aloud ἀνάθεμά τον many of the latter thrice repeating of it with vehemency. The French Embassador, and we Franks and many Greeks could not but smile. My Dragoman (a Greek) told me that if this one be turned out, and Parthenius restored, the other faction will anathematise him as much, and they served Methodius just soe. Then Παίσιος read a formall instrument, wherein he personally agreed to the censure; the like did the other two *ex parte*, and all the Metropolites, all ending with ἀνάθεμά τον. Then they proceeded to another part of their service, in which the new patriarch (another Διονύσιος) had a short part, which he said in sight of all at the door within the sacristia, where he was all the time. After it (half way in the choir, just against the Patriarch's seat) another officer of the Church (which is the μεγάλη ἐκκλησία, a grand chiesa), I suppose him the μέγας ῥήτωρ, mounted on a *scabellum*,[2] 1½

---

[1] The *Logothetes* corresponds to the Chancellor in the Greek Church.
[2] *Scabellum* or *scamellum*. Gk. ὑποπόδιον = a footstool.

foot high, made a very handsome speech in his commendation, pronounct it very plain and gracefully. He insisted upon a parallel between their hopes now and their former calamyties, though touch't but lightly upon Parthenius, I suppose for fear of his returne. He complimented the Metropolites and expatr. (ex-patriarchs) with the presage of future happiness, and their good choyce he commended, etc. The new Patriarch all the while lookt humbly down to the ground. After it, he returned a short and modest answer. Next came up toward the Sacristia (above the Orator a great deal) the Bishop of Heraclea, with a pastorall staff, and, holding it in his hand, made another pretty compliment, partly to the New Patriarch, partly (turning about) to the company, and then, going up to him, presented it to him, and kist his hand. Then he on his left hand, and another on his right, lead him along to his seat. In the midway, the ex-Patriarchs, rising from their seats, met him and kist him (*alla graeca, del un ed altro omero*[1]), then return'd to their seats; he goes on to his. Then come all the Metropolites, pass in order, and kiss his hand; returning to their seats immediately, they passe on towards high masse. The Gospels are bound very rich in Embroidery gold and silver, and have the crosse on the side, which, as it was brought back from the pulpit (in which it was read), the patr., ex-patr., and the French Embassad. kist. The host, before it is consecrated, is brought through the body of the Church, at which all the Patr., expat., Papa., etc., uncover their heads (and come downe), which at other times is cover'd with a black knit kind of Monmouth with eares, and a kind of course listany hood over it, which they put of and on upon many occasions. Before consecration and elevation, all adore to the ground, the patriarch, expat., etc. Masse

---

[1] "From one shoulder to the other."

being fully ended, a Metropolite went up and preach't 1st a very short prayer, then name his text Mat. 5-8, καθάρτατος, then saluted the Patr., expat., Metropolit., and the whole auditory, return'd to his text again, where the greatest part was reckoning up various opinions. He quoted Ignatius, etc., etc., and coming to speak of Parthenius, calling him bad enough, [amo]ngst the rest comparing him to Lucifer and the bad angels; he mistook, and said Παίσιος (who was there present, and hang'd down his head). Then we many cry'd out, *Parthenius, Parthenius*, at which he making a stand, said Παρθένιος λὲγω, and with much adoe went on. He ended his sermon with a short prayer. The greater part of his sermon was much about Parthenius's abusing the Church. At the door of the Church lay many thousands of candles, which were given by Greekes and others. First, before the New Patr. came from the Sacristia to his seat, every one lighted his candle, which made a brave sight from end to end of the church. Just as the New Patriarch took his seat, all cryed out (again and again repeating) ἄξιος, ἄξιος, ἄξιος.

After the Sermon was done, the Patriarch took down a small crosse (guilt with gold) that hang'd behind, and, holding it, he blest people (as he did once or twice in the office before with his hand, they all bowing at the same time). Then came out the *pane Benedetto*, and was carried to him. All the people came (thronging), kist his hand, and took some bread. The *Aqua benedetta* was not brought forth, as I saw. The French Ambassador invited me to dinner with him, as likewise to the Patriarch's House, but I excused myself, etc.

Nov. 21. we went (my Ld., etc.) to the Islands. We did not touch at any till we came to Principe.

Dec. 23, I was much indisposed; the 26th I fell ill of a continued feaver, which held me 17 dayes. I lost above 30 oz. of blood, reduc't me so low that (it being a very cold season) after my feaver left me I had much adoe to retain heat in my limbs; my right thigh was perfectly numb from my knee to my hip, but friction, and bathing, and flannel on my own head set me right. Dr. Alexander Maurocordato came (by D.'s kindness); he advised me, 1st, to eat flesh and goe colder in my very feaver. I a little inclined to his advice, but one poringer of strong broth increast it strangely, and I got a cold that I could not quit in 4 days. 2dly, he advis'd bleeding in the *salvatella*[1] (I starv'd my feaver out, eating nothing for 5 or 6 dayes, but dinner and supper, one little porringer of Eng. Gruell). 3dly, when I was out of my feaver, which he cal'd a miracle, he advis'd me to beer, forbad me all wine upon pain of relaps. I drank beer at dinner, found my stomach windy; at 6 o'clock I drank again with a tost, but it gave me a most intolerable fit of griping in my stomach, which, with vomiting, I got away in 3 houres. I recovered so well as to go to Chappell.

Feb. 7th, 1667, came a young priest—he wrote down his name himself, D. Hilarione Bubuli—to me from padre Jeremiah, to know if any letters were for Venice from my Ld., me, etc.; amongst other discourse he made a great discovery to me. He was a Basilian (a Greek), but in orders (by Rome) a Venetian, born and bred under the Greek Arch Bp. there. He was not inform'd well by Padre Jeremiah (who is a Greek of another stamp), and, taking me for a Romanist, told me there were many Metropolites now Romans in their hearts, and that some money would do anything amongst them; they question'd not but shortly to make Metropolites enough of their own way. He said this Patriarch was a lay man, cropt hair bare, but by money and friends he was made a deacon one day, a priest the

---

[1] The *vena salvatella*, a vein on the back of the hand much used formerly for bleeding.

next; a Bp. and metropolite of Larissa the third. The design was this: they underhand by mediation of the K. of France and his Embass. here, the Emperour and his resident at Adrianople, the Bailo of Venice, first calumniate the Present Patriarch, and are now plotting his removal. Next day they have here (now obscurely) the Metropolite of Paros and Naxia, who they designe shortly for Metropolite of Ephesus, a true man in his heart to them; next to make him Patriarch. The businesse is committed to the Italian Archbp. now at the new church (St. Francesco): he told me the Jesuits and the Capuchins know of it, and he knew I would be secret, too; he said Padre Jeremiah was ignorant of it wholly, though he knew him wel affected. I mentioned Panagiotes at Court; he said he was not acquainted with it, nor must be, but he had a very great kindnesse for this Metropolite, and he himself has copied out all their letters of late correspondency, and he will be ready to make him Patriarch they question not; his name was D. Hilarione Bubuli, as you may see his own hand on the first whole leaf of this book. He said the Greek and Latin Church differ in 5 things; 1st, the Holy Ghost; 2nd, The leaven'd bread in the Sacrament; 3d, Purgatory; 4, The Pope's supremacy; 5, The forme of Baptisme. He said they had all their services in Greek, but Romanized.

[Dr. Covel's Diary is here very obscure, and evidently intended for notes, which he himself only could understand.]

Copy of the Kaimacham's to our King at my lord's audience.

Directed thus•

To the glorious amongst the princes and lords of the Nation of the Messiah, Ld. of Honour, Charles the 2d, King of England, whose end be Happy.

To the Glorious amongst the Princes and great Lds. of Jesus, the supreme judge of the Nation of the Messiah, and governour of all the Nazareen affaires, Lord of honour, greatnesse, and respect, who is solicitous of honour, Charles the 2d, King of England, whose end God conclude with all happinesse and grandeur.

We signify unto you the purest sincere friendship of my most potent, great, and Majestick master, the Imperiall Lord of the pure Ottoman faith, which is our duty to doe (according to the office we hold in the high port) with all diligence and respect, because of the sincere peace that is between the two kingdomes, being desir'd friendly and with honour, we signify and sincerely relate how that the choice amongst the nobles of the people of the Messiah, Sr. Dan. Harvey (whose end be happy), your Ambassador sent to reside at the high port, being arriv'd at the Imperiall City frequented by all princes and great lords, we receiv'd by his hands your most courteous letter, and, according to custome, he came to the Imperiall Camp to have his audience; and, after the Imperiall manner, having been honour'd and received, he presented at the Imperiall throne your letter, and the translation of it, the sence whereof was well comprehended by our high Emperour, and the presents well accepted by his Imperiall Majesty, who has sent by his Imperiall letter an answer, hoping that the antient sincere friendship shall be alwayes continued on our part. My most honour'd friend then departed to renew the Imperiall capitulations; but the most honour'd and happy great Vizier being come to the Imperiall stirrop about the affairs of the camp, it was defer'd until his arrival. Then, if it please God, the happy and supreme vizier arriving, be assured he will not fail to renew them. Hoping from your friendship a continuation of the good correspondency and augmentation of the confederacy day by day, I remain with the desires of the same.

Dated in the garrison'd City of Salonica.

July 30*th*. Γεράσιμος μητροπολίτης Τουρνόβου for 20 purses of money bought the patriarch's place. Dionysius, Drista, etc., fled to the French Embassadores.

The G. Signor's letter after my Lord's Audience. Directed thus:

The Imperiall letter to the Glorious and great Prince of the Nation of Jesus, Ruler of Nazarene people, our friend Charles the 2d, whose end be happy.

To the glorious amongst the great Princes of Jesus, and reverenc't amongst the high potentates of the people of the Messiah, sole director of the great affaires of the Nazarene nation, Lord of the limits of respect and honour, of greatnesse and of fame, Charles the 2d, King of England, Scotland, France, and Ireland, our friend, whose end we wish may be happy.

Our sublime, high, and Imperiall signet arriving, you will understand how that the most respected amongst the nobles of the peoples of the Messiah, your Ambassador Sir Dan. Harvey, whose end be fortunate, did arrive with your letters at our happy port, and, according to the antient custome, our most honourable Viziers did bring him before our noble Throne. Being come unto us, he did consigne your Royal letter, which was received with all respect and honour, translated, and presented at our noble Throne; the tenour whereof was observed and pleasing to us. We received also your presents with satisfaction, and his requests and demands, whilst they are conforme unto our noble lawes, and correspond to the friendship between us, shall be consider'd, and for the time to come, you not permitting anything in the prejudice of the former peace on the part of our Imperiall majesty, there shall not be suffer'd any thing in prejudice of the same sworne league, which shall be undoubtedly alwayes preserv'd, and to conclude we wish you all health.

* * * * *

The Turkes at Biram, and at all victoryes and births of the princes, make great mirth. It happen'd the Sultana was deliver'd of a second son this last Ramas, Decemb. 1673. The mirth was put of till the Biram, and then it was doubled; all were mad for 3 nights and three dayes, every shop open and drest up with laurell flowers, etc., many candle machines with pretty figures, puppet playes, dancing, etc.; the Janisary's chambers was the finest sight. Almost in every shop was 1, 2, or more of these old mysticall figures of health. Whether it is of any meaning among them, or only taken up by chance, I could not be informed. In many of them was a sphere of 2 or three circles; if it signify anything of antient superstition, it must be endlesse or everlasting health.

1674.

Jan. 6th. Usually about 12 tide, beastly boisterous weather; few vessels at sea. 20th, we were kindly entertained at the Dervises; they play'd to us; the old supravisor beat the Tambur (the antient Tympanum); their tones were very passionate; the rest devoutly attentive. Many of them have a great 6 or 8 square Agat (with a hole in the middle) at their girdle. He (whome I ask't about it) told me that stone foretold the sicknesse of their friends by growing pale on the edges, and their death by growing pale towards the hole in the middle; he said it sweats against poison, etc. I remember two Kalenderis aboard the Viner had each such a one; they had the caps of a wandring Dervise, but in all things else like the habit of the Kalenderi, in Mr. Ricaut, he makes them Santons, but in good earnest they are meer Tomes of Bedlam. One had a horne tyed about his shoulders (like a wild goates, but longer); he blew it like our sow gelders, high to low. He had a great hand jar, a terrible crab-tree truncheon, a leather kind of petticoat about his middle, naked above and beneath. It was then in May or June. He had a course Arnout Jamurluck.[1] He drank wine (like a fish water) which we gave him to blow his horne.

Mart. 26, '74. Our King's letter for the G. S. directed to the most High and Mighty Emperour Sultan Mahomet Ilam, chief Lord and Commander of the Mussulman Kingdome, sole and supreme monarch of the Eastern Empire.

To the Vizier, thus directed to the high and excellent Lord the Vizier Arem.

---

[1] Arnout = an Albanian garment.

VOYAGE TO SMYRNA WITH SIR DANIEL HARVEY'S BODY, WHO DIED AUG. 28TH, 1673.

Apr. 10, 1674. At 8 at night we weigh'd (being upon the Dogger), and next day 3½ in afternoon we came to Anchor at the Asia side over against the little conduit within shot of that most innermost castle. We went on shoar and dispatcht our business with the Aga there. My Ld. had sent each of them a vest of cloth; we had our audience without the castle, in a house on purpose, by the draw bridge. Our Jew Druggerman, 10 or 12 dayes before, had shew'd some strangers up and down without the Castle, and at last, venturing to peep in, was catch't and soundly drubb'd. Notwithstanding this, I went round about the outside and past it.

Several guns on the ground play up and down the Hellespont; on that side are 14 port holes, where lye great guns chamber'd to shoot stone shot, very big, near 2 foot diameter, all fixt and immovable, and therefore to be charged only without. They will fling a shot crosse the Hellespont with ease. In the night they have lights on either side, and watch if any ship steals down; just as they eclips those lights, they can see them and so fire upon them. Bellonius makes it but ¼ mile over; it is near a mile at least. I was not on the other side Castle, but I counted just 23 gun holes and thre sally ports between them; it seem'd a farre bigger castle than Abidos above said.

12. By reason of our present, with leave, we weigh'd at 10 o'clock, and within lesse then an houre we passt the other outward castles, but at too great a distance to say any more then that they are fairer and greater, and built according to modern formes. At night we reacht the N. end of Mitilene about 8 o'clock.

14. At 4½ in the morning within sight of the Centurion

and Smyrna Castle. At 10 we anchor'd, and went on board. Capt. Wild thence to the Advice frigot (then there in port), thence to Smyrna.

26*th*. Put my dear Lord Harvey's body on board the *Centurion*.[1] The great Cabin was hang'd and the floor cover'd with mourning; round about were fasten'd scutchions; the Steerage was hang'd likewise. My Lord's body was taken of the Dogger into the Centurion's long boat, there cover'd with a rich velvet Pal, bordered with white Sarsenet and satin. At the Head of the Corps was fixt a Hatchment, my Lord's armes, in a square frame standing on one of the corners. At the head of the boat was his six trumpeters and his drummer. The Advise's long boat tow'd it forward, and in it was his 6 Trumpeters likewise, and his drum, all sounding a dead march, went slowly forward in a round; the Consul's (Mr. Ricaut's) boat followed; after that many of the festoons in other boates. At its reception into the Centurion there was 3 voleyes of small shot and 30 Guns fired. The Advice fired 28; all the General ships and others in port fired, some 12, some 14, some 16 guns. Worthy Capt. Hill, who brought him out, fired every minute all the while we were going on the Dogger. The Body was put down into the hold, and a Cenotaph stood in the great cabbin, cover'd with the pall. The great Scutcheon displayed at the head six great tapers burning by in six great silver candlesticks. I gave away about 40 dwt. weights among the officers of the Centur., and sent a cask of 19 Meters of wine among the Seamen. We din'd aboard, treated civilly. The Consul brought flasques of Smyrna wine; Mr. Temple brought 20 flasques, and several fresh provisions. At 6 at night we all returned to Smyrna.

---

[1] The *Centurion* was a fourth-rate ship of the line, of 531 tons; *temp*. Charles II. (*Archæologia*, xi, 183.)

22. Parted from Mr. Temple's seate at 21st, midnight, or towards one o'clock this morn. Got on board the Mary and Martha by 6. Out of the sandhead, lay becalmed all that day and night over against the w. end of long Island.

29th, Wednesday. Ashoar at Tenedos; gave the Aga of the Castle 1 oak case.

All the Greeks live the N.E. end of the Town. They goe in the streets cover'd with a petticoat over their head, gather'd in to a button above; their gown without a wast, hang'd on with two latchets on either side, girdle above their brests. A bullock there for 4½, kil'd, drest, cut out in the street in ½ an hour. Holy fountain at the N.E. end. No church, but several Papasses say masse in a little hole in a stinking house, which the padres make a Tavern about 8 yards square; the V. M. in a little hole, etc.

2, *Saturday*, came to the custome house by 12 o'clock. Saluted the Seraglio with 7 guns. Deo laus et gloria ex grato corde.

*   *   *   *   *

Apr. 1st was Maunday Thursday, to the Greek it is μεγάλη πέφτη.[1] At daybreak the Patriarch washt the disciples' feet. A great waxe candle was brought before him (instead of a mace). He came to his throne in the ordinary habit. Every Greek (that makes it right) makes his crosse leisurely, ἐν τῷ ὀνόματα τοῦ πάτρος[2] ✠ (the top of the brest), καὶ τοῦ ὑιου ✠ (the middle), καὶ τοῦ ἁγίου πνέυ (✠ on the right above the pap), ματος (on the left above the pap). All the Metropolites do it very gravely. There were, 1st (next to the preacher's throne), Heraclea; 2d, Cyzikos; 3d, Νικομέδια; 4th, Chalcedon; 5th, Philippopoli, etc., etc. The patriarch came to his seat (whilst the choir sang the

---

[1] Great Thursday.
[2] "In the name of the Father and of the Son and of the Holy Ghost."

GREEK CHURCH CEREMONIES. 157

Gospel out of St. John 13). Then there were the 12 priests (all maryed), which came two and two, and bow'd to the ground, and kis't the patriarch's hand, retired back, ador'd again, and retired into the Sacristia. Then all array'd in priests' cloathing proper, only upon everyone's neck was the apostle wrought in gold, whom they represented. First came a miserable poor wretch (without a cape, etc.) to represent Judas; then a good stretch after followed all the rest, and seated themselves before the Patriarch, who was at the other end. Then the Patriarch vested himself in his robes, στοιχάριον,[1] with a hole on top like a surplice with sleeves, body to the ankles; sallow green (or yellow green) tuffetay, Ωράριον,[2] a broidered tippet, ἐπιμανίκιον,[3] embroyder'd sleeves (he crosses and kisses every vestment, and he was putting on this and forgot, then pul'd it of), ἐπιτραχήλιον,[4] embroyder'd kerchief put about his neck, Ζώνη his girdle (alla turkesa), ὑπογονάτιον,[5] a square embroyder'd handkerchief (foot and half square), with 4 tassels; it hang'd by his right side. Then his 2 deacons help him down (4 staires); he begin with Judas, and the Third deacon in the pulpit (reading the same Gospel) repeat to every washing, "He began to wash their feet," etc.; he kneels down, and washes the right foot (which only is bare), his 2 deacons helping him with bason, Ewers, etc. Whilst the 3d Deacon is in the pulpit reading, he strips himself of all his robes (the στοιχάριον, ἐπιμανίκιον, ὠράριον, ὑπογονάτιον), but the ἐπιτραχήλιον, and another lose vest, half slew'd[6] to draw the sleeves (with laces), set with 3 bells on each side, and two to each corner (likewise when he

---

[1] στοιχάρι = mod. Gk. surplice.
[2] ὠράριον = a stole.   [3] ἐπιμανίκιον = a maniple.
[4] ἐπιτραχήλιον is also a stole.
[5] ὑπογονάτιον is a part of a priest's dress in the form of a diamond, which hangs below the knee.
[6] Slew'd = swung round.

vested himself he put of his monkes hood), τὸ ἀπάνω καμηλαῦχον,[1] and divel's cap (as the G. S. cal'd it) τὸ ἔσω καμηλαῦχον, and put on an embroyder'd crown set with diamonds and pretious stones, and quarter'd (with 4 glass diamonds and perls); upon the top a crosse emerald and sapphire. He puts on a blewish *pestemal*[2] before him, and a large Towel over his shoulder, with which, when he has wash't the foot, he wipes, then kisses, and the person at same time kisses his crown. He proceeds (beginning at Judas) till he come to St. Peter 12; there begins a Dialogue; the Deacon go on to (Joh. 13); he asks: Lord, will you wash my feet, etc., the deacon only repeating the passing words; at last he wash him, too. Imediately all the rabble strive for the water to dip handkerchiefs in it, and a Greek answer'd me (as I ask't) that it must be very pretious after so many good prayers. This done, the Patriarch returns to his seat, the deacon leisurely reading the same Gospel again. He re-vests himself, the 12 rise, and, reverencing 2 by 2, return to the Sacristia; after them the Patriarch, then there changing his clothes for his ordinary habit, he returns to his seat, and then the masse begins. When he went out of the church his 2 deacons bore up his traine, the candle going before him. He treated me at his lodge with coffee; invited me to dinner, but Draco and I would not stay. Many gatherings for Judas[3]; amongst the rest there were there the 4 treasurers of the Church, οἱ ἐπίτροποι τοῦ παγκυρίου. There is a great chest, fair and rich, on the right hand coming in, called the παγκύριον. Draco's brother-in-Law, who was at first a furrier, is the chief, worth, by common report, 600 purses of money (300,000 doll. = 75,000 lb.).

---

[1] καμηλαύκι is the modern Greek for a priest's cap.
[2] Apron.
[3] Refers to the Greek custom, still in vogue, when they assemble shoot at a dummy Judas.

The Prince of Moldàvia owes him 80,000 doll. ; Wallachia as much ; the church as much ; and every Metropolite something. He gave a silver broach for candles, worth at least 500 doll., to μεγάλη ἐκκλησία. He hath taken the debt of the Church upon himself, covenanting to be continued 4 or 5 year. Over against the Patriarch's seat are two other of states just together : the first Moldavia, 2d Walachias ; but they two never meet together, but dispute their superiority, and therefore alwayes one or both are absent. The Patriarch, when he blesses the people, or his own vests., etc., lays the thumb of his right hand crosse the ring finger, the fore finger streight, the middle finger bending ; the mystery in it is I.C. X.C.[1] The people bow to the ground, then kiss the Patriarch's hand, then retire backward, reverance a 2d time, then go away as they goe back; some tumble over the head of the others bowing behind them. Before the Patriarch came the priests were anointing poor slaves, which priests must alwayes be 7 in number, and pray'd over them. In the masse the bread and wine are caryed in procession alwayes before they be consecrated ; the Patriarch comes down, and every Metropolite and all adore low to it as it passe by. When all is done the bread left upon the *prothesis*[2] (after the piece for the Sacrament is taken out as is comonly distributed) was given by the Patriarch himself, some in their mouths, some in their hands.

* * * * *

Mart. 23rd, 1676. Holy week. I was at the Sermon at St. Francesco's ; saw Demetrius Simon wash 12 of the fraternityes feet. The priest reads or sings the Gospell out of St. John 13, and he rose from his seat at the upper

---

[1] Final letters of words, ʼΙησοῦς and Χρίστος ; Byzantine form of Sigma.
[2] The *Prothesis* is the altar for shrew-bread in the Greek Church.

end of the stalls, and put of his vest, put on sackcloth, and gird himself with a *pestemal* put before him, and a towel on his shoulder, came down to the 12, who were sat on two formes in the chappell just before him, at these words, "He put water into a basin" (for the priest stayes till he may be ready), he puts water into a great basin. At those words, "Lord, not only my feet", he comes to the first, and pouring a little water upon his right foot, washes it, wipes it with his towell on his left shoulder, then signing it with the crosse, kisses it, and they kisse his hands; this he doth to everyone, then returne to his stall, and puts off his sackcloth, and resumes his other clothes. Then they go to their prayers; a layman sayes and sings most of them; the Prior or sub-prior gives the benediction.

July 17th. There was an old Lady (daughter to a Sultana of some of the former emperours), commonly now called Sultana Sporca,[1] from her ill manner of life, for she kept about 30 women slaves of youth and greatest beauty she could provide, and these were all taught to tumble, dance, and sing, and act many tricks; and so, often going abroad to great Bassa's houses to shew them sport, brought their old baw'd in a great revenue, every one presenting them liberally, and what they got she received. Amongst the rest she was possest of one of the greatest beauty that then was found (as was said), not onely in the Court, but the whole Empire, if not the world. When we were at Adrianople the Grand Signor sent to demand her for his own use; the Sultana denyed her, saying she had made her free, and that she could not now be used by them legally, but as his wife; thus she avoyded the G. Srs. importunety. Here about 10 dayes since she (continuing on the dancing trade) with her companions were at a great Bassa's house to tumble and play tricks, and the Capitaine

---

[1] Italian, "dirty".

of the guards to the G. V.[1] (who had been with him, and
fought valiantly in all his warres at Candia, etc., and was
become his favourite) chanct to be there ; and when the
girl had done, he (which is unusuall for strangers) presented her 200 zechines, being smitten most desperately
with her, and two dayes after sent to the Sultana, begging
that she might come to his house, and he promised 2,000
zechines reward ; they came, and after some houres sport
he sent home all the slaves, but kept her all night, and
next day conveighed her to a friend's house in Stambal ;
she was thre dayes by Mr. Hyet's house. The Sultana
next morn made Answer to the G. S., telling him that the
girl was really her slave, submitting herself to his mercy
for having cheated him before, saying it was only because
she was then too young for him, but now the captain had
violently ravisht her. The G. S. was as much inflamed on
the other side, partly with remembrance of former love,
partly with madnesse that he lost one so sweet. He
went immediately to the Viz., commanding him to look
into the businesse as his ; he cals the Captain, demands
why he had done so, and where she was, etc. He denys all;
says he abused her not, nor knew where she was. He sent
to the Kaimachan of Stambol, and charged him privately to
watch the Captain, etc. In the third night the Kaimachan
took them both about 12 at clock in bed, or on a sofa
together, brought them before the Grand Vizier. The Sultana (infinitely troubled) sent the Grand Signor word. The
Captain told him she had been at 40 other houses as well
as his, etc.; he was not afraid of death nor the sword (as'
he very well knew), and therefore valued not one straw
what became of him ; but all that he desired was that his
Mistress should be spared, in whome he should live even

---

[1] Grand Vizier Achmet Kiuprili, who won Crete for the Turks in
1669.

M

when he was dead. G. S. sent word immediately to strike of his head, which was done (he was strangled : Soliman Basha saw him), and the body lay'd publickly open at the Tents, with the head under his arme all day (July 18), being pay day, for all the Janissaryes to behold it. He had been infinitely beloved by them and all the court, and 2,000 purses of money had been offer'd to save him, but all impossible ; the girl was immediately taken into the Seraglio. I fancy this was at bottome onely a deep policy of the Grand Signior's Vizier, " it is necessary that one die for the people." People began to be mutinous and rebellious, and by the process of the story (for certainly the Vizier might have hinted something to the Captain when he set the Kaimachan to catch him, and have advised him to let the girl be forth coming under hand, making peace with the Sultana, etc.), some great example was to be made, which was on the Vizier's own favourite, etc.; else I must count it a severe piece of justice upon the Captain, who dare do that against Law which the G. S. refrained from. The G. S. kept the law which the Captain dare break, yet he knew her to be a slave, which the G. S. knew not, and that might alleviate. The Sultana was punisht as well in losing her slave and future gain. Or, lastly, we may roll the exorbitancy of Princes last, who desire to engrosse all pleasure to themselves. This great Capt.'s death breads ill blood in many hearts : his good services in the Field of Mars might have interceded for one spasso (recreation) in the court of Venus.

July 19*th*. From St. Swithin's day, 15th, the ayre was cloudy, and upon this day at even began a mist which daily increast to that thicknesse as no man could se 300 yards at sea, nor at land (unlesse on the hills) as far again. It was not a moist mist; it continued vehement till 28th, then dayly abated. The sun continually rose and set like blood ; most part of this time the wind blew strong, which is more wonderfull; at other times it carying all mists away. It lay continually betwixt N.E. and N.W., yet more to the E., then the W.; all which make one conclude that this mist was brought and continued from the Palus Mœotis and Black Sea it self, and gave us a perfect taste of the Cimmeriæ tenebræ. The 29th and 30th days of June almost cleare.

* * * * *

Aug. 24th, '76. The G. S.'s Tents. I have seen them and the rest at Adrianople and at Maidan[1] here several times. He hath but onely the three; the rest are little tents for his servants' kitching. I saw the G. Srs. tent at the shew at Adrianople, which was much the same in make and dimentions, but this at Maidan being most perfectly set out with all its appertenances, take its description. First, then, there was a small stand about 8 foot square within, with a paire of small staires to mount it, was cover'd with reddish or inclining to purple cloth, with 4 golden balls at the corners and one at the top; the corners were to be lifted up, or, if he desired more fresco, the whole side, as all the rest could be quite taken away, the cloth being fasten'd above with loopes and buttons of wood. This Kiosk, or stand, they remove upon many occasions; he had a farre greater at Demirdesh[2] to see the horse races. This stood next the outward door of the tents, looking towards the place of execution, as likewise to the plain where the Janissaryes are pay'd, etc., and he is there present himself. At the sights at Adrianople there was another for the young prince.

The first tent is square, supported with 7 wood posts one way and 4 the other way; it was 15 strides long and 12 broad; the roof flat, kept streight with ropes; a large round

---

[1] Lit. market-place.   [2] Demir-tash.

flower in the middle. They have sides for this in cold weather, which they can open and shut at pleasure; on the outside upon every post stands a golden ball or flower-pot. The second tent is round, supported by one standing post in the middle, with golden ball or pot at the top, by which there is drawn upon a cord a curtain at pleasure crosse the tent, on the outside of which he gives audience to his own ministers of state, or makes his great divan, and sits in justice; on the in or back side he gives audience to Embassadores, or the like. The diameter of this tent (that is, from edge to edge of the fringe that hangs above as the eaves of an house) was 17 paces; that in Adrianople was 15, so that it is plain they are made of severall bignesses. The under sides of this likewise were to let down or up, take on or off, at pleasure, by such kind of loopes above and on the sides, the button being a piece of wood; the interstices between, if they were above, were cover'd with a fring, one within the other; without, if it was on the side to clasp the curtains together, one was made to lap over the other, so that they can shut a tent up most exceedingly close and warme. The third tent is his long tent, supported with three posts, and golden balls on pots; it was long (from the eves at one end to the other) 35 paces; at Adrianople, 37; by putting of it and extending it they may easily gain or loose a pace or two. At the middle post, to the outward side, was set a bed or broad couch, bolstered up at both ends, of twilt or ticking sattin; the coverings, silk, embroyder'd. At Adrianople it was ten times richer, with gold and pearls, for without doubt they have alwayes ready several coverings. The floor on this and the round tent is covered next the ground with a thick sort of course Yorkshire or Kidderminster woollen cloth, over which at severall times they spread carpets, or foot cloths of severall richnesse and value. At Adrianople I saw it once with Persian carpets; another time with sattin, embroyder'd with massy gold, as the floor likewise was where my Lord had his audience ; the bolsters and cushions were suitable. Behind this was a partition wall made of canvas, the ground and the flowers of bits of cloth ; the covering of all these tents was on the outside a pale green canvas ; on the inside the ground satten flower'd with bits of divers colours, some satten, some fine cloth, and all the edges and seems were wrought with gold and silver twist. All the flowers and Kiosks, etc., wrought are fancyes not at all according to nature, and though all together showes very glorious and stately, yet in the particulars it is very bungling and blockish. They often bring in round bits of satten or cloath patch't one upon the other in their fruits and flowers, and being of divers colours, represent so many Crescents. They make likewise the figures of some antick birds, few beasts, but no men. The panes of the inside are all arch't as the wall tents belowe ; at bottom a fring as on the side. The vallance was of the same make, and were of various sorts and fancyes in several tents of party colours. Passing through the Partition wall we came to the Gr. Sr. sleeping tent, or bedchamber, which they call *oda*[1]; it is square, with a ridge above like a house, which is supported with two long posts, four shorter being at the corners under the eves, which hang over like a pent-house, as the wals which were made lattice fashion, and richly gilded and painted, with doors to open on thre sides ; it was about 12 or 13 foot square, for we were not suffer'd to enter neither here nor at Adrianople. When it is very hot these lattices alone are used ; if it be cold it is wal'd round with red cloth lined with flower'd damask. We looked in ; it is floored in like manner with the rest, sometimes richer, sometimes not ; there is a bed stand crosse the door at upper end, bolster'd at each end ; the bed stood plain, but they can set it out

---

[1] *Oda* = sleeping-room.

with severall adornments. Upon a settle or little stand by lay the Al Koran and a whimsicall coat of a great Santon[1] dervish, which was all cover'd with green silk; this was not there at Adrianople. The santones coat I saw taken out about ten dayes after; it was like a *Taberd*.[2] There are therefore three courts, as it were, all invironed with a wall tent, embattled like the walls of a City, which none else can have but himself; the flowers and corners are red canvas, the lists of white girt web, the ground green canvas; all in this fashion, but 4 have some severall fantasyes in some suits, which are not in other suits; yet the severall suits are uniforme to themselves. In the first court, therefore, stood the Kiosk, the square tent, round tent, and the *Capagasi*,[3] etc., and Long tent; in the 2d Court the *odà*, and many tents at distance two *oghlans*, or pages; and others in the third court were all other offices, Kitching, sherbets, etc. One side of this outward wall in the Maidan reached 400 paces; but that may alter, according to the ground on which they pitch it, which may be lesse, or far more, and the figure may alter; the foreside was about 100 paces. They have many bales of wall tents to adde upon occasion. We went in at a side door, having obtein'd first leave of the Capagasi; before the great or common door stood six Javelings, which, with horse-tayles about their upper end, and a golding globe at top, about 4 yards high, and just before them was pitch't a round ordinary tent, where the hangman set, and all publick justice is done in the sight of the G. Sr., who stands in his little Kiosk.

Upon the right hand, going up from thence, stood the

---

[1] *Santon* = holy man.

[2] *Tabard* was originally a light vest worn over the armour; and generally embroidered with the arms of the wearer.

[3] *Kapougi*, "gate-keeper"; and *Kapa Agasi*, "master of the gate".

Mosäifs[1] tent with 3 horse tayles before it, as every vizier of the bench hathe; but they have but two great tents in their first court, to wit, the square and long one. Next to his was the Muftis,[2] then the two Cadeleskiers',[3] all with but two tayles before them; then several bashes tents, then the vizier's tents, in all things equall to the G. Sr.'s in pomp and fashion, onely his walls are plain (as the rest of the great men), without battlements, and the balls of gold are lesse. The bignesse likwise of his tents did not agree, though that may depend upon the pitching, for the square tent or portico was 12 paces long and 8 broad. These tents were canvas without and within the ground, but the flowers were bits of cloth, satten, painted and gilded leather, very little silver and gold about them. In the place of audience was a stool cover'd with purple velvet for Embassadores audience; befor his 3 tayles was also a round tent for Justice; there sit also his under officers, to write Ashrs.[4] One side of his tent reach't down about 330 paces, the bredth at head was 80. Next, at a good distance, was the Vizier's tent; a long one stood without, where he or his *Hasnadar*[5] gave audience to all that came. He has two courts within; one long tent for himself, with artificial gardens about it, and all his slaves and waiting servants in 7 or 8 more round about him; these in the first court. In the second his agà,[6] and other tents for other servants. I have been treated there several times by his *sherbetjé basha*,[7] who was my friend; his tent is full of fingians,[8] snowpit fountain water, etc., all ready coffee, etc. Never tasted such sherbert in my life. All these tents front to one center; in a circle in the midst are tents belonging to the *Dafterdar*,[9]

---

[1] *Moutessaref,* "sub-governor of a province".
[2] *Mufti,* "the chief lawyer".
[3] Judge-advocates.
[4] Penalties.
[5] Treasurer.
[6] Captain.
[7] Pourer out of sherbet.
[8] Coffee-cups.
[9] *Dafterdar*= President of the Treasury.

where stood openly many, many sopets with money and treasure. Behind Kaseamstapha basha the G. Sr.'s son-in-law, Kaimachan of Adrianople. When we were there I was informed that they alwayes pitch't in this form. Behind the vizier were all the other bashas, and many other officers and servants. When they are at war the Janissaryes are placed round on the outside.

Now, on the land by Chalcedon is built a lighthouse or Pharos, which they call (as likewise a little village by it) Pheneir, and Phenerè,[1] as at Pompey's pillar, which I question not was erected for the same purpose. Coming from thence, on the shoar towardes the factory seraglio is a fair large fountain; just by it a garden new empaled, and enlarged much bigger then it was. A great kiosk in it, then ready furnish't for the G. Sr.; under it, about 15 or 20 steps, is a fountain of delicate water, which the G. Sr. uses now daily. At Scutary there are very fine walks, all shaded with Cipresse (most), pine, firre, some oak, ash, Lotus, horse chesnut, cherry, beach, and other trees; there are new taken in two or three vinyards. There are several Arbors cover'd with vines of delicate grapes. The Bustange[2] invited us in, and treated us very civilly.

* * * * *

I was at the Dervises in Galata, which Dervise Mustapha the Näizam bashè, or head of the players of the pipe which they call Näi.[3] He hath been there 14 years, his pay is 45 aspers[4]; to the rest he payes 5, 6, 7, 8, or more, as they are deserving. They have 100 kilos of wheat per annum, 100 per annum vacoof,[5] 3,000 aspers per man; from the G. Sr., 10 sheep at little Beiram, 100 at Ramazam. They have usuall prayers in the houses, and he that is devout may

---

[1] Modern Greek, *Phanari.*
[2] *Bostangee* = gardener.
[3] *Naï* = a flute made out of a reed.
[4] *Vide* note, p. 145.
[5] *Vakouf* = money from the mosque property.

pray all night long, fast, etc. There are 4 Tekyes[1] or monasteryes, of them here one, two Kasoumpasha, 3 Bisicktash, 4 Yenicapon; on Stambal side there are eighteen sorts of them. These founded first by Molàh Hunkyòr, Harset meulanàh, for he goeth by both these names. Heretofore they preach't, danc't, and piped every Tuesday and Friday. 3 lye here buryed : 1. Arzéh Mahmet effendi, a great benefactor to them ; 2. Ismèl Effendi, who was once their sheik (or head, though it signifies prince) and benefactor ; 3. Ismaèl Effendi, another benefactor, who built them 10 chambers, and left them 1,000 dollars. They let their neighbours be there buried for their money. Formerly, the *Baltagee*[2] of Galata seraglio were buryed there ; now they have a corner apart. There Govisè Achmet is their Sheich now, who receives all the money, and hath himself $1\frac{1}{2}d$. per day. Their musick is a Tambor, and a long week small lute with wire strings, to which they sound their Nai or pipe, whereof they have two sorts, a base and a treble ; for the middle ones partake of that to which they are nearest. The little pipes have 7 holes on the upper side all in a row, and an eighth at the bottom, a little of one side, and just in the middle (measuring from that lowest eighth hole upwards) on the back is a 9th hole. Some of these are a foot and $\frac{1}{2}$ long ; some lesse, some more. The long pipe hath six holes, on one side three, and three at equal distances, and on the back side, just half way, there is a 7th hole. There is neither a fipple[3] above, nor noze[4] in the mouth, but the head is a horn sloped up and brought to a very fine edge, which leaning sidewayes to the mouth, gives the sound, as boyes (with us) used to whistle in acorn cups, this πλαγιαῦ-

---

[1] *Tekie* = Dervish's monastery.   [2] *Baltagee* = axe-bearers.
[3] Fipple = a stopper. "In recorders, which go with a gentle breath ; the concave of the pipe, were it not for the *fipple*, that straiteneth the air much more than the simple concave, would yield no sound." (Bacon, *Nat. Hist.*, § 116.)   [4] Noze = nozzle.

λος[1]; whence our flagiolet. Shepherds use smal pipes of wood with such mouths, and some I have seen of the wings and thigh bones of Crowes, Bustards, Pelicanes, etc.,[2] from whence of old were cal'd *tibia*. These dervish pipes are very dear, not one of twenty proving good and true. The smallest and deepest he ask 3 dollrs. for, and some of the largest he vallued at 20 dollrs. One (which had belong'd to the Convent these 300 yeares) he valued at 50 dollrs.; yet more for its sweetnesse, then antiquity. They play mournfull tones, but seldom any poynt of musick. They are all made of Indian canes, just such as we make our fishing-rods in England of; the workmanship and luck in proving good give them their price. At every joynt they are whipt with gut strings, more for ornament then strength. The present G. Sr. is much delighted with them.

We went to see the vaults under Sta. Sophia; they were full of water, then 17 ft. deep, and overhead from the water up to the top of the arch, about 2 yards and 6 inches. Every pillar is square 4½ feet, and distant one from another just 12 feet. The bricks very broad, thin, wel baked; not playstered within; the mortar very hard. They say it goes under Atmaidan[3]; we could not enter it. The wast water of the aquaeduct enters into it and out of it, passing through the Seraglio goes into sea by the dunghill. Severe punishment to have houses with offices into it, or throw any filth into it; the well of Sta. Sophia runs into it, and many wells in the Seraglio, etc.

---

[1] πλαγιαῦλος = Mod. Gr., a transverse flute.
[2] Still in use in the Greek islands.
[3] At Maidan = the horse-market.

AN ACCOUNT OF OUR JOURNEY TO ADRIANOPLE,
1675.

You must note that in Turkey navigators reckon their way by houres, not by miles; however, I have made an estimate of every dayes journey both wayes, reckoning 3 miles to the hour, and, truely, I believe that our pace in generall did come pretty just to that proportion.

May 2d, 1675. To *Ponte piccolo*, hours 7½, miles 23. Upon a Sunday, after morning prayer and a sermon, we set out, being about 100 horsemen. My Ld. and Sr. Tho. Baines[1] road in a kind of double horse litter, used by the great men in Turkey, caryed by 4 mules, cover'd with fine wrought cloath. The name for this thing is a *Takt-i-rovan*, which is as much as a running seat (*Takt*, "seat"; *reván*, "current") in Persian, from whence they have taken this state. There were four mulitecrs to attend upon it, and two *Mestagées*,[2] or fire caryers, to go before it; they carry upon a great staff, or short pole, an Iron made just like our beacons, into which, when evening is come, they put *Pinus sylvestris*, which they call *Sheráh*, or χερὰ, and being very fat and unctious, it flames and burnes well, and lasts long; but to supply their fire they have each man his bag full of shivers and splinters of the wood, with which they tend this fire. Wherever my Ld. (as the like is observed to the vizier, and all other great persons travayling) took up his lodging, so soon as it began to grow darke, they came and fixed these beacons, by irons sharpened on purpose at the lower end, just before his door (or tent, when he lay in one), and then began a short prayer for the Gr. Signor, the Embassador (or their patrone), and all the company, par-

---

[1] *Vide* Introduction for an account of Sir John Finch and Sir Thomas Baines.   [2] Deriv. *Mesh*, "a torch".

ticularly naming every one, the Treasurer, Secretary, Papas (or chaplain), Turgemen, etc. This is the use of the Countrey, and if the grandees travayl in the night, or goe but a street's length in their cityes, these *Mestages* goe before them instead of lanthorn men, or torches. I thought good to mention them thus fully here, because here it first occurres, and you will meet with them often in the insuing story. My Ld. had a coach also, which went by empty with six horses, postillions, trappings, etc., all *alla Turchesca* (as the fashion here); the coachman rides on one of the hinder horses, and not in the boxe, though sometime I have observed it. So likewise the chief *Turgeman* (or as we commonly call him, the *Dragoman*) had his coach and 4, large; all the principle attendants there had also their carts (or rather waggon coaches) with 4 wheels, and some two horses; some three horses all abreast. I fancy your *Trigae*[1] were such; for I have observed here many antient customs and fashions yet remaining. I, amongst the rest, was appointed to have one to carry my cloathes and other baggage, as likewise I had my servant, and a *seis*, or groom, to look after my horse. There were above 60 of these waggon coaches in all, with all this trayn, and about 20 or 30 strangers that went onely to set us out the Town. We left Pera, May 2d, and though our way from Stambul is direct and short, yet, we being on the other side of the water (the Sinus Ceratinus), we were forc't to go about by the meadowes, where, by the help of two bridges, we past the two streames (or cornua) that meet to make up the creek that separates Pera from Stambal. Within 1½ h. we came to the first rivulet, cal'd of old *Barbyses*. About a mile further we passed the 2d rivulet, of old *Cydarus;* both are very accurately described, with all the little hills and valleys about them, by *P. Gyllius*, in his Bosp. Thrace,

---

Trigae = three-horsed chariots.

l. 2, c. 3, onely *Barbyses* hath a stronger current, especially in winter. I have been often times *alla caccia* from one end to the other of it. A mile further we came to the suburbs of Stambal, commonly called Job's tomb, but it is the dormitorys or Mausoleums of severall Turkish princes, Viziers, warriors, and men of fame amongst them, one whereof was called Jüpe (as they now call Jacob, and the Armenians call him Agúp), which gave name to the place, and I veryly believe *Gyllius*, l. 2, c. 2, was either mistaken or misinformed when he calls him *Aibabarius*, for the Turkes call the place *Aiübazár*, which is the mercate place of Jüp (*Bazár* being in Turkish the Mercate place, as Balukbazár, etc., the fish mercate, etc.). I have been often there amongst the tombs. From Jüp bazár we came under Stambal walls, which are distant from thence about ½ mile, and, passing about a mile further, we came to Adrianople gate, from which we insisted on the direct great road, as followeth about three mile of; we crosse a little rill, not much worth your notice, but onely I resolved to set down every water run, that (if possible) I might give some light to your antient Geographers, our common maps (Ortelius, Ptolomy, Sansoin, etc.) being very false. We left two little Turkish townes on our right hand, *Dav'd Basha* (David Basha), a mile from Adrianople gate, and as much farther *Hasnadarcui* (Treasurer's town); *cui* is a common termination, as *ton*, *don*, etc., with us, and signifyes a village or town. A little beyond the foresaid rill is a very large *chinàr*, or plane-tree, with a square green bank cast up about it, and a very noble fountain by. Here in sommer many come to take their *spasso* and recreation in the shade (which that tree casts), sitting upon carpet with tobacco, coffee, and pure water, etc. Three miles farther we cross two other little rills, which meeting together (and, as I suppose, with the former), make a large stream, which enters the sea between Stambol and Cape

Stephano (the mouth being within 2 mile of this latter. About a mile farther is a brook (then it was dry) with a stone bridge of 6 arches, and a little farther a rivulet with a stone arch over it. I verily believe all these unite and enter the sea as above say'd, for all the way from the first to the last is low, flat ground, and these may very well meet there towards the sea; but I am convinct of it by reason I have been at *Ponte piccolo* by water many a time, and never observed any other outlet into the sea but in the place aforesaid. We come from Adrianople gate to *Ponte piccolo* in 4 hrs.; it must be about 12 miles.

Ponte piccolo is called by the Turkes K'ootchóok chekmejé (it is little chest or cabinet), by the Greeks μικρὸ χωριὸ, or little town. It is inhabited partly by Greekes, partly by Turkes, and is about the bignesse of Newmarket. It has one large street, through which lyes the road, in which are many shops of victuallers, Knackers, and makers of horse furniture, smiths, etc., all fitted for travaylers. There are severall (*Chans, or caravanserais*) stables, and lodgings for passengers: that is, roome and provisions for horses and mules, and by them room for men to lye down; but if you carry not your couches or quilts with you, you must take up your lodging upon the cold ground here, and everywhere else in Turkey upon the road; as likewise your victualls in some places may be had drest for you in such shops as I have mention'd, or else you must carry it with you, and cook it yourself, or live upon barly and chopt straw with your horse. Here our caterer (or purveyor) found very good fish of all sorts by reason of the sea and a lake being very nigh, but in other townes travaylers find nothing but leekes, garlick, onyons, bread, salt, pickled olives, cabbidge, cowcombers, melons, and the like, little bits of broyl'd flesse, which they call *Kibób*, but whole joynts nowhere, rice, pancakes, and severall kinds of pastery meates. We, being so many in number, had a man who alwayes went before to every *Conáck*, or stage, and brought in muttons, beafes, veales, and the like, what he could get, having two *Chiaúses* to assist him, else the people would in most places not afford us anything, the best Turkes, if they travayl alone, being content with the fare of the road above-named. At our entrance on the East side the town standes the Turke's *Mosché*, and a college, or hospital, both built by one *Abdisalláh* (*i.e.*, the Slave of God), *Tefterdóre* (Treasurer) to *Sultan Solyman;* (others say to Sultan Osman). There is there allowed maintenance for three learned men in the law, or Chiefes, at one dollar per diem, as likewise rice, butter, bread, etc., for them and twenty more students there under them, who have the salary of 18 Aspers per diem. There my Ld. and all us that belong'd to his court were lodged, and they, according to their statutes, at night came and brought us two or three great platters of their pottage (made of rice and onyons, etc.), and for everyone a loaf of their bread. Any great personage passing that way may lodge there, and cannot be denyed neither room nor this entertainment. They get well by it, for at parting every great man leaves some charity to them, as we also did. There is a pretty large court, as bigge as the second in Emanuell Coll., one story high, with cloysters and little chambers (with chimneys) round about, and a fountain in the middest. All passengers carry their own beds, or mats, or quilts to sleep on and set on, for, as is before said, you find room, but nothing but the bare wall besides. I and two or three companyons slept on carpets in the Cloysters, it being very hot weather; my Ld. and Sr. Tho. Baines had travayling beds to set up and take down upon all occasions. Our cookes and such like went allwayes before us, and in every Conack we had our provisions ready all the way against our coming in. At the end of the great street we past over a water and a moory ground by a long bridge and causeway, having a great lake on the right hand and the Sea on the left, separated by a small peninsula of land. The bridge hath 12 arches: the first, *Ponte piccolo*, very large, next the Town over the chief stream; then two lesse at a good distance; then nine more as much farther. These last serve only to let the water passe that fall from the hills in winter, and would be prest up by the bridge and caseway, and so otherwise would endanger both. The bridge is stone, rayed (striped) with slight timbers on each side. It is about 312 of my paces long, broad enough for 3 carts to passe one by the other; to it is joyned the caseway of stone 462 of my paces, and at the bridge foot it is about $2\frac{1}{2}$ foot high. I find this lake in Ortelius map of old Thrace to be cal'd *Myrmex Lacus*, but he hath not taken notice of a fresh water river that runs through it, which I have rowed up and down at least 5 or 6 miles. It runs with a small but very strong stream, so that at the mouth, where it empties itself into the sea, our boates from *Stambol* enter with great difficulty, as likewise it is very deep and very strong under the great Arch of the bridge, where, though the water continually sets out, yet the water in the lake tastes brackish. Up this fresh river, about 5 or 6 mile, is on the right hand a very high and steep mountain, with a most famous cave, which runs 10 or 12 mile underground, and is hewn in many places that two or three men may walk abreast at their full height.

May 3d. To *Ponte grande* $4\frac{1}{4}$ h., miles 13. Going from *Ponte piccolo*, so soon as you are of the caseway and past the moor you rise up an easy hill, at the foot of which, just by the corner of the lake, is a little village on your left hand call'd *Coomcui*, or Sand-town, from the sand hard by there in the lake; onely Greekes live in it, and have forgot the Greek name, or else it never had any. About a mile or two farther on the right hand, at the edge of the lake, is another, called by the Greekes *Cabárana*. Half way to *Ponte grande* you leave a little Greek town on the right hand hardly cal'd *Ahúrcui;* thence you descend a little but very steep valley, and in the bottome is a little river with a stone bridge of three arches. This valley is not much above one mile over, but is a very dangerous place for robberys and murders, and therefore is cal'd by the Turkes *Aram-derry*, or accursed valley. On the brow of the hill on the other side this valley stands a very fine but little queach[1] of popalar, cipresse, and some elme and willow trees very thick to-gether; it is paled in very high, like one of our parkes. In the midst of it is a seraglio of the G. Signor's, where formerly they came in summer for pleasure. Under the pales, upon the road, is a couple of clear and very large fountaines with severall cisternes, where some few comrades of us made a halt and took a dram of the bottle. *Ponte grande* is cal'd by the Turkes *Buyobk-checmedje* (or great-chest, abusing the word *checkmése* for a wooden bridge, as both these and the other bridges at *Ponte piccolo* at first were of wood), in Greek μεγάλο χωριὸ, or great town. The inhabitants are most Turkes, some Jewes and Armenians, but more Greekes mixt with them. The road and the sea makes this Town, as well as *Ponte piccolo*, flourish. This is bigger then it; there is likewise good store of excellent fresh-water fish, as likewise of sea fish. On the west side the town lyes a great Lake which hath communication with the sea, and seemes to have been an arme of it antiently, but now cut of from it except in 4 places which we passe by bridges, now of late yeares made of stone, but there remain ruines of wood, which show them to have been of old of timber upon stone cheekes,[2] to draw up and down and move into the Lake, we passing them to the right hand. The water, when we

---

[1] A queach is a thick, bushy plot, a *quick*-set hedge. "The fortresses of thorniest queache." (Chapman's Homer, *Hymn to Pau*.)

[2] Sides or supports.

N

past, was not very deep. These four bridges are joyned together by stone casewayes, which in winter, if more rain falls then is vented by the arches or covered with it, yet there being room for the water to play, all is with out danger or damage, the stones towards the lake being clenched with lead one to another. The first case-way from the street end is 60 paces, that bridge is 183 paces with 7 arches; 2d caseway, 39 paces; the bridge 166, with 7 arches; 3d caseway, 19 paces; the bridge 127 with 5 arches; 4th caseway, 14 paces; the bridge 233 with 9 arches; the last caseway about 30 paces—all soe wide as three carts may goe abreast. I am the more particular in these little things, that you may see the Turkes are neither niggards nor fooles in these public workes, for I assure you I never saw stronger work than among them; and some things are as fine and neat as we can possibly shew. There is a large river which enters this lake at the north, but runs not very swift. The Greekes call it now Μαυροπόταμι, the Black river; the Turkes very near the same, *Kará-sou*, Black water. Now judge you whether *Athyrus* runs here or no.[1] The sea comes up to the bridge; though it is very shallow, yet it is a pretty harbour for small vessels out a little farther between the two capes, and this little port addes to the greatnesse of this town above the other *ponte*, where there is none. My Ld. was Lodged on the side of the Lake, at the end of the Town; the weeds and dead carcases, and other filth which they dayly cast in, in the hot weather, made so foul a stink as we were all almost stifled with it. Here are in the town many, many *chanes*,[2] besides where we lay, and several pretty large streets. For building, once for all I must tell you there is none all over Turkey but what is very mean and beggarly, and for the most part dark and sluttish: I

---

[1] Marked on Ortelius' map. [2] Inns.

except your Moschés, Seraglios, and publick buildings onely. Some great men of late (as this present Vizier now at Stamboul) have ventured upon great buildings for themselves, but it doth often prove their ruin ; they becoming thereby suspected for becoming too great, and so the G. Signor cuts them of and seizes their possessions.

May 3*d.* To *Selibria* h. 5¾, miles 17. Going from *Ponte grande*, so soon as we had past the bridges and began to rise up the hill, there we past two little townes, both inhabited by Greekes ; one on the right hand called Πλάγια, the other on the left, by the sea, called Καλικράρια. We called at these by reason of the fame of good wine there, which we found true. About 6 or 7 miles from thence, on the left hand, stands a little town on a promontory looking into the sea ; the name I could not learn. About a mile farther we passe a little rill, and a mile beyond that (which is about half way to Selibria), we go by a little ruinated town, just in the very sea, the road lying upon the sand ; the town stands to the right hand, in Turkish *Koombúrgás*, or sand-burough[1] ; in Greek Κουμιὸ, a word corrupted from the Turkish *Kobm*, which is sand. We had very good wine there, especially a small sort of claret. There hath been formerly a little castle or fort there, but all the great stones are picked out and carryed to *Stambol*. The *Valedéh-Jámisi* and *Valedéh-Chane*,[2] *i.e.*, the Q. Mother's Mosch, and the Publick *Chane* or *Hostelry*, was built with part of them. As once for all, I must tell you that round Stambol for many miles the Turkes have taken almost all the fair stone they could find to rayse their buildings in the City, so that little is to be expected of inscriptions or monuments of antiquity ; especially in Thrace, or anywhere near the shore of the Propontis, from whence caryage by sea is easy. Nothing remaining in a

---

[1] Still known by this name. [2] Valedéh Sultan = Queen-mother.

manner but the inward part of the walls of old buildings;
the Maidan,[1] the case or outside of it was of good stone,
being pull'd down and disposed of. This hath been a pretty
town, but now it is nothing by its situation. About 2 miles
from hence we passe another, a pretty mercate towne, and
rich by reason of the road, and a little port for small boates.
It is cal'd in Turkish *Bogáthos*[2]; the inhabitants are most
Greekes, but in the great street are many Turkes. There
is yet standing a little tower with very thick walls, which is
now turned into a granary. About three miles from thence
we enter into a Moorish ground, which we passe by. A
caseway and bridges of stone, of one arch apiece, over as
many little streames, deep, but very narrow, which uniting
hard by, enter the sea (which is all the way in sight to our
left hand), in one pretty large channell; it being the onely
stream that deserves the name of a river from *Ponte-grande*
to *Heraclea* (Erekli).

* * * * *

May 5th. To Ciorlúh (Chiorlóo we pronounce it), 8½ h.,
25 mi.[3]

Going from Selibria,[4] we leave the Sea (having hitherto
had it all the way on our left hand), and mount, arising
well into a plain champion[5] country, as indeed all the way
to Adrianople is champion. Scarce a tree, unless some few
about *Chiorlóo* to be seen; by which you may imagine
what brave hunting and hawking the G. Signors have
there. Just under Selibria runs a small rill, which enlarges
into a kind of pond at the very town, over which we past
by a stone bridge of 4 arches; and about a quarter of a
mile further we enter a moorish ground, in which is a very
fair stone bridge of 32 arches, and with the ascents at each end

---

[1] Market-place.   [2] Modern maps *Boiados*.
[3] Spelt on modern maps *Tchorlou*.   [4] *Silivri*.
[5] Champion=champaign, a flat, open country. "The Canaanites
which dwell in the *champaign* over against Gilgal." (Deut. xi, 30.)

it is about 450 paces. The water under it was little and did not run, which made me conclude the bridge built onely in case of land floods in winter time, which must needs be occasioned by rain from the neighbouring hills, they being steep and enclosing this flat ground on every side. I could perceive this overflowing water enter'd the Sea in one mouth with the little rill before mentioned ; and besides this there is no other river near to *Selibria*. About 8 mile of from it by the sea side I crosst another little one as I came home. Out of this moor we rise (as is said) to the top of a hill, into a plain, which is a black spongy soil, and seemes to be very binding, for there we saw them at plow with 6, some 7, some 8 yoke of oxen in a plow ; especially where they were new breaking up. The first town we came at was called *Kinnekléh*,[1] a little Turkish town in a very fertile playn. About half way we crost a little river, which enters the sea about 3 or 4 miles to the W. of Heraclea, or rather is that just now mentioned 8 mile from Selibria.

* * * * *

Chiorlóo or *Chiorlúh* hath been a very large town, as it is yet most inhabited by Turkes, yet there are Armenians, Jewes, and Greekes too. It is not onely a great road town, but also a very great trade, and mercate is driven there for all sorts of commodityes. On the east side the town runs a great dry grasse, as big as the Divels ditch at Newmarket, in which are severall fountaines, yet standing, of excellent water. At the lower end (from the Town) it is crost with an aquaeduct of 96 paces long (the distance from edge to edge of the grass), with one onely little high arch in the midst. It is decay'd and dayly running to ruine, yet the earthern pipes on the top are yet whole, and the water runs still in them. It was a very antient way of conveighing water, and far

---

[1] Probably *Sinekly* in modern maps.

beyond either wood or lead. I saw several old ones at *Carthage, Ephesus, Smyrna*, etc., which must needs some of them have lain in the ground thousands of yeares unperisht. I shall briefly give you this description: they make earthen trunks about foot and half (sometimes little more) long; one end is made with a shoulder, the other end with a female grove (to receive that end of a second trunk). Now to close each joynt they have an excellent mortar, which they call *Lukiûm* or *Lookioóm;* it is made of unslaked lime and beaten brick, most finely powdered and sifted, cotton wool very thinly pul'd and strew'd on, and then all slaked with linseed oyle and mixt together, then they reject whilst it is fresh made, otherwise it hardens immediately. Then care is to be taken that the trunkes be kept from force, and they will endure to eternity. Beneath this dry grasse to the North are many vinyards, fig trees, etc. There have been within this 20 yeares here in town above 400 Greek familyes, now they are shrank to near upon 100; yet they are forc't to pay the same *Harátch* (pol money) and other dutyes (for *the G. Signor's lead cannot sink;* he will lose nothing of what once is settled to him), which comes to 1,000 dollrs. per annum, just as they did before; which makes the poor creatures yearly break and run away. They have but one Church, a little poor thing, but kept spruce and neat, there belonging to it a Bp., 4 priests, and 2 deacons. I was there at Vespers with them, and found them extremely civil, and they shewed me all the town. Over their church door they have fixt a pittyfull marble stone, which they saved out of the ruines of an old castle that was here; it was all flead[1] to build the Turkish moschs, which are at least 12 in all.

* * * * *

---

[1] *Flead*=stripped. " He ought to sheere, not to *flea* his sheepe." (Ben Jonson, *Discoveries*.)

May 6th. To *Karesterán*[1] 6 h., miles 17. Going from *Chiorloo*, about a little mile, we passe a little river; over it was an old stone bridge, almost broken down, which have had 4 arches. Just half way to *Karesterán* we passe a good large river, though in sommer it is almost damn'd up with sand; there is a good large bridge over it of wood, but slight timbers in it. All the way it was still Champion ground, most like a black moorish soyl, yet I judged it lighter than that on the other side *Ciorlóo*, because we saw severall ploughs with but 4 oxen in them, and those yoaked all abreast. The town has its name from *Karismack, i.e.*, to mingle or knead; for the least rayn (as we experienced when we were there) makes the spongy, soapy (fuller's) earth just like past. Upon the S.E. side of the Town, about one quarter of a mile, runs a small river, but very strong stream; there is a bridge there with 8 arches and about 100 paces in length. The river may easily in many places be leapt over; yet in winter the water overflows farre. From a delicate cleer fountain on the same side the town beyond this river, upon the side of the hill (to our right hand, as we descend to come hither), is an Aquæduct brought, and in the valley are three steps or pyramids built to divide the water into severall trunks, as also to let the overplus run in winter, without prejudice to the course of the rest. Just about the spring growes infinite of excellent *scordium*,[2] which I have found an excellent preservative against the plague. Here is a very good Mosch here, and a large *châne*. The town is enriched onely by travailers; at present it is but small, and built but in latter times out of the mines of Miso.

May 7th. To *Bourgas*[3] 4 h., miles 12. About 2 or 3 miles from *Carestéran* are several decay'd fountaines by the road side. At 4 mile is a very good fountain that runs

---

[1] On modern maps *Karitchtran*. [2] Garlic.
[3] Modern *Lule-Bourgas*.

plentifully, with cisternes for horses to drink. A little farther are several little rills, with one arch't bridges over them, and hard by a pretty big river, but no bridge. Just half way on the left hand, on the very road, is raysed a good great hill, with a *fossa*[1] about it, and an entrance on the side next the road up to it. I take it to be a monument of the dead, slain in some battle fought upon these plaines. We have observed many such, as shall be say'd : it was an antient custome and right paid to kings (as about Gallopoly) and inferior persons. It is as high as Bartlow hills, but the fossa is in a manner fill'd up. From the top we counted 12 villages spread round about ; it is seen almost to *Burgas*. Within two mile of *Burgas* the earth alters to a lighter kind of sandy soyl, yet Plowmen were there breaking up with 6 yoak of oxen in a plough.

Burgás is a pretty large market town. We passe over a pretty street or two ; then came a most stately *Châne*, having a fair square court and large fountain in the middest of it, and cloysters round about ; then fine apartments able to hold well nigh 1,000 travaylers with their beasts. This is joyned to a very brave *Mosch* by a large *Cupola* crosse the main road, supported by 4 arches (28½ feet wide) ; the street passe under two, and the passage from the *Châne* to the Mosch goes under the other. Entering into the Kháne (for you must pronounce it in the throat) sit many shopkeepers; amongst the rest, the finest Tobacco-pipe heads are sold there that are to be found in Turkey. The Town is all Turkish, and very populous for the bignesse. Mahomet, Vizierarém[2] to Sultan Solyman, had a son, Bassa of Morea ; complaints were made of him at court. The G. Signor

---

[1] Trench.

[2] *Mohamed the Bosnian*, better known as Sokolli, from the castle of Sokol, where he was born, retained the Grand Vizierate for fifteen years, under three Sultans, and did much for the then rapidly-decaying Ottoman power.

bid him advise his son to do better. He, without any more adoe, sent and took of his head and presented it to the G. S., who for his severe government in that point gave him all his son's estate (which otherwise falls to the G. S.), with which he built several noble buildings, whereof this *Khâne* and Mosch are none of the least. On the W. side the Town (which we past the next day) runs a small river, on which stands a Turkish mill, driving 3 pair of quernes (each mill grinding 10 *Kilos* or bushels of wheat in 12 houres), and yet the water there is not so wide but I could easily step over it. They are Greekes that forme the mill, which belong to 'Αγιαβαλάκ, a little town (concerning which more presently) hard by. There is also just by this town a tile kill, formed by other Greekes of the same place; though the soyl all the way hither is black and spongy moorish ground, yet here is so good a naturall mixture of sand as to make most excellent tile. Over the river, going out of town, is a bridge of 4 arches, long in all 146 paces; the stream is nothing in sommer, but the Town standing in a kind of pan in winter, it must needs be great. The stone with which this bridge is built is such a porous kind of hard *pumex* as I never beheld; it seem'd to me to have been made of clay and pills of sand, which afterwards mouldring away might cause those eyes. Down the river hard by is a Turkish town cal'd *Múctary*.

May 8th. To *Bobbás-cui* 4½ h., miles 13. About a mile from Burgas, standing upon a little hill on the left hand, we saw ἀγιαβαλάκ, a little Greek town (as is said), but very populous, there being now above 400 familyes in it, many of the men going out to work all the week (as before is intimated), and returning on Saturday, live very well, they being farre more industrious then any of the Greekes I ordinarily ever met with. About six mile of from *Bobbas-cui* we crossed a little brook; a mile and ½ farther another; as far again a third, with bridge, all almost dry. An old Turk took it from the Christians, and from him it is now so named, for *bobbá*[1] is the common name for *Father*, and is given to every old man in common discourse. He lyes buryed in St. Nicholas' church, the one thing remaining of the Greekes memoriall or building here. It is made a place of prayer, and he is reckoned a great saint amongst the common people. When we went into it to see his tomb we met another old Turk, who had brought three candles, and presented them to an old woman that looks after it, and shews it to strangers. He said he had made a vow in distresse to do it. The old woman told us: Yes, my sons, when ever you are in danger pray to this good holy man, and he will infallibly help you. Oh, fye! sister, quoth the old Turk, do not so vainly commit sin, for he was a mortall man and a sinner as well as we. I know it, quoth the old wife, that onely God doth all, and he doth nothing; but God for his sake will the sooner hear us; and so ended that point of Turkish divinity. This Church is standing pretty intire. It is but little (as I above said, I guesse most others were), but very handsome, in the same forme almost with Sta. Sophia, with a great *Cupola* over the body of it; but the outward wall is scaloped. On the east side the town as we goe in runs a little pretty river just under this church, and hath a very well built stone bridge as ever I saw for the bignesse, of a very hard freestone. It is broad enough for 3 carts to goe abreast. It is 232 of my paces, beside the ascents at each end. It hath 6 little arches in the midst, and severall little flood-gates on each flank. All stones are rob'd here, likewise to build their Moschs, which here are 3 or 4, one very fine one. The town is a pretty large town, and will dayly increase. *Ibrahim bassa* (now General of the Turks' army), in

---

[1] Or, rather, Baba, now called Eski-Baba. Ortelius calls it *Siki-baba*.

bringing an Aquæduct thither, the shafts were open'd not far of from the W. side the town.

May 9th. To *Háfsa*,[1] 6 houres, miles 18. Going a little out of Bobbas-cui, on the left hand, is another great hill, cast up, I suppose, on the same account with that between *Coresteran* and *Burgas*, but not so big, nor so high. Upon the Top of it lyes now a very long Turkish tomb. That I may here tell you the difference, you must know that they never lay anything over their dead but the earth. All the sides of their tombs are good stone, but above nothing but earth, except in your Royall Mausoleum or those of great men. There they place a cœnotaph over the grave, and a great candle at head and feet, and at the head the fashions of the cap he wore, by which is known whether he was a man of the law, or some civil magistrate, or souldjer or woman, etc.

About seven mile on the road we passe a little, little hamlet cal'd *Coopháteui*, or *coophas-cui*. About a mile and ½ from thence (I guesse it half way) we crost a little brook which ran plentifully, but as we return'd it was dry. When we came within 3 or 4 mile of *Háfsa* we saw the top of mount Rhodope, which lyeth beyond Adrianople to the west, as afterwards shall be sayd. This name is wrote severall wayes, but pronounced all alike. Here is a most noble *Châne*, farre better then that at Burgas, and likewise a *Cupola* crosse the street, and a fair mosch annext in the same manner there described; but these two latter are as farre inferior as the other is superior. All were built by the same Mahomet Vizierarem, who built those at Burgas; thence they were made in the same fashion. He lyes buried at *Jupe* (before mention'd) in a fair mausoleum which I have seen; and it is reported of him that he repair'd all the publick bridges in the Turkes' territoryes from Adrianople into the bounds of Persia; and built as

---

[1] Modern name the same. Ortelius calls it *Capsia*.

many Moschs and Chánes as there are dayes in the year; and by this means continued Vizier 40 years, an unusual thing in this court, for it is a wonder in this present *Kiuprili*[1] not so much that he succeeded his father, as that he hath staid in so long.

May 10*th.* To *Adrianople,* houres 5½, miles 17. Khavsa lyes S.E. from Adrianople. Getting out of town (which stand low) we again saw upon the first hill Rhodope before us; at 8 miles end we passe a little brook; at 3 miles farther another. With in 2 miles, or little more, of Adrianople is a very good fountain, and fine *Kiosk* or summer-house by it. Hither comes severall great men in summer to take their pleasure. The city begins to appear about 4 or 5 mile of, and indeed it shews gloriously, as all their citys doe at a distance, but within they are very mean and beastly. The Moschs and *Minarys* (or steeples), which are very stately, especially Sultan Selim's mosch,[2] which is the best here, of which more afterwards. The country (as is said) all the way perfect champion ground with pleasant easy hills and fruitful valleys; the soyle generally pretty good, but it is much neglected; and though I have all along mention'd several little villages, yet I assure you this part of Thrace (taken in the whole) is very little inhabited and lesse cultivated. About the townes and villages we saw good husbandry; but elsewhere, I am confident, above 2 thirds of the land lyes unoccupyed, and where they neither plough nor plant vineyards, they feed neither meat nor sheep, nor goat, nor anything else. In many, many miles riding we saw neither corn-field, nor pasture, nor flocks, nor herds, but onely wild neglected champion ground. I have a catalogue of many fine plants observed by the road, but I omitt that, and come now to tell you how we were receiv'd and brought into the city.

---

[1] *Vide* Introduction.   [2] Mosque of Sultan Selim II.

About 6 mile of the city we were met with all the French and Dutch who, belonging to Pera with us, were then at Adrianople to see sights. At *Soláck chesmi* (*or the Page's fountain*), which I just now mention'd, were provided 12 of the G. Signor's horses for my Lord and his attendance to mount and ride into city with all; they were all admirable good ones, and set out as rich as was possible. I left my own and took one of them, whose bridle, saddle, great stirrups, breast plate, buttock cloth, etc., were either all of beaten gold and silver, or else most richly embroyder'd. My Lord's horses furniture were set out with jewels and pearles most gloriously. There were groomes appointed to attend upon every horse. By that time we were mounted and got into the road and our ranks; we were met with the *Capigé-pasha* (the word signifys chief porter), whose office is much like our Master of the Ceremoneys, and the *Chiau's pasha* (or head *of the ciauses*, who are like our purcevants or messengers of the green-cloth); these two were in their court vests (Capsitans) of clothe and gold and silver, with rich furres, and horses and furniture suitable. After them followed 70 chiauses in their habits, and severall *cherbigées* (colonels of the Janizaryes). We all made . . . d till the ceremony of use and complement past; then we went into the city in this cavalcade; first the cherbigeés turned back, then the Chiauses, then the *Capigé basha* and *Chiaus basha*, then my Ld. (having the strangers that met us just before him), then all the English gentlemen, then the servants, then the *torch-bearer* with Sr. Tho. B., then the coach and 6 horse, then the other (Turgemans) coach; then all the Carts followed. My Ld. had three good horses (of the Companye), richly furnisht out, led by all the way from Pera. The first street was lined with Janissaryes. We were conducted with all this train to the house appointed for my Ld.'s lodgings, and that street had Janisaryes likewise on both sides. There the Turkes and strangers left us. The house we first were allotted was the damn'dest, confounded place that ever mortall man was put into; it was a Jewes house, not half big enough to hold half my Ld.'s family, a mere nest of fleas and cimici,[1] and rats and mice, and stench, surrounded with whole kennells of nasty, beastly Jewes. We made shift that night, and my Ld., sending to the Vizier, had another immediately, which proved very convenient; for here upon these occasions the G. Signor turnes out whome he please (of Jewes or Christians) out of their house, so that it is troublesome and dangerous to them for to have a good house, and in that end of the town there is none, being all Jewes, crowded two or three familyes into a house that hath not more roomes. If the old Jewes were such poisonous beasts, I must needs then allow their frequent washings, and think they needed not touch a dead body to be unclean, for they could not touch a living one without being so; but more of them anon.

* * * * *

An Account of Occurrences at Adrianople, 1675.

May 17th. The Ragusæan Ambassador visited my Ld. His name was Márin Cabóga. The Turkes call this Embassador (alwayes one being at Court here) Dóbra Benedíct, which is as much as good Venetian. He was a lusty, gallant fellow, and I got a very familiar acquaintance with him, and found him merry, cunning in his businesse, but most strangely superstitious as to storyes of witches and such like. One day, being to visit him with a friend of mine, he fell into such discourse, and at last assur'd us that he had met with a Jew woman who, for certain, was a witch. We desir'd to see her. She was cal'd; and when

---

[1] *I.e.,* bugs.

she came, she would not owne any such thing as that she could raise the devil, but she would tell us many charms and tricks : one was, this Signor Cabóga some few dayes before had lost some money, and suspected one of his servants for it. She comes with an Old Testament in Heb[rew], and, tying a key in it at the 51st psalme, hang'd it upon her finger on one side, and upon the finger of another old hag (her camerade) on the other side. Then he began to think of one whom he suspected, and immediately he reads that psalm in any other language which he understand (as he did it in Latine); if the person be guilty, the Bible turnes and drops downe whilst he reads ; if he be innocent, it hangs immoveable to the end of the psalme ; then he thinks of another, and so begin again. This so possest him as would needs have them shew it us, affirming that when he thought of one person (whome he therefore concluded guilty) it never fail'd. To work go the old hags; he reads; down drops the book. We laught and desir'd we two might hold it upon our fingers (for I perceived the juggle most clearly: it falls with pressing the finger a little stronger then ordinary); he consented, and though he thought of the same person, the book hang'd cleverly to the end in despite of Mother Mumpus.[1] I bad him think of any other person in his mind, as myself, or friend, or the old woman, etc., and before he had gone half way I turned it with as much dexterity as if Mephistophilus himself had been in my Elbo. My gentleman was amazed, but these cunning Jades put a neat conceit in his head. He told us this trick would not do unlesse we were both of us clean; for, said he, it would not do with me at first, for, to tell you the truth, I had been

---

[1] The term "mumpus" is derived from "mump", Dutch *mompen*, "to cheat". "I am resolved to mump your proud players." (Duke of Buckingham, *The Rehearsal*, p. 23.)

with a prettie girl, but, so soon as I had confest myself, it never fail'd, so that all we could say (if we had 10,000 compurgators, it had been all one) would not persuade him but one of us, or both, had been dabling. I told him of our trick with the Sive, and shewed him the very cheat, both in that and in this, and, with much adoe, we convinct him a little. At last I understood indeed what kind of Conjurers these two women were: they were famous, truely, for raysing (or bringing up) little Devils, but they were all in the shape of pretty wenches. One I had the fortune to see, one as like *Cis Archer*[1] as if some kind spirit had really conveigh'd her own very self hither; and in troth it might be she, for these fairyes, I veryly believe, had flesh and bones. He often recounted to me the dreadful earthquake that happened at Ragusa in Easter week, *1666*[2]; he, being himself in it, gave the greater light and credit to his businesse. He had kil'd a great man in a *rencontre*, and was imprisoned for it, and sentence past upon him to suffer death; he being at his prayers, expecting every moment to be cal'd forth to execution, was, at a suddain, tost from one side of the prison to the other, just under an arch, and that place from whence he was joulted was blown up into the Ayre, as if it had been done with gunpowder. After his fright

---

[1] Probably, as Covel was a Cambridge man, he alludes to the same lady as Mr. Pepys speaks of as Mr. Sanchy's mistress : "And there found Mr. Sanchy and Mrs. Mary Archer, sister to the fair Betty whom I did admire at Cambridge."

[2] The terrible earthquake at Ragusa is stated by Von Hammer as occurring in 1668. Five thousand persons perished in it; the harbour was destroyed ; "water, fire, air, and earth were mingled in a terrible combat, the result of which was the ruin of Ragusa" (Von Hammer). The Turks took advantage of the position, increased the taxes, and utterly crushed the place. In 1678, one Ragusan Ambassador was put to death, another put in prison, and 200,000 crowns demanded from the inhabitants.

was a little over, he got out, and in this sad juncture of affaires behaved himself so gallantly, as he was not onely pardon'd, but promoted, having been several times Ambassadore here before. The greatest part of the houses in the Town were shaken down, which was done at one blow, without any antecedaneous trembling or admonition; but after it follow'd a trembling, which ceased not perfectly in 4 yeares after. There were about 400 and odde noblemen before this accident, but not above 140 escaped; yet not one family of them was quite extinct. He onely was left of his. There are not above 18 familyes antient amongst them. From the harths that were in the houses over thrown broke out all over the town a most dreadfull fire, which continued 22 dayes; yet, notwithstanding it, and the other terrible shock of the Earthquake, nothing of their walls or fortifications, or any publick buildings, were harmed in the least, neither was one corn of powder fired, though all their magazines were then full. There was a poor woman servant after 15 dayes digg'd out alive; she had lived in a kitchen all that while, with a little dishwash and oatmeal left there by chance. He saw likewise a little child digd out hanging at the mother's brest (who was dead) three whole dayes after this sad hap; the child is yet alive. He is a very short man, and behaved himself bravely against the Venetians, who afterwards assailed the town. They pay to the G. Signor a yearly tribute of 12,500 Hungars at 2½ dollars apiece, with a *dazio* (as the merchants call it); it is often more, as now one is valued at 2⅓ doll. Besides this tribute they are forced to make presents at severall times of great solemnityes, as now the G. Signor sent to them to come and honour the Circumcision of his son and marriage of his daughter. They were much confounded, not having any precedent left of what ever had been pay'd before; but the *Chid* (or steward or deputy) to the Vizier favour'd them with a

O

record of what they paid about 80 yeares since in Sultan Morat's[1] time, which saved them much of what they intended to have given. I was very much obliged to him, for severall times he took me along with him to see sights, and to be treated by the Turks (as you shall hear anon), even to the envy of severall of our company.

May 19*th.* My Ld. had audience with the Vizier for the ceremony of it. It is the same with what is performed here at any audience with the *Caimacham* or *Bostanje basha.* We were conducted to his Pallace or Seraglio through the City. Two Chiauses (which by order waited upon my Ld. from Stambol continually till he return'd thither again) and all our janizaryes leading of us, and we all following on horseback, we were brought into a pretty large room with a *soffá*[2] (a square raysed about 1½ foot from the ground) covered with carpets very rich, and laid upon the 3 sides next the wall with narrow quilts, or little beds, and great bolsters round, all cover'd with cloth of gold. At audiences at Stambol we putt of our shoes, but here it would be an affront, as if we were afraid to spoil the Vizier's goods; the like is before the G. Signor. My Lord was placed upon a low stool upon the sofá, and we all stood there close at his back. Round about us stood many Chiauses and other attendants. After about ½ of an houre's stay in come the Vizier, and drops himselfe down upon the couch crosse-leg'd. My Ld.'s stool was put nearer to him. Just as he came in all the waiters cry'd: Whish, whish, etc., in token of silence (though I never saw such silence even to admiration (as hereafter shall be said) without this sign, and at his setting down they all give a great acclamation, as much as *God blesse the G. Signor and him, etc.* Being thus sat down, my Ld. deliver'd him the King's letter, and told him that his maister commanded him to do soe, and, with all,

---

[1] Amurath III died 1595.
[2] Arab. *suffah* is deriv. of our word " sofa".

to speak something more to him by word of mouth. Amongst other things, my Ld. urged very much the perpetuall friendship of the English, and that in the warres of Candia there appear'd not one English man against them amongst those many other strangers that sided with the Venetians ; to which the Vizier answered it was true, he himselfe was witnesse to it. My Ld. thanked him for so speedy an audience. He smiled, and said it was a time of mirth, and the great matters were laid aside awhile, so as he had that leisure. My Lord wish't it might ever be a time of mirth and joy to him. Many such complements past, though the Vizier was alwayes very brief and sparing in his words, whether out of a formall gravity, or the reall Turkish humour of taciturnity, I know not. He look't very pleasantly, and, as we were inform'd, with an unusuall sweetnesse ; though, at best, I assure you, I thought he had Majesty and state enough in his face all the time, being all the time of a very, very composed countenance, excepting once (as is above said) we fancy'd some shadow of a smile. He is but a little man, and goes (as I often afterwards saw him) a little lamely; and something stooping thereupon, which they say is from many issues which he hath about him for the Sciatica.[1] He hath a small round face, a little short thin black beard, little eyes, little mouth, without any wrinkles in his lips ; a smooth round forehead and an erected brow, with thick, but very short, hair on it. He is pockbroaken much. In summe, he hath an acute but morale and serious look ; and, if I can judge anything, I should think him a subtle cunning man, though I had never heard so much from the world. He is, they say, 44 years old, though, for my own part, I guesse him not above 40, if so much. He was then in a Chiauses Cap, but he hath severall, as I have seen him many times in them. At

---

[1] The Grand Vizier, Achmet Kiuprili, died towards the close of the year 1676.

all audiences, from the G. Sr. himself to the Kaimacham of Stambol, we give presents, viz., vests of cloth, silk, cloth of gold, silver, velvet, etc., and in most places we receive vests from them, which are a peculiar sort of garment, onely to be then put on by us, and the maisters of state wear them upon peculiar occasions up and down the Court. They are made like our sophisters'[1] gown, without a cape. The stuff is of white silk, flower'd with great branches, sometimes half moones (and the like), yellow or tawny, all with very great weales[2]; and, according to the dignity of the persons, they are of cloth, of silver, or gold, or with more or less gold and silver wrought in the silk. There were give 16 amongst us. I sold mine for 6½ dollrs. My Ld.'s was worth 25 or 30; all the rest like mine, except the Treasurer's, Secretary's, and chief Dragoman's, which were worth about 8 dollars a piece. I am confident this was a very antient custome, and is mean'd in scripture by changes of rayment, etc. We were with the vizier about ½ houre in all; my Ld. was with him in person not above ¼. After these little passes were over he rose up (the waiters making the same acclamations, and bowing a little to my Ld., past on, and we come out with my Ld. You must understand at all audiences (except with the G. Sr. himself, as you shall hear afterward) my Ld. is lead in and out by the Treasurer and Secretary: one on the right, the other on the left. The Cancellier to the Company, and one or two of the merchants, viz., Mr. Cook and Mr. Salter, were not vested, which you may imagine was taken amisse. My Ld. would have talked of keeping peace with Tripoli, Algiers,

---

[1] *Sophister*, a Cambridge term. Second year's men are called junior sophs.; third year's men, senior sophs.

[2] *Weales*. A weal is a mark or stripe. "Thy sacred body was stripped of thy garments and wealed with bloody stripes." (Bp. Hall, *Contempl.*, bk. iv.)

THE GERMAN AMBASSADOR. 197

Tunis, etc., as likewise would have desired to treat by proxy or in private, but it was not then thought convenient.

May 23rd. The Resident (from the Emperor) of Germany visited my Lord.[1] There had been a little *pico* taken. When Count Leshley[2] came into town Embassador from the Emperor some time since, our Embassador was then in town, and sent his secretary and court to meet him. My Ld. expected that this resident should have done as much to him. But he excused it, assuring my Ld. that he was that day with all his court call'd about businesse before the Vizier, and so all disgust was past over. His name is Giovanni Christophoro, and sometimes he wrote it Chinsberg; a most ingenious, courteous person; and as wise and cunning a statesman. I was most infinitely obliged for his civility, being often with him, and alwayes treated like a prince. He is an excellent schollar; mathematicks and history, and all manner of Antiquitys are his chief delight. I shall have occasion to say more of him anon; yet I will not omit one strange thing now. We had been informed here by a very worthy gentleman that at *Tocay* in Hungary the vine (which make the best wine in the world, if you believe the Concil of Trent) very often bears grapes with the *Acini*, or stones, of massy gold. I, standing by my Ld., and by chance hearing him mention the wine of this place, desir'd my Ld. to mention this story

---

[1] Count Kindsberg was Ambassador at this time from Germany to the Porte. He had a very difficult diplomatic game to play: firstly, to remonstrate with the Sultan for the tyrannies of the Pashas at the towns of Wardein, Erlau, and Debreczin; and, secondly, to counteract the influence of the French Ambassador, M. de Nointel, as France and Germany were at war at this time. Count Kindsberg died in the following year of the plague, or, as some said, of poison administered to him by one of the officers of the Janissaries.

[2] *Walter de Leslie*, Lord of Pettau and Neustadt, and Field Marshal of the German Empire, was Ambassador to the Porte in 1665. His embassy was noted for the pomp displayed and for the magnificence of his presents to the Sultan.

to him, and I assure you he confirmed it to be very true, but in a more modest way then we had heard it recounted before : to wit, that the wine was very heavy, and sometimes here and there will certainly be found in the grapes a stone of pure gold, as he himself was presented with two or three such grapes ; for it seemes they can know which are such grapes before they break them. Discoursing the point, he defended the possibility of it, asking how pearles sometimes are found in oysters, or little chalk stones in gouty men's hands, etc. My Ld. return'd his visit two dayes after, and there remain'd a good correspondency betwixt them ever after.

May 25th. We went to see the cavalcade made in honour of the young prince *Mustapha*[1] before his circumcision. You must understand that when any great man's son is to be circumcised, a day or two before he shall be cut he is caryed upon a horse up and down the town in triumph, richly clad, but accompanied with severall other poor youths or children, but finely drest, who count it an honour to be circumcised at such a time. There goe a great multitude with them, singing, dancing, shouting, and Turkish Musick playes all the way before him. This ceremony pay'd this day to the young prince was of this nature, but performed in a Royall manner ; for all the Court of the G. Sigr. appeared, and we saw much of the Glory of the Empire. All the great officers of State, as likewise the Mustafaraca's[2] (which are the *Lancie sperrate*, the G. Signor's life gard, for I was well acquainted with one who was a Renegade) and other chief officers, had all *chiaus* caps, as the Vizier himself, etc. They were most excellently horsed, though now Amblers and middle-sized horse are all in fashion. Most were in rich furre vests, the

---

[1] Prince Mustapha came to the throne in 1695, after his two uncles, Solyman II and Achmet II. His reign was singularly unfortunate, and he was deposed and imprisoned in 1703.

[2] The *Mouteferrika* was the quartermaster.

outside cloth (it is a dishonor for great men to go without a furre vest, though it be in the heat of summer) ; some the outside silk, satin, velvet, cloth of gold and silver. The horse-trappings extream rich ; the buttock cloth embroyder'd with gold, silver, pearles, etc., at the meanest wrought with silk ; the saddles in like manner ; the stirrups, many of silver, some guilded ; the bridles plated with gold, or silver and bras ; and many set with good stones and pearl, especially the peak on the forehead, and at each ear, etc., this in general.

First come by severall companyes of Janizaryes, with their Cherbigées or Colonells on foot. Then past the Vizier's pages in a company distinct and distant by themselves ; all very proper, stout men, in crimson velvet floured *Delaman's*[1] (they are exactly like our cassocks), with very large silver gilt embost girdles. Then follow'd severall companyes of more Janizaryes, with the Chiaus of the Janizaryes on horseback in the reer, who had a girdle all embroyder'd at least 1½ foot wide. After them, as many more Janizaryes, with their Cherbigées on horse back. Then as many more Janizaryes, with the Janizary Aga (a devilish severe fellow, both in shew and in nature and practice) in the reer of them on horseback. Then followed another company of the Janizaryes, with the *Chid*, (or you may call him) Lieutenant to the Agà, who is their head. One thing is remarkable, that whereas our swordmen never goe in companys thus but armed, as if they were ready to meet an enemy, here the devil of sword, gun, or weapon, should you see. Some companyes of the Janizaryes had each man a little switch or stick in his hand, the rest nothing in the world about them ; and in the whole cavalcade not any armes in the world were ever seen, except a cimeter and pole axe, which every horseman, let him be

---

[1] French *doliman*, derived from this Turkish cloak, a light overcoat with straight sleeves, buckled by a girdle.

who he will (as I myself have had many times), wear, the first fixt to his saddle under his left thigh, the latter to the pummel over his right knee; and yet for all this security there is no mutinying, no *embroglys* or tumults, but the best government in the world. Next come severall companyes of Armorers (Jebejées) in green caps, edged with gold or silver, as their purses would beare; (chesmejées) victuallers with red caps like Janizaryes, onely the flap stands higher above the head piece. Then came severall Cadyes[1] and Cadeleschiérs (men of the Law), with their *Naïps* or Secretaryes, or rather Scriveners. They were all in a sort of sophisters (or lawyer's) gown, without a cape, short sleeves, and of severall colours and stuffs, richer or baser according to their ability, silk, satin, etc., all fur'd; these are Cadyes, captains, or *divan* habits.

Next followed the Vizier's Guards in green vests and caps, which differ'd much from what Consul Ricaut made them; their vest was closed together with monstrous great buttons and tassels; they were at least 300 lusty stout fellowes, all *Albaneses*. After them came more of his pages clad like the first. Then follow'd he himself, the *Mufti* and *Mosaïj*, or great favorite; the Mufti in the midst, in a white cloth vest and ermine furre; on his right hand the Vizier in a white satin sable furr'd vest; on his left hand the *Mosaïf* (or *Cooloqlan*), the favourite, in a green sattin sable vest. Then were caryed by 40 *Naculs*, 20 on a side, which are divices made upon a large pole in forme of a pyramid or cone (rather) of wire, painted paper, beggars batten (such as we trim hobbyhorses[2] withall), and flowrs and fruit of wax work, and painted paper, etc. At every wedding and circumcision such toys as these are carryed before the partyes concerned; but these were more

---

[1] Kadi.
[2] " Bring me the bells, the rattle bring,
And bring the hobby I bestrode."
(Shenstone, *Ode to Memory*.)

large and costly. Then were carryed by two more *naculs* of incredible bignesse; it was the most gaudy magnificent peice of (Hobbyhorsism) folly that ever I saw. It was continued in quite another kind of frolick upon a large mast of a ship;. it was 27 yards long, and the lower part was 5 or 6 yards diameter; the ornaments of it were much like this here described, onely between every sphere were square cubes furnisht out with the same fancyes, especially wax work. Now you will say: How could this colossus be moved? At the bottom were eight or ten large bars of wood fastend parallell (as the strings or bars of a sedane and betweene these were harnest above 100 slaves; and before it (upon these bars) stood (or road) a master of a galley, who menaged the Slaves, they resting and reering it up and down at the noyse of his whistle. Now, for fear it should overset and topple down, there were four long pikes of wood fasten'd about half way up, and as many ropes came from the top, by which other slaves (taking hold of the lower end) guided the top and kept it alwayes right up. To let these walking timber-trees pass by the streets of the city many houses were untiled, and some in part pul'd down. I went to view them whilst they were making. They broke down a great stone wall of the publick *Châne* in which they were made to let them out. The story of the walls of Troy and their Hobby-horse is to it as Tom thumb[1]

---

[1] The origin of the diminutive Sir Tom Thumb is, like that of the Teutonic myth, *Jack the Giant-killer*, to be found in the earliest annals of our race. An old ballad, written in 1630, commences thus:—
"In Arthur's court Tom Thumb did live,
A man of mickle might,
The best of all the table round,
And eke a doughty knight.
"His stature but an inch in height,
Or quarter of a span,
Then thinke you not this little knight
Was proved a valiant man."
Probably the Tom Thumb alluded to by Dr. Covel is the one who, in 1588, fought a duel on Salisbury Plain with a noted giant.

to Bevis of Southampton.[1] I must here tell you a story. The Vizier sent an expresse to the Bailo of Venice, commanding him to send for all the actors of their operas to come with their scœnes, musick, etc., to grace the G. Signor's solemnityes. The Bailo excused himself, urging it was impossible (besides of the inconveniences, etc.) to bring all that lumber and trumpery by land and Sea in due time. The Chiaus (the messenger) storm'd and swore: what was impossible for the G. Signor to do? *Walláh* (by G.), my maister, if he will, can fetch your whole city hither just as it stands there; streets, houses, churches, and all. The Bailo, with much adoe, got of; but, ifaith, when I saw this moving wooden steeple so easily menaged, I began to think the *Chiaus* had some reason in him. The little *naculs* were afterwards set before the G. Signor's tents: the two great ones before the Queen-mother's Kiosk (or sommer-house or Balcony), all in the place of sports, of which more by and by. After these *Naculs* were past, came young prince Mustapha, surrounded on every side before and behind, with a brave troop of *Cherbigee* (Collonels), all on foot, in their caps and feathers. The prince himself was mounted upon a lovely beast, which was, in a manner, nothing but jewels, pearls, gold, and silver from head to tayle, and led by two mighty, lusty Cherbigées richly clad, on each side one; two more in like manner went fanning him all the way and shadowing him (for it was about ten o'clock, and a most excessive hot day). They have large fans made here on purpose for great

---

[1] Sir Bevis, who conquered the giant Ascapart, and kept him as his slave, was the hero of one of the most favourite old legends.

"Of Hampton all the baronage
Came and did Sir Bevis homage."

Mr. Pepys alludes to the figure of him over the gate: "At Southampton . . . . Bevis's picture is on one of the gates."

personages of bustards' feathers, contrived from 1½ to 2 or 3 foot wide. Whether it was by chance or on purpose, I know not, but he made a stand just before us, where I view'd him wel (as I have done oftentimes since), being within 3 yards of him at most, now I was about 5 yards distance. He is in generall an ugly, il-favour'd (and I guesse very ill-natured) chit; he hath a perfect Russe face (as I have seen enough to be some competent judge) as may be; he hath a beetle brow, a short, flat, saddled nose, with a little cop[1] at the end; a roundish flat face, low forehead; eyes and eyebrowes fair, the latter inclining to a sandy colour; his eares very large, as much as can be seen; his hands (as all Turkes are brutish and carelesse of them) tan'd and swarthy. His mother is a Russe, and his father of a Russe extraction. He had a plain Turbant on, like a common Turk, and a black single feather on the left side, at the bottom of which was a diamond of about 40 (or, as they say, 43) *carats*, sent home from the K. of Persia of old to a young prince of this Empire. He had likewise two others, very large, on each side his vest, to clasp it before, and instead of buttons were large pearls set al down the edge. His Delamon under his vest was cover'd all before (instead of buttons and loops) with broaches of rubyes and Emeralds; his vest was a white cloth of silver sables; his delamon purple cloth of gold. He road to his father's tent; there he was received with a kisse, and sat down by him. After the young p. and his attendance follow'd his Musick, Ten Pipers, 6 Drumes, 4 trumpets, 2 kettle-drumes, and 4 tamburs (or tympanums), like sives cover'd with parchment at bottome; all these were mounted on camels. The streets were lined with women on one side and men on the other. The women of quality came coached, and the chief had stands, or shops, or chambers, on purpose provided. All were vailed, yet I took notice

---

[1] Cop=lump.

of many delicate persons that would now and then be
peeping, and some slipt down their vail very farre, which is
accounted (if observ'd by the rest) a great peice of impudence. The streets were continually kept swept by broom
men that waited on purpose ; and they were every foot and
anon between company and company refresht with water,
which *Sackals* (budget men[1]) brought and sprinkled on
purpose. Amongst so many people it was most wonderfull to see order and strange silence, not the least rudenesse
in boyes or men ; yet, to keep the crowd of people of and
in good order, there are men on purpose in all these public
meetings appointed, cal'd *Tooloonjés*, from skins of sheep
(cal'd Tooloons) blown up full of wind, and all dawb with
oil and tar, and in leather jackets besmeared in like
manner. The Turkes (who are very spruce and chary of
their fine vests) run from these people as from the Divel,
who upon occasion will strike them with their *tooloones*,
which will break no bones, but onely daub them ; they
have leather caps with bells all down the side. There were
about 200 of these Raga-muffins, and their two Bashas, or
capes (heads), on horse back commanding them. In the
furniture and ornaments of men and horse that day
Diamonds, rubyes, emeralds, gold, silver, embroyder'd
work, etc., were common things. The slaves employ'd in
the *Naculs* before said had all their liberty. This day was
the 11th of their moon *Rebiul Evil*[2] (or the first Evil), the
next being *Rebiul acker*. One thing I will here conclude
this paragraph withall. You can imagine what strange
prodigious civility all Franks (as they call us) found everywhere at these festivals. I have been twenty times myself
caryed in to see the sights, when all Turkes have been

---

[1] *I.e.*, watermen.
[2] *Rebi* is Turkish for spring. *Rebi-u-l-evvel*=the first (*evvel*) of
spring, *i.e.*, the 3rd month. *Rebi-u-l-akhir*=the last (*akhir*) of spring,
i.e., the 4th month.

huncht[1] away. They took the greatest pride that we should see and (at least seem to) admire everything. I have been many times very, very near the G. Signor himself (sometimes ½ an hour together, as long as I pleased), with my hat and in my hair, both which they hate as the Divel; and have return'd quite through the City (once or twice al alone) in the midst of the great multitude of Turkes, and yet I assure you I never met the least affront in the world, but rather extraordinary kindnesse, as shall be hinted particularly afterwards; and amongst these vast multitudes all are as husht and orderly as we are at a sermon. I could not possibly believe it till I found it alwayes so, and from me you may believe this wonder.

May 27th, and the 13th of their Moon, is Mahomet's birth day, which they solemnly kept, for they have severall holy dayes as well as we, besides *Birâms*, etc. This day the G. Signor went to Sultan Selim's Mosch (which is the chief Mosch here); we went to see him go by. There was no great state or train; most of the great men came scattering. The Vizier came riding by himself, with about 20 or 30 of his pages before him in crimson velvet (as before is described), on foot before him, and about 8 persons on horseback about him; to wit, his *Kihiá* (or deputy or steward properly), his *Agá*, or chief Governor of his household, etc. The Vizier[2] was very plain, his vest green cloth, with ermin's furre, and, a distance being kept between his pages before and his attendants behind, he rode alone in the middle. About an hour after (it was near 11 o'clock) came riding in front about 10 *Bostanjés* to se the street clear'd and water'd, as before is said; they speedily

---

[1] Hunched=pushed. "Then Jack's friends began to hunch and push one another." (Arbuthnot, *Hist. of John Bull*, ch. xiii.)

[2] *Achmet Kiuprili* was the real ruler of Turkey from 1661 to his death in 1676. He defeated Sobieski on several occasions, besides winning Crete for the Turks.

rode back again and joyn'd with their company, who made up about 50 in all. After them follow'd the G. Signor's pages on each side the way, in cloth of gold, dark sky-colour'd *delamons*, with broad embroyder'd girdles, and every one a *jint* (or small javelin) in his hand of black ebony inlaid with mother of pearl ; all were on foot in two files, about 60 in all. Immediately followed the G. Signor himself, very plain, in an ordinary *sarick*, or *shash* (*his Tiara*), and purple *cáook* (his scul-cap, about which his shash is wound). His vest was very plain likewise, onely two good large stones were set in brocades to clasp it above before ; the two tips at the bottom before were born up by two footmen, and his garments underneath were very ordinary as might be. I have seen him many, many times (as is said before) ; but take this little description of him once for all. He is a very swarthy man, his face shining, and pretty full eye, black and sparkling ; his nose something long, and beetled[1] at the end, a full, roundish high forehead, a severe brow, his beard black, very thin, and not very long. The Vizier's beard is much thicker, but they say he does not wear it longer than the G. Signor's ; his hand big, but very rude, *alla Turchesa ;* the upper part of his face something resemble Mahomet the 1st in *Knowles.*[2] He hath a great deal of Majesty in his countenance, and terror, too, when he please to put it on. He hath been very lean and sickly (3 or 4 yeares since), but now he is exceedingly plump and hearty. I have been certainly informed by *Grerúch basha* (a Renegado, and his cheif Chirurgion, who circumcised the young prince, as by and by you shall hear more), with whome I was well acquainted, that the onely Physick (in a manner) which he used was Issues (whereof he hath had 8, nay 10, at a time upon him) (they are much used by all people here, especially

---

[1] Beetled = projecting. [2] *Vide* Knolles' *Hist. of Ottoman Turks.*

in the Plague) and exercise, especially hunting,[1] which he followes still most extravagantly, many times going out two or three houres before day, and it may be not returning till as late at night; sometimes (as this last winter) summoning in all the *Villánes* in 20 mile compasse to drive a whole wood or forest before them. They tell a good story of him (but I have also heard it of one of his ancestors), that many of the poor *Villánes* dying once for hunger and cold, the *Bostanjé Basha*, or some other officer, caused 8 or 10 of their bodyes to be laid in the way where the G. Signor was to passe. The G. S. seeing them, askt what they were; the officer told him Poor Villánes starved and perisht in his service, adding what pitty it was, etc. The G. S. immediately swore they were all rotten, and he would hang him for providing noe sound men, so his pitty had like to have cost him his head. Pardon this digression: now we return to the story.

Just after the G. Signor followed the young P. Mustapha, very plain likewise, with two servants on horseback attending, on each side one; after followed several Bashaes and other great men, all in plain clothes. There was a Sermon there, and prayers (as is usual); and after 2½ houres all returned. The young prince with his father went to the Seraglio, and about Kindí (the 9th houre in the Turkish account of the day), he was circumcised by the Chirurgion above said (whose new Turkish name is *Onufé*), who had for his paines 10,000 zechines (about 6,200 lb. sterling), as he boasted to me; but I am confident it was much lesse. It was

---

[1] Spon and Wheeler say, vol. i, p. 242 :—" Sultan Mahomet IV, who now reigns, has so keen a passion for the chase, that for long he has made it his occupation. It is for this reason that for seven or eight years he has made his residence at Adrianople, for the environs are most suitable to give him the pleasure that he loves." Mohamed IV was also of a decidedly literary turn of mind.

presented him from the Q. mother in a large silver bason. He was an Italian, ignorant enough, but bold and ingenious. As at other circumcisions (as is before hinted), many accompany the great man's son, and take it as an honour, so here were severall 1,000es circumcised at this feast; an account see afterwards amongst the generall notions. I now will begin with the festivalls in honour of the circumcision, which began May 15th, they counting it the first day of the moon (from the *Phases*), whereas to us the day before was our new moon, which they reckoned the 29th, but in reality was the 28th, on which night the rising in a little thin cloud appear'd bigger then ordinary, and gave them the greatest pleasure and occasion of rejoicing that could be.

After these solemnityes were past, in the beginning of the next moone (June the 14th) began the solemnityes of the Mariage of the Mosaifs (the bridegroomes) house, of which in good order. First, then, you must know that going into the Seraglio here there are two buildings which meet at the great gate almost at right angles, before which lyes a delicate plain, wherein they had pitch't these Tents so in a rank as to make up a third side, and inclose between the two former walls and the tents a large quadrangle, which they left open on the 4th side for people to come and be spectators. Here every night come the G. Signor and the Prince, the Sultana and ladyes, and all the court to their proper places to see the sights. The company never come together till about 2 o'clock after dinner; for, setting up and spending all the night in revellings, the forenoon went to recruit them in sleep. About Kindí (which is the 9th hour) were brought presents to the G. Sr. dayly; for all great men throughout his whole empire were compel'd to present him and the sultana: and many about the Court not giving so liberally as was expected, were forced to second presents; some were *manzoold*

THE CIRCUMCISION CEREMONY. 209

(turn'd out) for their niggardlinesse. It is commonly reported that the cost of all these sports, etc., come to 12,000 purses of money, whereas his presents come to at least 32,000 purses, each purse being 500 doll.; so he gain'd 20,000 purses, or 10,000,000 dollars, which, at 4*s*. 6*d*. the dollar, makes 2,250,000 lb. sterling. These presents were carried by publickly to the G. Sr. tent, and there the chief of those that brought them were vested by the G. Sr., as is said in our audience with the Vizier. When these presents did not come by there was continuall dancing or variety of sports, either before the G. Sr., Vizier, Sultana, etc., some or other, all the afternoon, of which by and by more particularly. About a full hour before sunset (sometimes sooner) were brought into the ring every day many, many young lads to be circumcised in honour of the G. Prince, or, rather, the honour was their own in being his companions; and every one has a pension as long as he lives of a certain number of aspers (I heard 3 named, but that is too little) per diem, and are call'd the Prince's pensioners. This circumcision last 13 dayes, till the P. was cut. That night the G. Sr. and Sultana stay'd within to comfort him, yet we had the old sports before the G. Viz. and Testerdare,[1] etc. At the time abovesaid all the persons to be cut that day were brought round the ring, singing a Turkish song, being onely some words of the Al Koran, and rejoycing with musick and clapping of their hands; then they were brought to the tent, where they were cut publickly. I saw many 100es of them (there being about 2,000 in all the 13 nights) cut, and the Turkes would be so farre from hindring your seing, as they would make way for you. There were many of riper yeares, especially renegades that turn'd Turks. I saw an old man which they reported to be 53 yeares old, cut. The

---

[1] *Defterdar*, High Treasurer.

P

common way there of turning was (as I saw severall) to go before the G. Sr. and Vizier, and throw down their cap, or hold up their right hand or forefinger; then they were immediately led away by an officer (who stands by on purpose), and cut with the rest. I saw a Russe of about 20 yeares old, who, after he had been before the Vizier, came to the tent skipping and rejoicing excessively; yet, in cutting he frowned (as many of riper ages doe). One night we met a young lad, who askt us the way to the Vizier. Being a country boy, we askt him what he would with him. He told us his brother turn'd Turk, and he would goe find him, and be cut, too; and two dayes after he was as good as his word. It is very dangerous meddling in these cases here. There were at least 200 proselytes made in these 13 days. It is our shame, for I believe all Europe have not gained so many Turkes to us these 200 yeares; for, though the Ch. of Rome boast their Emissaryes here (as, indeed, there are many, many), Jesuits, Dominicans, Franciscans, yet, believe me, they have other designes than converting of Turkes.

* * * * *

There was constantly a Mezin[1] (or cryer, or steeple man), which call'd to prayers from behind the G. Sr.'s tent, as I thought, out of the Seraglio. Besides those who call to prayers upon every steeple, every great man (as the Kaimachan Bostangebasha, etc., at Stamboul) has his Mezin, and by consequence the G. Sr. must have his. Then, indeed, it was wonderfull to see with what reverence, uniformity, and most admirable devotion all (especially the men of note) betook themselves to their prayers in publick; the chief men in their stands and tents, the others (everywhere round the ring), 20 or 30, or more or lesse, in companys abroad upon carpets or the bare ground. We were permitted

---

[1] *Muezin*, the call to prayer from the minaret.

to stand by without the least disturbance. I had seen their manner before, and have all their prayers (which are in Arab) by me. Sometimes they stand, sometimes kneel, oftentimes bowing their head to the very ground and kissing it. I was once within 5 yards of the G. Sr. all the time.

There is in all *Mosches*, and in most great men's houses, and was here likewise in the G. Sr.'s and others tents, a *Imaun* (Imam), or learned man (for they have no such thing as orders or distinction between clergy and laity), who did *praise*, or rather speak out the prayers, the rest keeping a profound silence and imitating him in their bowings and postures. I should heartily have commended their piety, had I not seen in the very same place all the roguery and beastliness, and the like, acted there publickly with the applause and approbation of the chief men amongst them as well as the rabble : as shall be by and bye recounted. Devotion being ended, which never lasted above ¼ of an hour, imediately strike up the *Capagası's* musick (the head of the white Eunuches), and the Capigé basha's musick.

The G. Sr., Vizier, Kaimachans, etc., musick is all alike. 1st, there are trumpets, which come in onely now and then to squeel out a loud note or two, but never play a whole tune. 2d, pipers—their pipe is much the same with our trebble shaurne[1] or Hoóboy ; these play continually without any pause. 3d, great drums, but not bract[2] as oures, nor corded at the bottom ; they beat them at both ends, the top with the right hand with a great stick at every long or leading note, the bottom with a little in their left hand at every small or passing note ; these have their pauses often. 4thly, little kettle or dish drums (for they have both) dissonant one to the other, for they are in

---

[1] Shawn or hautboy.   [2] *I.e.*, metal-plated.

paires; these rest sometime likewise. 5thly, they have 2 brasse platters about foot wide, which they hang loose in their hands, and clatter them one against the other.

I am very inclinable to believe all this Musick old, and mention'd in Scripture. These last either were the cymbals mention'd in Chron. 15, 19. At the sounding of the Musick above 200 Mestejés (or firemen) came from the G. Sr.'s stables (which were hard by) into the Ring, bearing their Beacons upon their shouldjers, and singing all the way a prayer for the G. Sr. in such a dismal tone, which, with the noyse of the musick before named, and all the lights and fires, and the black *Tooloonjés* muving up and down, gave me the perfectest representation of Hell that ever I yet saw upon earth; yet the Turkes count it a heavenly thing. I do verily believe our custome of pulling of our hat, and bidding good evening at lighting up, or bringing in of the first lights or candles (as like wise all Greekes, Jewes, Armenians, and the Italians here give the *buona sera* at the first light), was a very antient custome all over the East, and this prayer of the Mestejés is nothing else. They set their lights round the ring and tend them with fuell. Those before the Sultana, G. Sr., Vizier, etc., wer 6 or 8 branches upon the same stalk; the others were single. This shewes you something to conceive the double ones by. There were about 200 *Tooloonjés* to keep of the rabble, continually waiting; and though they suffer'd no Turke to go in, yet we could passe and repasse without the least difficulty imaginable. All the lights placed and orderd, besides the light of the moon assisting, the sports and dances begin afresh, which continued commonly till midnight; sometimes much longer, seldome lesse.

On May the 21st was nothing to doe, for just about sun set was such a terrible *Burasca* of wind, thunder, lightning, rain, and hail (very great) mixt together, as almost blew down their tents, beat out all their lamps, and spoil'd all their machines, and the sand, which is round the city in many beds before the rain, was roused in such a prodigious manner, as being that night on horseback I could not see his head ; it was a perfect Ægyptian mist of dust. The G. Sr., Vizier, and all the company were forced to retire for that night.

After these dances and sports were over, about midnight (as is said), began very excellent fireworks of all sorts, which continued till towards morning, and then all retired to their repose. Now for the dances and sports. You must understand that from all parts of the Empire were summon'd all (his subjects), Jewes, Greekes, Arabs, Armenians, Turkes, etc., that were any wayes excellent for any sports or entertainments of delight, and truly I do not believe these Eastern Countryes can afford any thing more in that kind then what I have seen here. First, your dancers were for the most part young youths, very handsome generally; most Greekes, yet some more Turkes, Armenians, and a few Jewes.

The best were clothed very rich, either cloth of gold, silver, or rich silk. They had on a *just a corp*, as we say, coming to mid thigh, close button'd at the hands, and girt about them with rich girdles as their purse and fancy led them ; under it (over the rest of their cloth's) they had a petticoat, which was very large, and hang'd very full, down to their ankles ; this was very rich, and of some pretty light merry colour. These clothes were given them by the G. Sr., or Sultana. Their heads are not shaven quite close, but very lovely locks are left round, which at other times they wear up close, and are unseen ; but now they let them down, and set them out to best advantage, sometimes disshevel'd all about their shoulders, sometimes braided and hanging at their back. They commonly wore over their hair a plain cap of silk (small, or scull fashion'd) or (which is more gentele) a fur'd sort of cap, cal'd here a *culpáck*. There was a delicate lovely boy, of about 10 yeares old, had as comely head of hair, long as most women. With him danc't a lusty handsome man (about 25), both Turkes. They acceded all the roguish lascivious postures conceivable with that strange ingenuity of silent ribaldry, as I protest I believe Sardanapalus and all the effeminate courts of the East never came near them. They pleased so extremely that there was scarce a night but they acted in some place or other. I saw them severall times before the Sultana doe as much as anywhere else. The rest danc't 4, 6, sometimes 8 in a company. It consists most in wriggling the body (a confounded wanton posture, and speakes as much of the Eastern treachery as dumb signs can), slipping their steps round gently; setting and turning. Never is their arming, or any figure, or handing; yet one night before the Sultana they danc't in hats and perukes, and Frank habit, but could not imitate us in anything. I never saw them a second time, which makes me believe they did not please. They allwayes come before the person (where they dance) running (as all other that have occasion to passe and re-passe, unlesse in the bringing of presents or the like solemnity); then they fall either into a semicircle or whole round, and so continue falling out of one tune and humour into another, till at last, with a merry wherry of their musick, they turn round (as the Dervises) a long time, and so stopping they bow, and away they run to their musick, which are always hard by. These differ from the other Musicianers, and may be cal'd the private musick, being commonly Pans pipe of 20, 25, 30, (at most) 32 reeds, placed in order, lesse and shorter each than another as the notes rise. I have heard it plai'd on three or four times since I came into Turkey, and fancy it certainly to be the most enravishing tone in nature; yet the notes are fixt, and cannot be alter'd flat and sharp *ad libitum*, and therefore cannot be brought into the canon of musick to play anything that is appropriated to some peculiar lessons. 2d, a little pittifull instrument with three wire strings, which every fellow thrums ordinarily about the street. I take it to be the *Pandura* of the antients.[1] 3rdly, Turkish and Arab lutes of 5, 8, sometimes but 4, double strings, with a little neck a yard (the least), sometimes more, long. They have severall sorts of them—all not worth a lowse. 4, a sort of Dulcimer with gut strings, touch't with both hands, as the Harp, onely this lyes flat and Horizontall. The Jewes have a kind of fiddle of 4 guts, tuned like a violin, but (that you may know the excellency of it) the back and sides are commonly made of the bottome of a gourd, the belly of a dryed film, or skin *hornifyed*[2]; the neck is of a piece of broom stick. Lastly, to crown the Consort, you have every where a *Tambúr*, of which something is said above, is well known in Italy. These minstrells set all down crosse leg at a convenient distance on the one side of the persons before whome they plaid. The dancers have in each hand two peices of Ebony, 3 or 4 inches long, which they knock and charre together in time to the musick. I fancy they are every whit as good as our castenettas. They call them in Turkish *chalparéh*, in Greek παιξάρι. Next there were many actors of little playes or interludes; all in the most beastly brutish language possible, as I was sufficiently informed by my companions, and there actions fully confirmed it. The actors of men were Armenians and Turkes that came from the borders of Persia, and several times acted certain conceits in Persian habit, which was very becoming, being far more rich and gaudy then the Turkes wear. They often

---

[1] Pollux (iv, 60) describes the *Pandoura* as used by the Assyrians, consisting only of three chords.
[2] Hornified = hardened.

mix, as is said, severall sorts of beasts in their gambals, and in every play alwayes enter'd in a large Dear (like our hobby horses), whome they call'd *Hóo*, which is a name of God; but there it stood for a Robin good fellow, or hobgoblin, pulling them, and biting them, and playing a 1,000 freakes. In sume, the best of them did not exceed our ordinary Christmasse gambals.

There was one acted there very often not much unlike *the old man with 7 Sons, so good, so good.* They acted two drunken men, two young whores, and an old baud, and a gallant, and a souldjer; a cuckold and his three wives; wherein all the tricks and wayes of making love here in Turkey, and the extreame jealously and severity of these people were excellently well expresst. They acted a horse courser, a barbier, a butcher, and several such conceits. In Persian habit, with every one his plume of feathers in his *Turbant*, they acted an humour which pleased mightily. They begin in a ring, and what the cheif does all the rest are to imitate, or run the gantlet. If he turnes to the right, left, forward, or round, sculk down, start up, etc., they immediately do the like. Such pour pastorals we had in great variety, and they passe here for greater ingenuity than your playes can doe in England. Their tiring place is always behind the Musick a convenient distance, from which and to which they alwayes passe and re-passe running, as before is said of the dancers.

Next I must recount the Maisters of activity. First there was a *bastanjé*, a middle-sized squad fellow, who shew a vast strength in tossing about weights. Upon sticks or steales,[1] about 4 foot long, were fasten'd at the end round stones, each weighing from 26 pound to 50 pound a piece. Beginning with the least first, he would take in each hand one, and swing them about his head, under his armes,

---

[1] Steales = stales, handles or sticks of a rake, etc.

behind his back, over his shoulders, many strange wayes with the greatest dexterity and agility imaginable ; then setting down them, he would take the two next, and so change on till he come to the last, which (as is said) weighed at least 50 pound apeice; yet he would tosse them about with ease, even to admiration. Some of these he would hold steady and strong at his armes end. Having laid them by, he began with single ones of like fabrick, but weighing from 60 lb. to 120 lb. a peice, being equall to our hundred weight. Fastning the steel or handle to his wrist with a leather thong, he managed all the smaller first in like manner with one hand, still rising till he came to the greatest, which to my amazement he tost about likewise. He had others with a vast piece of iron at the end loose, so as lifting up the steal it would slip to the handle ; thence he would throw it out to the end again with a great slap or crack. These he first managed likewise double, then single ; but they were not so heavy ; the biggest of these weigh'd not above 50 or 90 lb. at most. Lastly, he had a round stone weighing a Kintal[1] and half, just our hundred and half, fixt or hang'd to two steales with two short chaines ; this would he tosse about at a strange rate, swinging it behind his back, his head being between the sticks and his armes. His right arme was alwayes braced with a fillet very hard and close above the elbow. There are many of these stone balls (or shot) with Iron steales or handles in many places here hang'd up, at which I have many times wonder'd, the Turkes telling ridiculous fables concerning them. There are two by the great *Bagno* in *Scutary*, and severall hang'd up over severall gates in Stambol with Turkish writing ingraved upon them, yet none of them exceeded (if they any wayes can equall) these which this fellow plaid withall.

---

[1] Quintal.

I made an exact enquiry since I came home, and understand that these here at Stambol have been in like manner menaged,[1] and the writings speak by whome and before whome it was done, as particularly one of them over Adrianople gate (in Stambol) was menaged just before Mahomet 3d, who took the City, and being infinitely pleased with the strength and activity of the man (whome report made a Bulgarian), he rewarded the man well, and caused the stone ball with the Iron in it to be chain'd up there in memory of him. Some of these in Stambol have a crosse peice of Iron at top, which make me inclinable to believe that the Greek Emperors had this sport before, and the Turkes learn'd it from them. There were vaulters there good store; but, indeed, I think we out doe them all.

This Bustanjé would do prettily well. I see him stand upon the edge of two Cimeters (each foot upon one) barefoot, and swing about one of his greater single stones without the least harme. There was an Arab likewise would lay his bare back upon one, and at the same time a great, lusty man stood on his belly, as likewise he would heave on 2 or 3 vast great stones by the help of a pulley, and yet his back never was hurt. I confesse to read this story in Busbequius made me amazed (as this may you); but when I saw the height of it, I counted it a poor thing; for by his buttocks, and his head, neck, and shoulders, he bore up his belly so as the cimiter lay under the hollow of his back, and a strong man may easily bear a vast weight in that posture. The same man took the Cimiter with his hands at each end, and, laying the edge to his bare belly, moved it very hard from right to left without any harme, onely making a little red line where the edge past. He

---

[1] *Menage*, here, means manage, control.

"He the rightful owner of that steede,
He well could *menage* and subdue his pride."
(Spenser, *F. Q.*, II, iv, 2.)

would fasten a pulley to a gibbet, and through ran a rope, fastend at one end to a ring, to which all his hair was tyed at the crown of his head; the other end was in his hand, by which he would pull himself up a great height. Sometimes he did it with another man at his back; once with an Asse fastend to his shoulder; once with a young camel. I have made some conjectures upon it, but I will not anticipate your mechanicks about this φαινόμενον, onely tell you it seems a pretty one. He took a great pole, about 3 yards long and ½ foot thick, but broader at each end, and setting one end upon the teeth of his lower jaw, he danct with it in this posture upright without touching it, but clapping his hands to his musick, by then he put another frame upon it with 8 or 10 branches (or he could adde more) upon it by a hole that was in the top. Upon every stanza he would set a cup of water; then raysing it, he would dance with all these in like manner without spilling one drop. Then by a stick, which he would put into the same hole, he set a little boy crosseleg'd upon it, and danct with him in like manner. Lastly, he would set a great pitcher of water up on the upper end, and dance with it; then all of a sudden, with great force, he would strike away the end at his mouth from him, and catch the pitcher in his armes. We saw most of these tricks upon the road acted by him, and all again repeated in the Ring.

Some yeares since there was an Arab at Smyrna did all these tricks much more dexterously; instead of a pitcher of water, he would lay a little child flat on its back upon the upper end, and bidding it shut its eyes, would dance with it a little while, and at last, striking away the pole, would catch it in his armes safely. He likewise would place a *handjar*, or Turkish dagger, ¾ foot long, upon the ground, with the poynt upwards; he layes himself on his back with his head close to it, then raysing up his heeles, and his body poysed, his body upon his head and neck, and then with a jerk would turne himself quite to the other side the dagger without the least harme. This fellow did the like, but more bunglingly. The Smyrna man would likewise place three swords with their points upwards, and upon them a little piece of dirt or such a thing; then fetching a run, he would passe them on the ayre, striking of the pieces of dirt, and with the fourth step come to the ground. This logger-head did not doe it, though he said he could.

Jugglers were many likewise, but the generality were loggerheads to what we have in England. There was one, an Arab, so ill-looking a fellow as you would have sworne that he was elder brother to the Divel himself. His face exceeding black and shriveled much (for he was old), blear-eyed, his head bald and shined like soot, being well baked in the sun; he had short, crisp'd hair, black and massy (like a black moor) round about like the Corona of the fryars; and he was accordingly clad just like a Dominican in a white serge vest or gown closed before, with open sleeves covered with another black one like it in all things, excepting that it was not closed before.

The common people here are the most superstitious, credulous, fabulous creatures alive. I speak of all Turkes, Greekes, etc., and this man by his lookes, and garb, and tricks had so imposed upon them as severall had represented him to me as if he had been one of the old Magicians in Ægypt risen from Gehenna. I was big with desire and expectation of seeing him, for he seldome (as the best of his jibes being common) shew'd his tricks publickly. At last I laid out for him, and he was brought to my Ld. He shew'd little then, but I saw all he could do afterwards, which truely was not much, and being so old, he slubber'd[1] his businesses over so as I could discover

---

[1] *Slubber* is a variant of *slabber*, to do a thing carelessly. "*Slubber* not business for my sake." (Shakes., *Mer. of Ven.*, ii, 8.)

all he did. He had 5 or six snakes tam'd, which were kept under the white frock, and with these he would make good sport. He would pull one from your buttons, nose, bosome, etc., and taking any thing of the standers by, as knives, handkerchiefs, bals, etc.; going to returne them, he would drop you a snake. Now, no people in the world being more fearfull of such things then these, he past for such a miracle-monger amongst them as I fear they of Ægypt were little better, especially considering how highly his conceits might be improved; for here are dayly snakes carryed up and down, tamed, of all sizes almost, and I did not question amongst the vulgar even in England to make thousands of them believe I could turn almost anything into them by sleight of hand, with a little thought and practice. By help of his under frock (closed before, and with wide sleeves), with his left hand he could give and take anything from his right hand unseen; by which he made many pretty conveighances, though none very fine. Had. you heard the relations of the people (some understanding men), you would not wonder at my relation to you. One came and swore to me that he pul'd a snake a yard long out of his nose; another that he put a little small ball under a cup, and it was turn'd into a serpent; another gave him a cup of wine, and he drank and return'd the cup, and going to fill one more for himself, swore there leapt out a great snake, etc. I got so much liberty as to see all his contrivances under his frock, which are too tedious to be repeated.

I saw another which thrust a Iron (which I had in my hand all the time, and it was really done) about 10 inches (at the least) long in to his nose, up to the hilt, and may easily be done with a little practice by anybody. Many more such tricks I have to communicate to you when we meet.

There was wrastling every day, according to the old way, which is yet peremptorily retain'd. They are naked, all but a short pair of drawers put over their middle. There is nothing of play, but onely meer strength required. Nothing is accounted of unless the vanquished person be laid flat on his back, and therefore they fall worrying and tumbling on the ground perhaps 1½ hour till one be rowled on his back. Many come in oyl'd all over, that no man's hand could hold fast any part of them, and therefore the wrist, or ham, or ancle, if they can be grasped, are the onely places of laying good hold. It is well pictur'd in a late author (Potinus), treating of medals, but it is nasty sport at best.

About mid-night, as is said, all the dances and other sports being over, began the fireworks, which, indeed, very much delighted me. The chief contrivers were two (a Venetian and Dutch) Renegadoes, there being appointed all materials in a large Chánc, and at least 200 stones to beat and prepare their compositions. First there were several figures of monstrous giants, many-headed and deformed. They were hollow'd and framed with little hoopes, and paper'd over. These were hang'd all over with crackers, serpents, sausissons,[1] etc., and after these were fired (which alwayes was done with excellent time), out of their heads, and Eyes, nose, eares, flew severall rockets, and, last, out of their mouths gushed streams of fire. Some had charges in their hands, which fired in the last place, and the armes being continued loose, swung them about very dexterously. Severall of these machines were contrived to turn upon the pole or spindle on which they hung, and were caryed round by a blind rocket attacht to the hem of their garments, for you saw no legs—nothing but a long coat cover'd their lower part. What was burnt of the frame was infallibly repair'd by next night.

Next there were Pyramids (slightly framed, all to be caryed and recarryed dayly, which was done by Slaves) of

---

[1] Fr. for *sausage*.

at least 10 or 12 yards high, hang'd in like manner with fireworks all over, and after they fired, remain'd upon the sides little cotton stoups[1] innumerable, which, being prepared with a composition of camphore, etc., burnt a full quarter of an hour after the others were past, like so many pure white flames or tapers, in due rank and file from bottom to top. At last, from the top, flew a volley of rockets, crackers, and other wild fire altogether, with very wonderfull delight.

There were contrived severall trees (as I may call them), or stands branched and hollowed, and filled with a nimble composition which gave fire from bottom to top to severall canes attach't to the sides (at holes on purpose) and charg'd variously with all manner of fire workes. Coming into the branches were discharg'd severall hundred of them together. There were severall large paste boarded castles, charged within and without with the like workes, which discharg'd in like manner. There was a high, large fountain, which, when it had discharg'd all his fire-workes, left four double rowes (at convenient distance) of pipes, which cast out streames and drops of fire in exact resemblance of the naturall fountaines of water; and, at the top, four large pipes, and, in the middle of them, a fift, very big, all which cast streames of fire (which was whiten'd with Camphora) upward. It dured a long time, and ended with a volley of rockets, discharged all at once into the ayre. There was a round fountain, contrived to move upon the pin or staff (on which the whole machine hang'd), in 4 or 5 peices, which, by blind rockets attacht to them, moved contrary wayes, though at a distance they all seemed to move the same way, the angles in the eye being the same. In all things else it was like the former fountain.

---

[1] *Stoups*=a vessel or receptacle; cf. Holy-water stoup.

There was (May 28th) a very large castle brought forth, intended to represent the castle at Candia. After an infinite of fireworkes discharg'd from it, and God knowes how many guns fired from within (by men on purpose, who withdrew afterwards at a port hole), it took fire at last (designedly) in so admirable a manner as no naturall fire could seem more reall. The combustible matter was made with so exquisite a composition, and the ribs so well contrived, as though the flame burst out in many places about the bottom of the roof; yet the top took fire in due time and burnt with the body, and dropt down first peice by peice. Then the sides began to let the fire break out through them, and by little and little the top parts of them fell down first, and then the wals wasted in order, till all was dropt down in one heap of fire. All this was done with that leisure, as it lasted at least an hour, and made the goodlyest bonefire that ever I saw.

There was severall men with hobby horses about them, and other figures, cover'd all over in like manner with fireworkes, which taking fire, ran up and down and encounter'd one another bravely. There were great timbers placed up like gallowes, and to one another were fasten'd ropes in such a manner as upon them were hang'd little ships, galleyes, etc., able to hold two or three men (but many, many made of paper, and the like stuff, represented a whole ship's crew), who managed the guns and fireworkes within, contrived most dexterously; and with other ropes pulling these vessels backwards and forwards, they represented a sea-fight very naturally. One was betwixt Capt. Georgio's ship (a famous *corsair*, about 10 yeares since taken by them) and two galleyes. It was late every night before this trade of fire was over, but then for an hour, some times, it was a great deal more. The *Mestegées* from all quarters of the Ring, at their fires, fir'd severall thousands of rockets (especiall 28th of May, the last night but one, and the best), which certainly are the best fireworkes to behold in Nature. Some of them discharg'd about 30 starres, and as many little camphire bals of pure white fire. There was a sort (which I confesse I doe not understand well) which flew up all wayes without any fuse, but onely one visible dull coal (as it were), till they broke aloft and discharg'd their starres, and with a great report, as many of the others likewise did. All these, when they were discharg'd, were levell'd to fly over the people's side; for at the festivalls at the birth of this prince, a Jew (that made the fireworkes) shot one large rocket towards the Kiosk, designing to have mounted it over, but it chanced to fly right into the Kuzler Agà's[1] lap, and burnt up all (if any little was left). The poor Jew was first drub'd 150 drubs on his feet, but the black devil, the gelding, would not rest satisfied with that, but got him cut of.

All these were shown the (28th May), but every other night we had enough, though not such variety. There were several Iron charges much like the chambers of *Pettarders*,[2] but farre bigger and longer. These were fasten'd into the ground fill'd with a slow composition, which being fir'd, cast up one continuall stream of fire (with dreadfull noyse) at least 20 yards high into the Ayre. The first night I went to see them on horseback, being caryed by an Italian Count (his name formerly Bocareschi), now a *lancia sperrata* to the G. Sr., with whome I had the luck to be very well acquainted some yeares agoe. He was infinitely civill to me (though a damned rogue all along, and I was alwayes aware of him), yet I shall tell you of him more by and by. He caryed me (being on horseback himself) between the G. Sr.'s and Vizier's tents within 8 yards of either of them (at severall times), without the

---

[1] The chief eunuch, who looks after the harem.
[2] Petards = metal boxes, loaded with powder.

least molestation or difficulty. I was round with him in twenty companyes of Turkes, and houses and places; but that is not now to be insisted on.

When the lights began, I and he went on the People's side, where were many more horsemen besides. My horse snorted and trembled, so I suspected no good, yet I was resolved to stay and see all. Just as the fireworkes began, he and many other horses by, ran mad, and rising up fell on his hams, then, trembling, on his side, fairly layd along and run away as if the Divel had drove him. I was getting up, but seeing many, many mad Jades coming, I fell flat on my face, and committed the event to God. His name be ever praised! for though I dare sware at least 100 horse and people came over me, I got not the least harm imaginable in the world.

You must understand this Bocareschi was a very parasite as lived, an excellent wit, and some little learning, the Latin toung perfectly; but for his damned traiterous perfidious tricks, was kick't out of all publick ministers' companyes. And for my own part I knew him well, but caressed him onely to make my ends of him at this time; which I did, for he had come and made a little interest here with my Ld. and Sir Tho. Baines. We went for Adrianople, and there he come almost every day, and eat and drank wine with us. Now he kept alwayes fair with me, for fear I might doe him some discourtesy. I alwayes gave him good words, though in good earnest every one else hated him. That you may see once for all what a beast he was, he came and eat and drink at my Ld.'s Table with the Plague upon him twice, and at last dyed of it, within 8 houres after he went from us.

I was with the Ragusean Embassr. (as is said) several times to see the sights. We always had a cherbigee or two that look't after us, and would not suffer the greatest Turk whatever to molest us; but we sat on a cushion with bolsters and cushions, very near the Vizier's tent. Once

THE BRIDEGROOM'S PRESENT. 227

Bocareschi had promis'd to shew Sr. Th. B. the sights (for my Lord never saw anything). One night he came with some servants, and one or two of the nation with him. *Bocareschi* seing the Embassdr. of Ragusia there placed (with whome I was at that time present), out of a pico (for the Embassr. hated him to death, and had affronted him highly) brought in Sr. Tho. B. and his company, and placed him just before us. The Embr. was divilishly displeased at it, as likewise the Turkes that waited on him. But *Bocareschi*, being a Metafaraca,[1] would not make any stirre, but came and desir'd the Embr. and us to rise, and so removed us to a better place, just under the G. Vizier's tent, where we rested in spight of him, till all was done. The Vizier wears severall caps (as is before mention'd). Once I saw him at the sights in one which they tell me is used in time of warre, but he soon chang'd it for a common one. As for all sorts of rope dancers, here were the best in the world.

June 10*th*. The present of Cool-oglan (the *Mosaif* or favourite), the bridegroome, was carryed by ; we went to see it. First went by severall companyes of janissaries with their cherbigées, then many more with their chief officers. The jannisary *Aga* in cloth of gold, the *Chia beghi*[2] in green velvet, the *Janizary Effendi* (or Lawyer), secretary or clerk ; the *Bashé chiaus*,[3] his cap little and short feathers. Then severall companyes of spahées.[4] The subbasha (or chief constable) of the Suburbs of Adrianople. These were all in court coates, like Chaucer's taberd,[5] armelesse, yet little hanging sleeves as the picture of the Virgin

---

[1] *Vide* note 2, p. 198.
[2] The Chiabeghi is the grand master of the court attached to an ambassador.   [3] Chief of the Chiaus.
[4] *Spahis*, a division of the Turkish army, consisting of light horsemen, generally chosen from the upper classes.
[5] *Vide* note 2, p. 166.

in C. Ricaut's book, p. 43, fur'd within and without, either cloth of silver, gold, satin, velvet, etc., all in chiaus caps but the Effendi, whose cap was lawyer-like At last came 30 mules handsomely trimm'd and furnisht, each loaden with two little painted chests or boxes in which was gold and silver, as is reported good store; next came in two rowes (on either side the street) one 112 persons on foot, in chiaus caps and well clad, bearing presents upon their armes (some one, some 2, 3, or 4), distinctly wrapt up in linnen, but every one was seen. They were peices for vests of cloth of gold, silver, satin, velvet embroyder'd works, pearl'd work, etc.; then a company of Janizaryes and Cherbigees on foot; after them were led by foot stately horses, and a strawish-colour'd bay was in the last place, as delicately limm'd, as I declare it, I never saw the like, with a curious starre on her forehead, about 15 hand high, as we guest. These were designed for the G. S. to dispose of as he pleased. After this came two little *Náculs*, and then three or four artificial gardens, about 3 yards square, with pretty knols and walkes, full of floures and trees, with their fruits all of tolerable waxe work, with *Kioskes* (or summer-houses) in the middle, and severall birds and beasts placed here and there amongst the plants and trees; two had artificiall fountaines in them, which were supplied with the same water by an engine of clock-work contained within them. All these were carryed by slings in the slaves' hands, who were (as aforesaid) menaged by galley-whistles; then followed, in two files on each side of the way, one 120 sugar-workes, borne on frames by two slaves a peice, sedan wise, made from $2\frac{1}{2}$ foot to a yard and half high, some more or less as the fancy required. They were Ostridges, Peacocks, swans, Pelicans, etc., Lyons, Beares, greyhoundes, dear, horses, Elephants, Rams, Buffaloes, etc. (it is unlawfull to make the figures of men); they were done brutishly and bunglingly. Then came a new set of Janizaryes and Cherbigees, and after them a present of all things necessary for a Turkish lady in her dressing-room; caryed open by men well clad, in two files as before, viz., a paire of bootes (for here all women do ordinarily wear such), a pair of *papoutches*[1] (sorts of shoes), slippers, chioppines[2] (or pattens of wood): all these wrought and cover'd with pearl of the bignesse ot ordinary cherry-stones the least, and intersperst with Diamonds and rubyes, etc. It was a brave time for Jewellers; any trash, if it made but a fair show at a distance, was vendible at good rates.

Next came a sable embroyder'd vest with 9 large button and loopes, Persian fashion, al set with pearl, rubeyes, and a great diamond on every button; the 2d button and loop, which serves for a clasp, had on either side a very large table Diamond. Next followed severall round looking-glasses with gold frames and cover (or door), and stydded with pretious stones; then several mighty rich girdles of stones set in gold and enamel; likewise several bracelets for the hands, answerable to them. Here you must understand that even women must have girdles, bracelets, and topases, or else they are no gentle women, as in England they are not without a black bag; the bracelets are wrought of gold wire, sometimes gold plate, from 1 to 4 or 5 inches wide, etc. There were two or three gold chaines with large brooches of Diamonds (and the like); at the end severall pair of earings, one amongst the rest of 2 Emeralds, pear fashioned, very large, valued by the Greeke that sold them (and shew'd me them before) at 5,000 zechines, or near upon 3,800 lb. sterling at 4s. 6d. to

---

[1] Turkish word for shoes; Mod. Greek παπούτσια.
[2] Old English form of Spanish *chapin*. "Your ladyship is nearer to heaven than when I saw you last by the altitude of a *chioppine*." (Shakespeare.)

the dollar. In a pretty christall glasse, with a little golden open frame, was caryed hanging a plain gold ring, with a rose diamond of 11½ carats. Severall cabinets and dressing-boxes adorned with pearl and jewels, severall Essence boxes, and the like, set out in the same manner. At last came a little crown all of beaten gold, studded with jewels upon the fringe. Then came the Testerdor (or Lord Treasurer) on horseback, who was *Vikéil*,[1] or deputy, for the *sposo*. He strew'd whole handfulls of aspers among the people as he went, which was but very slowly; all the presents being caryed in state, and as easily as foot could fall; they were lay'd all upon fine handkerchiefs in silver dishes. After the Testerdor rode his musick, 12 pipes, as many drums, 6 trumpets, 6 kettle drums; four cymbalists, all on horseback. After them come many, many servants leading and riding their masters' horses, who went before in the shew on foot.

Take here, if you please, as exact account as I could get of the manner of the Mariage and espousals. First, you must understand all was treated by proxeyes (which they call *Vickeel*), to the making of which two witnesses also were appointed, all by the G. Sr., to wit, two *Cadeleschiers*, one of Europe, the other of Asia. The proxeys were the *Kuzleraga* for the *sposa*, the *Testerdore* for the sposo, and thus they were made. The *Kuzleraga*,[2] with the two *Cadeleschiers* as witnesses, went to the *Sultana's* door, and knocking, said: Sultana, are you content to make me your *Vikéel* for marrying of you with Mustapha (the *Mosaïf* or favourite)? She answers: Yes. He ask her this thre times (on the other side the door, which must not be opened by no meanes), likewise thre times the same. This is immediately recorded by the two *Cadeleschiers*, and (as to the Sultana) is irrevocable. Then the same witnesses goe with

---

[1] Turkish *vekil* = a deputy.   [2] Chief eunuch.

the Testerdór to Mustapha or *Cool-oglan*, the *sposo*, and face to face the Testerdor ask him the like words (*mutatis mutandi*) thre times, and to each he answers : Yes. Then away these go to the *Mufti* together ; there they set down in his court (of which afterwards), the *Mufti* in the midst, with the *Kuzléraga* on the left hand (being the chief in Turkey) and Testadore on the right, and the 2 Cadeleschiers before them *alla Turchesa*, or at there feet *alla Franca*. The Mufti asks wherefore they call'd him ; they answer : To perform a worke of Paradise, to wit, the marriage of the *Sultana* and the *Mosaïf*. The Mufti asks who are *Vikeels*; the Kúzlcraga said : I am for the *Sultana*; the *Testerdor:* I am for Mustapha ; the *Cadeleschiér:* We be witnesses to it. Then the *Mufti* made the *Kuzléraga* and *Testerdore* to set one over against the other, and asks the *Kuzléraga*: Are you content to take *Mustapha* for your husband ? This is done thre times, to each of which *Kuzleraga* answer : Yes. Then he askes the like (mutatis mutandis) of the Testerdor, to which he likewise three several times answer : Yes. The Mufti then demands the Testerdore what dowry he will promise to make her ; he answer : a yeare's revenue of grand Cairo ; which is 600,000 zechines, at 4s. 6d. the dollr. ; it makes of our sterling money 33,750 lb. (I must tell you, by the by, that the greatest compliment to a fair woman in Turkey is to tell her her eyes are worth a year's revenue of Grand Cairo.) Then the Mufti asks the Testerdor : Will you give it ? thre times ; he as often answers : Yes. Then he asks *Kuzleraga:* Will you accept it ? thrice ; he answers as often : Yes. Then the Mufti sayth: *Bismillah* (in Dei nomine). Then all standing up, he blesses the mariage ; and so entertayning them with Coffee and sherbert, etc., dismisses them. The G. Sr. immediately vested these with cloth of gold and sables to the value of 1,000 dollrs. ; the other two (witnesses) with vests of 500 dollrs. I had not car'd if I had been *Mufti;* I am confident I could have made as good a marriage. During the festivalls of the circumcision, one day, all publick tradesmen were forc'd to go in procession with every man his wagon locked, in which he publickly labour'd at his trade—shoemakers, taylors, weavers, etc.; so much as Bakers had an oven, smiths their ittle forges, butchers flead their sheep, etc. Which you may imagine such a piece of glorious madnesse as Europe elsewhere cannot pattern. Every wagon was set out with tokens of their art, and boughs and *bandiéras*[1] of silk or painted paper at least.

June 19*th.* The *Dote* (or the dowry) was carryed by from the Seraglio, which was given by the G. Sr. to the sposo, as in all your ordinary weddings, before the bride is carryed her portion, which chiefly consists in vests and clothing. There went many by towards the Seraglio to come with the rest back again, as Janizaryes, Cherbigees, the Vizier's guards, Armorers, Cadeleschiers, and other officers, Topgées (or gunners) in red caps. Their Head men or bashas wore a furre cap, distinguished by the cock's feathers in the top; these being white and red intermixt, the other all of one colour. The *Mosaïf* himself came by, with the *Mufti* on his left hand.

We staid there about 1½ houre; then they all came back in this order: First, the Topejées, Armourers, the Vizier's guards; then the G. Sr.'s. waiters in Caphtans (or court vests): these serve him at table; then 4 or 5 Companyes of Janizaryes and their Cherbigées, all in Caphtans, sattin or velvet furred; then the *Aga* of the Janizaryes, with his crew; next came many, many Pioners with shovels, broams, etc.; then as many more Janizaryes with the Janizary Aga, whome they repute a very severe man, who never gratifyed any man that askt him anything, but

---

[1] Flags.

doeth all things of curtesy of his own head, or not at all ; any body is capable of that office, though he never was Janizary before.

The Janizary Aga had now his *Santon*[1] (or Tom of bedlame[2]) with him, with a strange kind of axe (or as they call it, Balta) on his shoulder. Then severall companyes of Janizaryes and Cherbigees ; then about 100 chiaus's with their feathers of distinction, just before on the left side ; then 8 or 10 Executioners on foot. Then followed two gardens in wax work, caryed by slaves as abovesaid ; then 40 little *Naculs* carryed by two files of Janizaryes. Then followed 86 mules, some laden with two long square sapets apiece, cover'd with *Caphtan* stuff ; some laden with 2 beds a piece with bedding, left all a little open to be view'd by the standers by, and were all cover'd with cloth of gold or sattin or velvet, richly embroyder'd, some with silver, some with gold, some wrought with pearl. A third part of the mules had two lesser square sapets (or leather hampers) a peice, cover'd with black leather. Then ten men bearing severall pieces of household stuff, as furniture for beds, green satin foot cloths, plated with beaten gold, several leather and velvet carpets, plated some as the foot cloths. *Mum-sofras* (round leathers to set candles, pots, etc., upon), plated likewise ; 4 very large silver lanthornes, the ribs gilt with gold. Then came by in like order, as is before said, bootes, papoutches, slippers, chioppines, set all with pearl and Diamonds ; hand bracelets, girdles, many pair of each, all gold and pretious stones ; Looking glasses, 4 close cabinets and 6 large open ones, such as stand in Goldsmiths' shops, all set out with jewels, pearles, gold wire, etc. A little stool of pearl and jewels ;

---

[1] Holy man or dervish.
[2] Bedlam, contracted from Bethlehem, because the hospital of St. Mary Bethlehem was used for lunatics, and anyone escaped or let out of this establishment was known as Tom of Bedlam.

a coronet of beaten gold. Some say all these were onely the *Mosaïf's* present (before mentioned) brought back again, which is most likely, they now being part of the Sposa's accoutrements; though others would needs have them all new.

After those came the Rice Effendi, with a Cadeleschier on his right hand. Then the Testerdar, with another Cadeleschier on his right hand. Then the Vizier, with the Mufti on his left hand, of whome more hereafter. There was also in the train, a little before the Rice Effendi,[1] the Vani effendi,[2] the greater preacher who prated down all the coffee houses and Taverns, and, upon my life, it was well done. More of him anon. Then, in the reer of them, were the musick—pipes, trumpets, etc., on Camels; after which followed many Janizaryes, and after them came many women slaves, in 12 close coaches, with 2 black Eunuchs before each coach, some of them inclining to tawny, whereof three were very well featured youths, all admirably well mounted, and exceedingly richly clad. After the coach rode 12 blacks more, in one body, like the rest—on horses, and habit, etc. All these were peculiar to the Sposa, and were reckon'd as part of her goods; for in many points the Civil Law of the Romans is here observed, as above you may see, no marriage without a *Dote*. Then followed about 40 servants on foot, leading as many horses, laden with these slaves' goods. Then followed the Rabble.

Jun. 23. The Sposa was carryed home, for, as I told you, every wedding hath something of this formality. The bridegroome sends presents with Naculs, etc., then the Bride's trumpery is brought in state, and she followes it, allwayes hid under a square pavillion born over her, or a

---

[1] Reis Effendi = Minister of Foreign Affairs.
[2] *Vide* note, *infra*.

THE BRIDE'S PROCESSION. 235

Canopy at least. After the procession were carried two gardens of fruits and floures in wax-work, with *Kiosks* in the middle, caryed as before. Then 2 great Naculs caryed by 160 slaves apiece, besides the guiders of the ropes and stages as above. Then two little Naculs of silver, with each of them a great candle at Top, which then were not lighted (the fashion before the Armenians and Greekes is to carry them lighted), but were to be lighted and renewed and kept burning during the whole festival, something in imitation of the old Hymenai ; these were caryed by slaves, likewise being very ponderous. Then came crab-faced Kuzleraga and after him followed immediately (Dulcinia del Tobosa) the fair Angelike *Agazé Sultana*, or, as others pronounce it, *Hatajé Sultana* (the present Emperor's eldest daughter), in a coach plated all over with silver, and garnisht out with gold, the wheeles and all other underwork (of wood and Iron) richly guilt or varnisht; a covering on the Top (as the fashion is) set with pearles and diamonds, six fair white horses, all the harnesse plated with silver and gold, and adorned with jewels. In their Tops each had a plume of feathers hanged with jewels. A postilion rode the forehorse on the near side, and the coachman the hindermost of the same side. The covering of the coach was, in part, tuckt up to show the beauty of the work, which was so close a lattice as you could perceive nothing but some opaque body by help of the little light that crept in from the lattices on the sides. There were several Eunuchs attended it, whereof the first two strewed Aspers on both sides the street amongst the people (whereof I have some to make you a present of, if it please God we ever meet). One was very well favour'd, a tawny, and the bones of his face in very good symmetry, inclining to a tawny. I heard a pleasant story of him, and once met him at a garden at Adrianople, but I must let that pass now. Two more very rich coaches, with 6 horses, plumed and bespatter'd with jewels, followed, in the latter of which (which was cover'd with red broad cloth, and set out nobly) a very fine woman opened a little hole at the fore end, and peep'd out at us. Her face and head tire were very plainly seen. I dare not say no lesse then that she was lovely. Her fingers and part of her hand were peeping a good while before her face, and her nails were stein'd (as the custome is here) with *aleanna*[1] of a golden red (there were 4 blacks attended each of these). Then followed two more ordinary coaches with 6 horse, and two blacks apiece to attend them. Then 21 ordinary coaches more, many with 2 horses, most with 4, with one Eunuch to every of them. Then followed servants with horses, and cloathes upon them, led by. About half-an-hour after came the Sultana's mother, in a very rich coach of silver, and embellisht with gold. There were 4 Eunuchs to attend her, and a great company of *Baltajées* axe men; as likewise 4 Eunuchs went a little before it. Then followed 6 good coaches with 4 horse, and each had a Baltaje riding in the Rose[2]; and one other by on foot. Then came three more rich coaches with 6 horse, and two *baltajées*, as the others. Lastly came one coach with 2 horses, and one *Baltajé*. There were many Blacks to accompany these on horseback, beside the soe named, onely they went straggling, and kept no order. In the rear followed the rabble.

Now, you must understand, all these coaches are made in the fashion exactly of waggons, onely they use cover'd over head, and hang'd by slings so close as the body have no room to swing, but jolts as hard as if it were fixt upon the axletrees.

After the *Rebuil*[3] *evil* moon was ended, there were every day at *Kindi* (the 9th houre) sports at the Mosaïf's house

---

[1] *I.e.*, henna. [2] Circular seat behind.
[3] *Vide* note 2, p. 204.

(which was in the city), and they lasted till midnight sometimes. They began the 14th of June, when they first saw the new moon, though it was a day old, it being by our account two dayes old then; they ended the 28th day. There was a very large square yard; at one end was a fair apartment of two chambers, where the Mosaïf and his friends continually were spectators; at the other end was a large, high, single room, to which oftentimes resorted the G. Sr., young prince, and many other favourites. After his sposa (as is said, the 23d day) was brought home, there was another square room in another corner with lattice-windows (*gelosie*), through which she and the Q. mother and others of the Ladyes saw all, being unseen themselves. The door was kept very strickt, that no Janizaryes or Turkes of fashion might enter, yet all strangers might go in without any difficulty in the world. I was there many times, of which some account by and by.

First, of the sports. We had every day the very same dancing as before; the same shewes at interludes. There were monkeyes, and dull Arab dancing, to entertain the people; for on one side were pitched tents in which the people stood, and the duller sports were before them. We (Franks) had liberty to go up and down as near the G. Sr. or Mosaïf as we pleased, and to stand and stare upon them as long as we pleased. They, in like manner, went to their devotions at *Kindi* (9th hour) and *Ack-shám* (the 12 hour), and yet immediately in their sports they should applaud the same beastlinesse. 20 or 30 couple of wrestlers every day with their skins oyled all over; they alwayes touch the ground first with their hands, then put them to their head, then shake hands, or rather take their hands flat wayes one between the other, then kisse their own hands, and so begin; they say it is to call Heaven and Earth to witnesse that they meet good friends, and if any mischief happens it is beyond their intention.

There were tame bears played their tricks; once I saw a little boy stark naked wrestle with one (taught on purpose), which pleased mightily, and was shewn severall times to the G. Sr. there. By the by, my Ld. caryed to Adrianople a large English mastife, which had fought in private with the biggest bear, and worsted her in single combat; he made a present of him, which the G. Sr. took mightily kindly. They call our mastifes *Samsons*, and the G. Sr. nourishes severall, and hath here hard by our house a sommering-house for them; but this dog was half as high again as any of those which he had (which I have seen severall times), and that made him more acceptable. There were the same tumbling, stilts, and the *Bostanjé* with his stone Bottels, and the rest; but the best entertainment was rope-dancing, whereof there was but little in the other place; but here every day as good, and in some things better than all that ever I beheld in my life.

I shall now conclude with something that I am sure is not ordinary (if ever it was done) in England. From the top of Sultan Selim's Mineret or steeple (which, as I measured it, is about 84 yards high, but the place I now shall speake of was 70 yards and 1 foot high) was stretcht a rope right over the houses down into this yard; there were two men came sliding down with pulleyes, one tyed to the hair of one of them, the other fasten'd the pulley to his ancle, and holding by it with his hands, sometimes slid soe part of the way, sometimes hanging at his length with his head down. The first time they tryed, the rope yeilded so much as if some men had not stood on purpose to catch them they had been beaten to peices upon the tops of the houses and trees that stood about that end of the Musaïf's yard, which was under the Rope; they then lengthened the rope and stretcht it very tight farther into the yard. This Rope was 460 yards long at first; they lengthen'd it to 480. Every day somebody or other slided down thus, or upon their breasts. One day a lusty fellow would needs slide down with a boy at his back, with a drum and a stick and switch to beat it ; just as they came half way the rope broke, and down they fell upon a poor Armenian who was standing in the garden amongst others to view the sight. All thre were prety hurt and bruised, but it pleased God all thre recover'd. The G. Sr. paid for their cure, and offered the Armenian a pension of 20 aspers per diem as long as he lived ; but he, thanking him, sent him word that he desired nothing else but that he might have 12 purses of money paid him which a great Basha had owed him a long time ; but if he dyed he bequeathed it freely to the G. Sr. The G. Sr. gave orders that it should be done forthwith. He had only his shoulder put out of joynt and his body bruised ; but I have seen him since well recovered. The other two were rewarded too ; the man with a pension of 40 aspers per diem, the boy was taken into the Seraglio. Upon the 27 day (which was the last day that they could use this rope) two men walkt up this rope to the minaret ; one came foot by foot back again down into the yard, and the other stay'd at the top of the *mineret*.

Now if any one in England had a mind to break his neck dexterously and *secundum artem*, I have told you how (if he have not very good luck) he may do it effectually. Every night there were fireworkes here of the same nature with the forementioned. There were here two Elephants and Castles encounter'd, with all sorts of wild fire, very curiously ; but there were no great rockets or fire that would mount, for fear of firing the City. Here were several sorts likewise of your lamp work. Still we found the greatest civility imaginable, and were severall times treated with sherbert of lemmons (once with coffee and sweet meats in a low room ; the Aga who carryed us in telling us that it would be a shame for us to come to the wedding of the G. Sr.'s daughter, and neither eat nor drink).

We were commonly carryed into the Ring, and seated by ourselves, and many times had a Cherbigée or a Janizary to keep the crowd from coming near us. I suppose it was more out of ostentation than any great love to us; and dayly came *Sackáls* or budget men with a budget of sherbert, and cups into which he fil'd it out, and gave to us constantly, amongst the rest of the people of any fashion.

I (as is said) was severall times as near the G. Sr. as I pleased, and saw the manner of his state. He commonly sat upon a rich wrought or embroyder'd silk quilt, and sometimes the Prince was here with him (but we could not tell what here they sat on, they being so high above us); and about him were 8 or 10 handsome young men continually fanning him by couples. He never here appear'd in any rich or gaudy apparell, seldome smil'd; few courtiers near him in publick, and those but a very little, little time. Once the Vizier sat and talk't with him in view about a quarter of an houre. The Mosaïf had continually company with him—the Testerdare, Kaimacham, sometimes the Vizier. He is a black man, sharp, descreet (or streight) nose, yet sadled a little between his eyes, some what beetle browed, broad flat faced, Russe-fashioned, but onely his hair is black, whereas their's is red, white, or fair colour'd; his eyes pinking and smaller then proportion, and they are something hollow.

About *Kindi* come up severall of the G. Sr.'s Fakoners, with their Spaniells and severall most excellent hawkes; as certainly the whole world have not better. They seldome keep a Hawke above one season, but turne her out loose, and every year have new birds taken in plenty. They fist their hawk on the right fist; they serve their hawke with the lower joynt of the legge (instead of the head, after our manner), and therefore not a Phesant is to be bought in the mercate (unlesse it was caught some other way) with two legges. For you must understand in Asia

side are many men keep hawks to get a livelyhood ; and
they furnish our Mercates. There are such every where,
but onely they are not suffer'd near his court least they
should spoyl his game.

One of our Merchauts and I were walking out one night
by the river side, and the Vizier's Aga came by with 3
casts of Hawks and spaniels, and at least 16 or 20 men. I
had chanc't to kill a snipe crosse the river, and I had an
old dog of my Ld. Harvey's, which I sent for it. He was
the most pleased with the sight that could be ; we walkt on,
but as we return'd we found him setting in the shade under
a tree. We would have avoyded him, but he sent one of his
men to call us ; we obey'd. He had now sent home his
dogs and hawkes, and most of his company ; and he had
gotten from a little town hard by a great bottle of wine of
at least 5 or 6 quarts. He made us set downe, and there we
drank out every drop of his wine ; onely we three setting
down. His servants, which there were not above 5, stood
round us. He made two of them pipe to us all the time,
which I swear was so sweet, as I never heard the like in
Turkey. Their pipes were the true Tibiae ; being made of
the shank bone of a Bustard (as we guest at his description
of it). He courted me extreamely for my dog ; but I told
him he was old and now worth nothing, and besides, it was
the remembrance of an excellent friend ; with which he
was hardly satisfied. After he had gotten his *Keéf, or
Keph* (his heart and head merry), we parted with all the
civility in the world. There I learn'd a great deal of
Falconry ; which made me here bring the story in.

THE PLAGUE AT ADRIANOPLE.

About the beginning of July happen'd a very grievous
plague at Adrianople. It was very rife round about us,
and so drove us out of town to a little village about a mile

and ½ of to the W., called *Caragatch* (or black tree). It is in vain to tell you the many, many perills I was in, and it would be too troublesome for you to heare them, and for me to tell them. I shall onely say that, by constantcye, the Plague and all discourses about it grew so familiar to me as I was no more moved at them then at the newes of agues, or the new disease in autumne. My Ld. had a house here for himself, but all we were lodged, one here, another there, as we could procure single rooms. In the Towne are most Greekes, and the parson was infinitely civil to me, and got me a little room to myself, hard by my Ld.'s house; but within one month the plague set into this town likewise, and first seized my Land lady's onely daughter, who every day I used to prattle withall. Our Tents were set up, and I removed thither, rather then come near any body to fright them; but in 5 or 6 dayes it come every where so fiercely, that it drove my Ld. and all the rest downe into the tents to me, and I, lying in my Ld.'s tent before, was now disappointed and forct (with two more companions) to go to town again, where I and they lived (till we were coming home) in the parson's stable—and, faith, we past our time like princes, for we were within two bowes shot of the tents, and there we went to dinner and supper, and retired when we pleased. With carpets and mats we had made as good a sleeping hole as could be of it. There dyed at one time about 900 per diem in Adrianople, and above half this town dyed or fled. At last my two companions returned for *Stambol*, and then my Ld. would not let me stay there alone, so I had a little tent provided for myself and my man. Within one week the plague got into our tents amongst the servants. My Ld. and Sir Thomas fled to the Town again, the Plague being somewhat ceased at that end about their house. We endur'd at the tents, and I assure you there is no preservative like a merrie heart and a drame of the bottle. We lost our Baker, and 3 or 4 more of our servants, but the rest escaped—blessed be God. I was forc't to remove my Tent twice, for it was gotten in the next tent to me, within 20 yards, amongst one of our chiause's servants. There was not a man of us but was amongst plaguy people dayly. Count Bocareschi (as is said) came and dined with my Ld., and drank with us, with a plague sore upon him, of which he dyed the next morning.

This village has a little church dedicated to two saints,[1] ὁ ἅγιος Θεόδωρος ὁ τηρῶν and ὁ ἅγιος Θεόδωρος στρατηλάτης. They are famous for curing sore eyes, and, therefore, there are infinite little silver plates sloped and hollowed like eyes, and hang'd up as the antient ἀναθήματα.[2]

The River Arda and Meritch (Maritza[3]) joyne a little mile of, and then come running under this town; and here it is very sandy, and seldome clear in summer, for all the ground about it is very sandy, which, being dry in summer, upon every wind is carryed into the river, which makes it very shallow and broad. It is here fordable all the summer, but in winter, by floods from the hills, it overflowes into many outlets, which are dry in summer, as you may perceive the pricked[4] river next to *Dimirdesh*.[5] The fish are few and unwholesome. I saw a carp taken just 33 inches and $\frac{7}{10}$ long. I saw one at Stambol once somewhat above 36 inches, and my Ld. Harvey assured me he had one at his audience in Salonica about 40 inches long.

There were 50 Greek familyes in town, and about 10

---

[1] St. Theodore the Guardian, and St. Theodore the General. In the Greek Church hagiology, St. Theodore, with varied epithets, is always the healer of diseases.
[2] Votive offerings.   [3] The ancient Hebrus.
[4] Pricked = dotted on a plan.
[5] *Demirtash*, lit. Turkish iron-stone. Demir in Central Asia becomes Timur. Cf. Timur, the great conqueror.

Turkish *cheflicks*,[1] or summer houses. The best sort of people fled to other places, as the Turkes likewise themselves did from Adrianople to their houses here, for that same is a story that they are not afraid of the plague, because their fortunes are wrote in their forehead; for all fled, but such as were poor, or had offices about Court, and could not get away. There dyed that year about 100 persons out of the Vizier's own house; and really, those that are forc't to stay by it value it no more then we do an ague. But this is the same amongst Jewes, Greeks, Armenians, and every body else.

Mr. North[2] staid in Adrianople all the time, and come to us every day; I went to him severall times, and as I live I valued no more to meet a dead corps then a dead calf. Yet I have met above 20 in a morning, going from our tents to Mr. North's house; and there is more danger in passing by the clothes of the living then in touching the body of the dead. All slaves and poor people, so soon as they are dead, are wrapt in some pittiful covering (perhaps nothing but an old mat), and so laid upon a *Hamál's* or porter's back, and caryed away to his grave, without any more adoe. Infinites of Turkes came out of the Town and lived in Tents, as well as we; yet many Turkes came or sent out their women to their countrey houses there. I chanc't to see a couple of very lovely women severall times, which came and lived in a fine house just by me, and being under the government of onely one poor silly old man, they would get out into a great garden there hard by, and romp and play the rogue like little sprites; but more of that between ourselves.

This whole town live by selling of wine, and every day

---

[1] *Cheflick* is Turkish for a country house or farm.
[2] Afterwards Sir Dudley North, and Ambassador to the Porte. (*Vide* Introduction.)

come hundreds of people from Adrianople to be drunk ; so that it was impossible but that the Plague should be brought thither. The Janizary Aga gets at least 10,000 dollars a year out of them for selling their wine ; and yet he came there many times in show of severity, but notice was alwayes given at least an hour before he came, so that he alwayes found the coast clear. By the by, I must tell you that the Turkes love wine, and drink as much as other people ; I am assur'd not one person in 5 (throughout all this part that I have travayled) refuseth it; at Court (excepting the G. Sr. himself, the Mosaïf, and Kaimacham) not a man but will take his *Keiph* profoundly. I have seen the Vizier himself, *Mamúr* that is, crop sick[1] severall times. All the Greekes and Armenians (not daring to be merry in Adrianople in companyes) come here to feast, and I have been severall times by when 200 or 300 persons have all been setting together feasting and drinking like fishes ; and the Turkes observe the same freedome, or rather take much more.

My Landlord (the Parson) was the greatest vintner in the town, and to secure his wine he put the greatest part of it into a place in the Church ; and in the yard by us the chief Turkes of the City would come and be merry publickly ; the common Turkes never drink but to stark drunkennesse. The Parson had a kinswoman that lived but on the other side of our hedge ; she was the onely child of her father, who would come and be merry with us, and we went thither to him often. This man was very rich and had promised his daughter and all that he had to a young silly fellow in town. She was extraordinary handsome and ingenious, and cared not for her lover. I know not how it came to passe, though they lived alone and had no neighbours, but yet she got the Plague, and dyed. I could tell

---

[1] Crop-sick = sick with repletion.

you a most passionate story of her, but let this suffice. There were about 500 Greekes came to her buryall, notwithstanding the Plague, and the Metropolite of Adrianople came to burye her; and the chief of the Town, which were fled, came back to the funerall. The young fellow was in a manner distracted, and came constantly every morning for many dayes, and mourned over her grave.

The manner of the Christians buriall here is much the same; all have the *Praeficae*,[1] who sing (or rather howl and snarlle out), which they begin at home and continue to the grave. The weather was excessive hot, and the air stagnated in a manner, we being placed in a pan or flat; so that it was plague enough merely to stay there. Whilst we were in Adrianople the rats and mice, and fleas, and rumbling of carts al night long, and brawling of curs (great numbers being nourisht in every street), and the stink of the Jewes, did give us no small purgatory; but coming here, where we thought to have had braver accommodations, we found it worse. The terrible heat of the sun reflected from a dry barren sandy soil, and the fulsome foggy aire, broyled us and choked us.

We stayed there about 3 months, and returning to Stambol we found the plague as hot there; and we lost one of the servants that waited in my Ld.'s chamber (within a fourtnight after we came home) of it, and since we have found that another had it, but conceal'd it. For my part I am not so Calvinized as to say our Fate or Fortune is wrote in oure foreheads; but this I will say, I think verily it was God alone that hath preserved me from so many deaths. Some that knowe me, I believe, may wonder what the Devil bewitch me to stay in this Hell of a place; and in

---

[1] The *Præficæ* were hired mourners who sang the *naenia*, or death-wails. The custom is still prevalent in Greece, the hired mourners being called *moirologistæ*.

good earnest I have wondered at myself, but that Fate (I think indeed) was written in my heart, and now begins to be obliterated ; but so moch for that. Now I will give you a little account of the country round about, as farre as I have been.

The River Vardar and Meritch (Maritza), as is said, before they came to this town, meet; and a little above, upon the side of a hill betwixt them, is a pretty little countrey town most Greekes called *Marás*. A little further under the hill, next towards *Meritch*,[1] is a little pit of a blewish sort of clay; here a company of old gossips at the 15th of Aug., which is the Assumption of the B. V., bring water from the river and mix it and the clay together into a perfect pudding or stodge ; and on that daye infinites of people, Turkes, Jewes, and Christians, resort thither and goe in, and tumble in the mire, which they believe will cure any sort of infirmity; and without doubt it often happens so.[2] These old Hags tell how in the night before the water springs out of the ground, and how it lasts till the Octave (that is, the 22nd day), and then dryes up ; both which I proved to be a notorious lye. Yet the people are so zealously bent to believe the story, as I had liked to have *been imbroglid* for disputing of it. The earth is a kind of fuller's earth, or very obstersive, and may doe good in many cutaneous diseases, without the help of the Παναγία,[3] as they call her.

On the other side that river, under a great ridge of hills or mountaines, is another pretty Greek village cal'd in Turkish Cadun-cui (Khanoum-cui), or Ladyes town ; there is excellent wine there. Over the mountain is a great Turkish Town, famous for a Seraglio of the G. Sr., whither

---

[1] The Maritza.
[2] Washing in sacred streams on this day is still frequent in Greece.
[3] The Virgin Mary.

he retired in the Plague, leaving the Vizier to act all. It is call'd *Ack-bonar*[1] (white fountain), and seemes at a distance a brave place.

Acrosse the river from our town (Caragátch[2]), upon the top of a high hill, stands a little (but very curious) Seraglio, or rather Kiosk or sommer house, whither the G. Sr. retires for a fine girle sometimes ; and it is contrived very convenient for the purpose. I have been in it ; it is the best prospect about all Adrianople; they call it *Khiderleh*, which is the same with St. George, it having been formerly a Greek church of that name. You must know St. George is a great saint even amongst the Turkes, and their galleyes commonly set out that day to the White Seas. I have been many times reflecting on the name which they give him, *Khiderleh* (and very commonly *Khidreleh*), the *Khi* being pronounced strong in the throat like an aspirate, and I have fancy'd it to be taken (as is perhaps the whole story) from ὕδρα ; and both that tale of Hercules and the Hydra, and Apollon and the Python, from Eve and the serpent. I may venture to give my conjecture now Dr. Haylin[3] is dead, and I shall be obstinate in it too.

At the bottome of that hill, next Adrianople, is a large suburb cal'd *Ildrém*,[4] or thunder. Round about *Khiderléh*, and all the waye upon the mountaines betwixt *Ack-bónor* and Khanoum-cui, are planted vineyards most plentifully ; the Turkes by their law may eat what grapes they please (it being the greatest part of their food from August to

---

[1] *Ak-bonar* is ten miles north of Adrianople, in the Tondja.
[2] Two miles S.W. of Adrianople, on the Arda.
[3] Dr. Peter Heylyn, the theologian and historian, who died in 1662, was noted for his captious criticisms. He wrote a life of Archbishop Laud, which Mr. Pepys thus criticises :—" It is a shrewd book, but that which I believe will do the Bishops in general no great good, but hurt, it pleads so much for Popery."
[4] *Ilderim* is Turkish for a thunderbolt.

Christmasse), and now (as is said) they freely taste the blood likewise.

On the North-east of Adrianople stands the Seraglio, which is very large, and on one side of it runs the river Tunza,[1] on the other side is a plain where we saw all the sights. There is a very stately bridge, or rather pile of stone, built over the Tunza from Adrianople to *Ildrem;* it is at least 970 of my paces long, and was built by Michael Waivod of Moldavia, as is cal'd Michael's[2] Kupru, or Michael's bridge. Tunza under it meets with a branch of Arda-Meritch; over Tunza by the Seraglio on the Town side is a very strong stone bridge; on the other side, about a mile and a half from it, is another bridge of wood. Upon that river on the west side, a little farther, *Backstrevacui*, where they make very good tiles and brick; next stands *Carajauis*, on the other side about 2 miles distant; and the mountaines on the east side of it have many quarreys of soft spongy stone, yet they use it in many buildings. It stands over against *Ack-bonar*. About 2 or 3 mile farther is *Corojecui*, a little village, and about a mile farther is a very fine lake call'd by the Turkes Gióle-babba, or father Lake (Giole being a lake); it stands with Tunza on the West, high hills on the E., and *Corojécui* to the S. It is well stock't with fish (and fowl in the winter time); we saw there in August multitudes of Pelicans, swans, and some Ducks. At the East end of it, at the foot of the hills, stands a summer-house of the G. Sr.'s, furnisht allwayes ready. There are many excellent fountaines of very good water; there are some few houses about it inhabited by

---

[1] The Tondja.
[2] Michel, the celebrated Waivode of Moldavia, aroused great animosity against the Ottoman rule in the Danubian districts at the close of the sixteenth century. In 1598 he became reconciled to the Porte, and invested also with the Governorship of Wallachia; but he was assassinated in 1601.

Turkes; we found them civil, and had liberty to go in and see what we desired. It is seated very pleasantly, being overshadowed by many Chinár (or Plane) trees. The Lake is round about environed with a great quantitye of sedge, which yearly yeild a plentifull crop.

The river Tunza comes from a place cal'd now *Yianobole*,[1] but I never was higher upon it then this place; all the way hither it runs very crooked and winding, and the hills on both sides lye in like manner winding in and out, and make a crook'd but large meadow or plain, in which the G. Sr. or Vizier, drawing out their forces for the warres, first pitch their tents. We saw all along the *vestiges* of them, and many, many ovens and kitchings framed in the earth, to make ready their bread (the true staff of a Janizaryes life), and *pelów*,[2] or Boiled rice.

From Caragatch to Adrianople we passe thre long bridges, the first of wood, serviceable onely in winter, the water being little or nothing in sommer; yet this bridge is the longest, and the river under it is nothing but sand. The second bridge is likewise wood, over a branch of the river that runs all sommer; for after Arda and Mellitch (Maritza) meet they go in one stream to the city, where meeting with Tonza (Tondja), they again divide into two streames, making severall very pleasant little Islands. About 2 or 3 mile of the City, to the South, is seated a large town call'd *Bosnacui*,[3] where the French Ambassadore was seated when he was at audience; and he tells me that upon that Island are about 9 or 10 such villages more. The rivers running on either side about 10 or 12 mile unite into one again, and the broad sandy brook

---

[1] *Ianboli* is now a town of six thousand inhabitants, on the left bank of the Tondja, on the frontier of Roumelia.

[2] Pilau.

[3] *I.e.*, Village of Bosnians, three miles south of Adrianople, on the Maritza.

to the W. enters into the same channell likewise ; of these three the first is call'd (likewise on this south side the City) *Tonza*, the middle one *Merrich*, the sandy one *Ardar;* as if the 3 streames after that had met at Adrianople, sever'd themselves intirely again. By this you may see the error of our common maps placing Adrianople upon the *Hebrus*, which cannot be properly said to be till all these three meet again beneath *Bosnacui ;* at least the currents are falsely there by them laid down. *Mellitch* comes from Pilippopoli,[1] Arda comes from Sta. Sophia[2] ; upon which, next to *Caragátch*, stands *Chorbocui*, or rotten town. About it are many long (but narrow) lakes, which may give the name in Turkish; and there growes infinity of *Tribulus aquaticus*,[3] which the vulgar Greek calls ἀγριοκάστανο, or wild chestnut, and from thence they call the name of the town in Greek Καστανοχωριὸ. Southerly from the river Arda is another village, cal'd in Turkish *Ishék-cui*,[4] or Asses town, in Greek Γαιδαροχωριὸ, which signifyes the very same ; it was cal'd formerly ἀηδονοχωιὸ, that is Nightingale town, but (as the Greeks now tell the story) a great lord of this countrey whom they call 'Ιουλιανούφερα, whom they make a Turke, sent for the Bishop of this town, who chanc'd to anger him highly about a *Cheflick*, or summer house, which he desired of the Bishop there ; and therefore he swore that whosover cal'd it hereafter otherwise then γαιδάρο-χωριὸ should be hang'd.

As much farther, just at the foot of mount Rhodope, and

---

[1] Capital of Eastern Roumelia.
[2] If this refers to Sofia in Bulgaria, Dr. Covel's geography is rather astray. No maps give a Sta. Sofia near the source of the Arda.
[3] Dr. Covel here probably refers to the *tribulus terrestris*, a caltrap, which is supposed to be the *tribulus* translated "thistle" in Matt. vii, 16, and Heb. vi, 8. It grows in quantities in the East, and is also known as "the Turkey plant". It is very prickly, and the fruit is used medicinally.
[4] Turkish *eshek*=a donkey.

very near Arda, is *Orta-cui*,[1] in Greek βουλγαροχωριὸ, whether the Germane resident went to avoyd the Plague. I was two or three dayes entertain'd there like a prince; and observed this and what followes: and, believe me, I will take it upon my credit to maintain this to be a pretty exact map of what is here set down. *Orta-cui* is a very populous town, built thre quarters round a very steep hill, like an Amphitheater reinverst or imbost. There are about 1,500 familyes in it, all Greekes. There crept in some few Turkes, but all the town setting against them, and playing them scurvy tricks, made them soon weary, and they have not of late had any, though it is a very paradise to live in. All the hills are cover'd with vineyards, which make a pleasant red wine, which we might buy anywhere for 5 aspers per *Ook*,[2] that is, about 3 pints. The valleyes grow either very good corne or pasture. On the south side the village, about ½ an hour, is amongst the hills a most pleasant clear fountain of purging waters, but they work without the least offence. On the North side, towards the east, is a great plain, very fruitfull in all manner of corne and flaxe. The town stands within ½ houre from the Arda, which runs amongst the mountaines most clear, and very deep. Just against this town it hath a mill set on it, on the side of which, towards the hills, it is very deep, and full of great rocky stones, those hills being nothing else. On the other side it is very shallow, with a small stream, and little pebbles at bottom, but no sand till below *Ishek-cui*, where the land round about is sandy; which confirmes me in my opinion that the river by Caragatch and Adrianople is so foul and sandy from the sand driven from shore by the wind; though beneath Adrianople, towards *Bosnacui*, it is foul by reason all the dunghills

---

[1] *Orta-cui*, lit. "middle village", is twenty miles S.W. of Adrianople, on a hill three miles from the Arda.
[2] The *oke* then equalled half-a-pound. (Ricaut.)

THE SOURCES OF THE ARDA.   253

(the Turkes using little manure or compasse¹), and carryon, and filth, and dead men (many whereof we saw dayly thrown in, being either executed, or perhaps dead of the Plague) which are continually thrown in. Here likewise are taken as good and sweet fish as may be—Carps, Roach, Dace, Pikes, and (above all) a pale-flesh't trout, which are good, from the stony bottom; whereas, about Adrianople, from the sand or otherwise, all fish taste fleshy and beastly.

A little above this mill, next the town, amongst the hills, hath been a large old castle; part of the walls are yet standing. The high mountaines, quite above, are now cal'd Θεοβουνὸ, or God's hill. I guesse not but these ridges of mountaines are the true *Rhodope*,² for the great road from Adrianople to *Salonica* lyes over there, and all travaylers assure me that on the other side are no other hills at all till they come to Hemus, which they still call ἀμομὸντε.³ There is but little earth and few trees upon these mountaines that I ever saw. The stone, where it is naked, lyes many times Horizontal, but oftener declining. Arda comes running from the S.W. amongst these hills, having his head about 4 dayes journey (as they informe me) from *Ortacui*, at a place called *Darovasi*,⁴ not farre from Sta. Sophia. Here are many, many houses built of wood entirely, the walls being made of whole trees hewn down and clench't⁵ at the

---

¹ Compasse = compost, in agriculture. The term for a mixture of earthy substances suitable for manure.
² Rhodope, now called Despotodagh, lies almost due west of Adrianople.
³ The Hemus range corresponds to the modern Balkans.
⁴ A branch of the Arda rises at Dari-Dere in the Rhodope range, about that distance from Ortacui.
⁵ Clenched = clinched, or clincher-built, lap-jointed work—a mode of building in which the lower edge of each plank overlaps the next one below it.

ends. There are a few such at *Caragatch.* I am informed that in Poland almost all mean people's houses are such.

All the people of this town seem to live well. We chanc't to be there after harvest, when they were treading out their corn. That fashion, and the threshing floores (as we translate it), or publick places to which they bring their whole crop to tread the corne out, are still here every where in use, no other way being known to Turke or Greek but that, and no barnes being to be found, but so soon as ever they have cut down their corn, they tread it out immediately, which is likewise done with oxen yoked to a great thick plank (which these people and the Islanders call ροκάνη[1]) about a yard and a half long and a yard broad. The bottome is all filled with sharp flints stuck into it.[2] Upon the top stands a person, who also guides the oxen round, and pricks them forward with a goad. In a great floor you shall have 2 or three of these, and as many yoke of oxen at a time. After they have trodden, or rather bruised, one flooring out, they lay another; thus all the strawe is broken to pieces like chaf, and thence it is call'd chopt straw. What from the slovenlinesse of their dressing their corne, and the badnesse of their mill stones (they being onely some pieces of very hard stone joyned together with a strong mortar, and collar'd in a hoop of Iron), there is no bread or meal in this part of Turkey but what is very gritty. Some of the Turkes do muzzle their oxen, but not all. In sharing their corn they have a kind of wooden glove on the 4 fingers of the left hand, which

---

[1] Ροκάνι, mod. Gk., is literally a carpenter's plane.

[2] These threshing-machines are still used amongst the tribes in Asia Minor: a board of pine-wood set with flint stones at the bottom, fixed along the grain of the wood. Cf. Isaiah xli, 15: "The new sharp threshing instrument having teeth."

in Greek they call παλαμαριὰ,[1] to guard their hand from thistles and the like.

You cannot imagine the strange superstition that is generally amongst the people of this countrey; Turkes, Jewes, Greekes, Armenians, all have their amulets and Telismes (talismans) and φυλακτήρια about themselves, but especially about their children, their horses, their houses. Nightingales are very commonly kept in cages and let out to sing by so much per diem, but you shall not see one but shall have a deal of this trumpery about the cage. The Turkes have commonly their Telismes engraved on silver or gold; I have seen 10,000 lye in goldsmiths' boxes to be sold upon all occasions; there are peculiar arts of making of these, but I count them all meer old wives' conceits. There was a Scotchman here who much delighted and practised in such mysteries, and gave me the best account he could, but I will assure you they are more absurd and nonsensicall then figure flinging[2]; and since he was gone I chanc't to dine one day with the French Ambassador,[3] when he had on purpose sent for the most noted Turk in all these parts for such things. It will be tedious for to recount you all that past, but we manifestly proved him an impudent imposter. He got his *Keiph* there sufficiently, and that was (I believe) his chief design. Your Greekes count nothing more sacred then the ἀντίδωρον,[4] the bread (not the sacrament), which is blest and distributed amongst the people upon Holy Thursday; this they call ὕψωμα, perhaps from our Saviour's ascention. At *Ortacui* you would scarce see a little child but it had

---

[1] These *palmaria*, or wooden reaping-gloves, are still common in the highlands of Asia Minor.
[2] Refers to the old form of magic of sticking with pins or knives a figure made to represent an enemy.
[3] Marquis de Nointel. (*Vide* Introduction.)
[4] Wafer given in return for a coin.

some of this either in a little silver box about their necks, or stitched up in a bit of silk, or tyed in a little rag; I have observed the like in many other places; many carry wolves' teeth, or the bones of their toes, etc., set in silver or gold; bones or parts of frogs, mice, lizards, Hippocampus,[1] etc.

As we went home from Ortacui we were driven into a town by a storme, and laid there the most part of the night. Our Janizary chanc't at our going into the house to catch a bat; he rejoyced exceedingly, and borrowing a zechine of me (the ceremony must be done with gold or not worth a farthing), he cut the throat of it therewith, pronouncing the name of God and some other conceits; he saved every drop of the blood in cotton, and kept it as a most divine thing. By this, he said, he could make friends with any one; love in a woman; in fine, preserve himself and us from all evil.

We set out from that little town, and were overtaken in a most dreadful tempest of Thunder and lightning; just getting up a steep bank a flash of lightning discharged a sheet of fire, which fell on the ground and rested there a good while, within lesse then two yards of me and Dr. Pickering (we two being foremost), and huft[2] my hat and vest like a mighty gust of wind; our horses trembled and stood as half dead, but presently we got forward. All the world will not persuade that fellow but that the blood of his Bat preserved us. I have now been too, too impertinent, but yet could adde much more to this purpose about your Greekes or βροκόλακα[3] (the walking of dead men), and their solemne prayers and exorcismes of their church in that point. Also

---

[1] The sea-horse.

[2] Huff=blow or puff. "The said winde within the earth, able to *huffe* up the ground." (P. Holland, *Plinie*, bk. ii, ch. 85.)

[3] Βρουκολακες. A common superstition still all over Greece is that dead men return as ghosts, and suck the blood of the living.

concerning the Armenians' *caracóngilas*[1] (or hobgobling, or kind of Robbin good fellow), which is universally believed by them, and on the 13th and 14th of Feb. have a solemnity on purpose about it. Likewise about witches (which certainly, if there be any in the world, they are here) I can tell you storyes which will much amaze you ; yet I must confesse I am very slow of belief in that point. I have likewise a strange Greek MS. presented me concerning such whimsyes ; but enough of this matter. Before the Plague I walk't about all the town ; the old city (as is said) is not above a 3rd part of the whole, and the walls are pittyfull thin brick work.

* * * * *

July 27th. My Lord had audience with the G. Sr., notwithstanding the height of the Plague. He came from Ackbonar to the Seraglio on purpose, for my Ld. was very pressing for it, and in earnest. We had stay'd a longer time then ordinary for it. It was performed as followeth : The time being appointed two days before, that morning, an hour before day, came two Chiauses to Caragatch to call us. We went suddainly to the foot of the 2d wooden bridge before mentioned, and there stay'd in tents till the rest of the chiauses came to conduct us, about 50 in all (they are paid by us a zechine apiece, and therefore we may have as many as we please, if we count their number a glory). Thus we passe to the Town side, where my Ld. mounted his best horse, and rode quite through the City upon him ; and we came to the seraglio gate about ½ an houre past 5 in the morning. After a little stay there, the *chiaus basha*, and *capige basha*, and *Peskeshjé*[2] *basha*

---

[1] Evil spirits called Karakongilas, or Kalkagari, are still believed, in remote parts of Greece, to haunt the world and play all kinds of pranks between Christmas and Epiphany.

[2] *Pishkesh* is Turkish for a present.

came to my Ld. to conduct him in. We past from the gate directly to the divan upon a stone caseway, through a square court, which I guesse every way is about 160 of my paces. The *Peskeshjé basha* is the same, in a manner, as our maister of the ceremonyes. *Peskesh* signifyes a present, as if *peskeshjé* were one of the Maisters of the presents, and *Peskeshjé basha* is the head or chief of them all. This man walkt with a great silver staff in his hand (as bigge as the Cambridge beadle) before my Ld. to shew him where to make his reverences: for you must understand all the sides of the court were lined with Janizaryes and other souldjers; therefore, as my Ld. past, he bowed to the Janizary Aga, *Bash. Chiaus, Chia Beghi*, and other great officers of the souldjery there. We came at last to the large Divan, which is just in the same fashion as that at Stambol (which I have seen), onely the side at Stambol hath no seates as this hath. The seates (or bench from which the inferior viziers are named of the bench) round the three sides are cover'd with embroyder'd silk, as likewise the whole floor of the same. Under it, upon the benches, is one continued quilt, or kind of cushion, quite round. In the middle of the side was a rich foot cloth, which reached from the back of the bench (or wall) down into the floor. Here sat the *Nesharjé basha*,[1] who (is a principal secretary, and) writes the Grand Sr.'s Firme[2] (or Fiat) to all his commands. There enters a little door on one side, where is such another foot cloth, onely every way larger. There sat the *Vizier Azém*. Over his head was a *Gelosia*, or lattice (as at Stambol), where the G. Sr. is often (as he was then) present, but incognito; and, as we guest, the Sultana was there once, yet some say it was impossible. On the same side sat 2 Cadeleschiers on

---

[1] The *Nischardji-baschi* is equivalent to the Secretary of State.
[2] Firman.

AUDIENCE WITH THE GRAND VIZIER.   259

another foot cloth. The other side is open from the bench up to the top of the roof. Here sat the Testerdare upon such another foot cloth. In the room behind him sat severall men of the law, who, upon occasion, could speak or receive any writing, or other matter, into the Divan, that side, as is said, being open, onely two wooden pillars supporting the roof. The Divan might be about 8 or 9 (at most) yards square. There is a stone gallery open into the court, out of which we enter'd, then into the Divan, which is open into the Gallery and court. My Ld., making his reverence to the Vizier and the rest, was placed in the corner upon the bench, without a foot cloth, beneath the Nesharjé, which was the lowest place, to wit, the right hand. *Mauro Cordato*[1] (the Vizier's Dragoman) and my Ld.'s two Dragomen in chief stood next him. Then all we stood with our backs to the court; we might turne side wise to look out, but one or two turning their backs to the Vizier were reprehended as guilty of too much rudeness. All of us being thus disposed of, immediately were brought in 320 purses of money, and lay'd in 32 heapes upon the floor, before the Vizier, a purse being 500 dollars. There were two little bags that were layd by themselves. You must know that the Janizaryes and souldjers about the court are pay'd once a month in this manner, publickly, before the Vizier and the Divan. But now the pay day was put of till my Lord's audience, it being a thing usually done at all Embassadores audiences, merely for to show the grandeur and glory of their Empire, though sometimes it happens otherwise. The Testadore therefore, after the money was lay'd down, gave up his accounts to the Vizier. He, kissing them, sent them to the G. Sr. by the *Peskeshjé basha*, and by him they were presently return'd again to the Vizier, who received them with a kisse. Then the

---

[1] *Vide* note p. 272.

severall chambers of Janizaryes (which stood round the court) were call'd in order, the word being given by the *Peskeshjé basha* very loud. The whole chamber comes running together upon the case-way to the door, where they received their proportionate bagges to be divided by themselves or officers. And, after the first chamber was paid of, they past away, and the next was call'd ; and so till all was paid out. Then the Cherbigees (the colonells) and other head officers came into the Divan, and, kneeling down on the Vizier's left hand, kist the left corner of his vest, and put it to their head, returning (as all the rest, that make reverence by saluting his vest, doe) three or four steps backwards and sideways, get out of his presence, he all the time sitting like a statue, neither bowing nor taking the least notice imaginable. The Testerdare (who many times had occasion to whisper with him) went alwayes to him without any ceremony at all. All this being over, basons, and ewers, and towells were brought in, and the Vizier, Testerdare, Neshanjé basha, and my Ld. washt severally, severall servants waiting upon each of them. Then were brought in 3 little round tables, all of them were alike, and they were cover'd with leather carpets onely (without any table cloth) ; then little flat loafes of bread (like pancakes) lay'd round in heapes, 3 or 4 one upon another, and severall broken in peices and scatter'd upon the table. By each heap, between, lay a coarse little wooden spoon, four little saucers of capers, olives, sampier,[1] parsley—the two first pickled, the other two in sugar lickquore—one little salt seller, one little pepper box. These 3 tables, thus furnisht, stood respectively before the Vizier, testerdare, Neshargé, all being exactly alike furnished. At the Vizier's Table was set a velvet stool for a seat for my Ld., over against the Vizier, who sat on the

---

[1] *Vide* note 1, p. 33.

bench. Three other such seates were set at the Nesharjé's table, where dined Mr. North[1] (the Treasurer), Mr. Hyet (the antientist merchant here), and Dr. Pickering (a Physician of Smyrna). Three more were set at the Testerdare's table, where dined my Ld.'s Secretary, Mr. Carpenter, Mr. Cook (the Companyes Councillier), and my self. The rest of the Merchants and gentlemen dined some in the next room with the *Rice-Effendi* and the Vizier's Secretary. Some else were with the Chiaus-basha. All our tables were served exactly alike with just 20 dishes of meat, which were set on but one at a time; and so soon as that was scarcely tasted, it was shifted away, and another placed in the room, so that we made a very short businesse of it, and, all along, the waiters at each table kept all so good time, as we began and ended just together. You must understand the Turkes make the supper (as the antients did) the best meale, and seldome eat at noon, but in the morning—and this was about $8\frac{1}{2}$ by the clock. We had a long course Towel layd round the Table in common (as the fashion is every where) upon our laps, instead of napkins. It was wrought and checker'd like a barber's apron. This was to wipe our hands, for, by every one, after we were set, on our right hand, into our lap or on our knee was laid a muckender[2] (of the same cloth, but finer) to wipe your mouth and beard.

I cannot give you an exact bill of fare, but as well as I can remember it was thus at every table: first we had 6 rost chickens brought pil'd one upon another, without sauce; we had no such finicallnesse[3] as knives or forkes

---

[1] Afterwards Sir Dudley.
[2] *Muckender* is derived from Spanish *mocador*, French *mouchoir* 'You knew her little, and when her apron was but a muckender.' (Dr. Corbett's *Marriage*, 1658.)
[3] Finicalness = foppishness. "Gray's finicalness about expressions was excessive." (Hall, *Mod. Engl.*, p. 123.)

onely the weapons that nature gave us, our hands and teeth. The Testerdare began by pinching the flesh with his fore finger and thumb, and invited us to fall to; I having seen the way of it many times before, fell on and brought on my companions. We had a dish of roast pigeons, which we eat in the same manner, nipping and tearing them apieces with hands and teeth, in any fashion. We had *Kibôbs*, bits of flesh, the first roasted, the last boyled; this was ready mammockt,[1] and cut to our hands. We had several sorts of *Dolmáh*,[2] which is minc't meat stuffed into peices of gourds, or gobbeted[3] in vine leaves or the like, and so boyl'd. We had several *Cherbaws*, pottages made of rice, wheat, etc., some sweet, some savoury; we had *Pelo*, rice boyled with peices of a hen; *Rice gellyed*, a perfect *fool* in a platter; another slip slop[4] of Dates and pine kernells; at all these we ployed[5] our wooden artillery of the spoon. We had a great *baked pye* in a platter, with puff paste above and minced beaten meat, wel season'd underneath; a puf past pudding in a platter, plain; *another*, sweeten'd with honey. About half way of this horse feast we water'd with a hearty draught of excellent Lemmon sherbert, which was brought in a *fingeon*,[6] or Polish glasse, gilt on the verge at the top. The Testerdare began, and we caryed it round, then it was

---

[1] Mammock = to tear in pieces.
  "He did so set his teeth and tear it; O, I warrant
  How he *mammocked* it."
                    (Shakes., *Coriolanus*, i, 3.)
[2] *Dolmades* is a common Greek dish now.
[3] *Gobbet* (cf. Old French *gober*, to devour greedily) here means made into mouthfuls. "Down comes a kite powdering upon them, and gobbets up both together." (L'Estrange.)
[4] Slip slop = feeble composition.
[5] *Ploy*, abbreviated form of "employ". "Twa unlucky red-coats were up for black-fishing or some siccun *ploy*." (Scott, *Waverley*, ch. lxiv.)
[6] *Finjan* is Turkish for a cup.

whipt away, and we saw it no more. We had my Ld.'s 2d Dragoman by us all the time, and the 1st Dragoman and *Mauro Cordato*, dragoman to the Vizier, attended my Ld. I sat so near him as I could have touched him, and I heard every word that past betwixt the Vizier and him, which was not much, but what it was was nothing of private businesse, but newes or such discourse ; all past pleasantly.

The onely thing of notice was this : talking of the stirres that have been made at *Fustenberg*,[1] between the Emperor and K. of France, the Vizier, laughing, askt why they did not cut of his head at first? then, says he, there had been an end of all the embroglios that happen'd after. We were all served alike in costly (lordly) dishes, which are used every where at court, and I saw them at the Vizier's and Mosaïf's houses. They come from India, and are all in use in Persia, for the G. Sr. nor any great Turkes can use silver dishes by their law. They call the mettal of them *Martabáni*[2]; they are very dear and much heavier (in proportion) then China, which they call *Phorphoré* (I suppose from πόρφωρα) ; their platters, which they call *Taback*,[3] of *Martábani*, are worth some of them 200 dollars. China is not half so dear here ; your little sherbert cups and coffee dishes are made often times of the same earth ; they ring like a bell ; the earth is darkish, but the outside glazed colour is greenish. The last dish being taken from table, we all rose up together ; the Grandees washt, and then my Ld. and me with him were caryed into the gallery, and there he sat on a long bench. Presently we were vested with Caphtans, which we wore all the time we were afterwards in the Seraglio ; there

---

[1] In Feb. 1674 the Imperialists carried off the Prince of Furstenberg, a plenipotentiary accredited to the Court at Cologne. This outrage broke off negotiations between France and Germany.

[2] Deriv. Persian *martaban*, a glazed vessel.

[3] *Tuback* is a Turkish word for "plate".

were given but 19 in all; my Ld. Harvey had 22 when he was at Salonica, and the G. Sr. spoke to him a great deal; but now (as you shall hear immediately) he said not one word.

The meat which went from our tables was caryed out amongst inferior officers, where was such scrambling as I never saw. I saw much, much better order once at a feast at the Kaimacham's of Stambol. The like was where our servants dined; yet all passed in silence, as the whole businesse above said was likewise acted even to a miracle, all being done with a nod or private sign (at which they are the best in the world) to the attendants and waiters, who stand like images with their hands acrosse before them. The same silence, gravity, and decorum is alwayes practised in all other places of justice or businesse throughout the whole Empire; *whish, whish, whish, whish,* or *kish, kish,* etc., is sometimes used if there should happen any the least *cavgá,* or disturbance. The Merchants that din'd without said some of them were hunch't[1] about and *Heyda'd*[2] (a word which signifies *get you gon*') with some rudenesse, as I am apt enough to beleive the rabble Turkes are like enough to do it.

After my Ld. and we had weighted about ½ an hour in the gallery, where Mauro Cordato had the impudence to sit by my Ld., the Vizier and the rest rose and past by us, and went into the G. Sr., who was in a low room. There was another doore going into some other room, and forwards run a high wall to the corner of the court. A quarter of an hour after they past by, my Ld. was cal'd; all we accompanyed him almost to the outward door, then he went forward with

---

[1] *Hunch*=to shove with the elbow. "Then Jack's friends began to *hunch* and push one another." Arbuthnot's *Hist. of John Bull,* ch. xiii.

[2] Usually written *Haïda* in conjunction with the word *ghit,* "go away".

onely six persons who were appointed to accompany him, viz., the two chief Dragomen, Mr. North the Treasurer, Mr. Hyet the eldest merchant, my Ld.'s Secretary, who carry'd the king's letter upon his head, and the Companyes Cancelleer.

My Ld. and Sr. Thos. B. promised me before we set out from *Stambol*, and all along assured me, that I should infallibly be one that should goe in, and no lesse then three dayes before did again secure me the same favour; but it happen'd otherwise on some other occasion, which I shall afterwards make you laugh withall. For my own part I repine not at it, for I have seen the G. Sr. again and again, and those that did goe in can onely say they did do so; for as to any thing that they saw there, the divel of any the least account could they give; onely something look't like a thing they call the G. Sr.; yet the whole account I coul'd get from them, or observe myself, is this fully and exactly. My Ld. and all the rest were led in by two *Peskeshjes* or *Chiauses*, one holding them under one arme, the other under the other, through the part of the court were we left them. So soon as ever they entered the room, their leaders, laying their hands upon their necks, bowed them down (my Ld. himselfe very low, the rest to the very ground); immediately Mr. North, Mr. Hyet, and the Cancelleir and the 2d Dragoman were hurryed out again so soon, as Mr. North, who was first, swore he observed nothing, onely in general that it was a very rich room, but in particular he remembred nothing in the world. The poor Cancellier, being a little man, was crushed quite down at the entrance, and Mr. Hyet had like to tumble over him as he lay sprawling on the ground: so they saw lesse then Mr. North. The Cancellier remember'd nothing, and Mr. Hyet said he had a pittyfull glance at the G. Sr., and indeed it was impossible they could look about them, these thre gentlemen being in (at that outward door, where we lost sight of them) but 48 of my pulses, which is not much above ½ a minute, as I have tryed by a half minute glasse at sea severall times. My Ld. stay'd after them about 200 of my pulses, so that in all he could not be there much above 4 minutes at most. He being led in and bowed (as is said) *pro more*, the chief Dragoman read his speech (and yet was out about the middle of it, as my Ld. himselfe told him before me afterwards), which I saw and was just 12 lines and a half in a small quarter of a sheet. That ended, the Secretary gave the king's letter to the Dragoman, and he to the Vizier, and he lay'd it by the G. Sr.'s right hand upon his bolster, who cast a kind of scornful eye towards it. The Vizier immediately told them: It's well, and he as Vikiel or deputy should take care of their businesse; and so, without one word or complement passing, they were all led out again. This my Ld. himself told me, and his Secretary and Dragoman confirm'd it.

Now for grandeur and state of what was there, my Ld. himself gave us this account. The G. Sr. was set leaning upon a bed, and had put on a most severe, terrible, stately look. The bed had four posts, like ours, but whether with silk curtaines, valence, etc., is not sayd. The counterpane was of crimson velvet embroyder'd and flour'd with pearl, and round the edges went eight rowes of the same, all as bigge and as fair as ever he saw in a necklace. The floor was crimson sattin, embroyder'd likewise and wrought with gold wire, which in some places was very big. The G. Sr. had a small, plain Turbant on, with a little feather in it; at the bottome it had a brooch of Jewels, amongst the rest one very large diamond. At the feet of his bed stood a large cabinet all cover'd over with jewels, which he first valued at 100,000*li*. (but in a second relation at 200,000*li*.) sterling; he judged it to be full of jewels. His vest and delamon,[1] from his neck down before,

---

[1] Cloak.

were all set with fair large diamonds and pearles. What the roof of the room had, the walls, windowes, and the like had, or whether there were chimney, chimney-piece, balconyes, stooles, chayres, etc., he could give no account; onely he said he thought the windore was but small, for the room was dark, so as he wonder'd the old Dragoman could read at all. You were out a little (quoth he to him), but you soon recover'd yourself; in fine, my Ld. said in generall that it was the richest room for certain in the whole world; but I question much whether he could make out the particulars.

Now I declare to you the chief thing I desired to see was the furniture and embellishments of the room; for (as is said) I have seen the G. Sr. again and again. Here are adornments in building very costly and comely, utterly unknown in our parts of the world, of which I am able to give some pretty account; perhaps the sight of this might have added something to my observations. So soon as my Ld. come out, we all accompanyed him through the great court to the outer gate. There we mounted, and stay'd about half-an-houre, till the Vizier and Testerdare came out; after them came out all the *Chiauses*, who again conducted us out of the Town.

Aug. 10*th*. My Ld. went to visit the Mufti. He had audience, in the very same manner as before is said, with the G. Vizier[1]; and, after a little formall complimenting, we return'd. He was a swarthy man, yet a good-natured countenance; his beard somewhat grey (being above 54 yeares old, as is commonly said), the left corner something longer than the other; a full eye, lean, discreet nose, well-fashioned mouth and teeth; his forehead of a middle height; serene brow, cheekes enclining to leanesse; but no wayes a mortifyed look. He gave us no vests, but received

---

[1] The Grand Vizier, Kiuprili, died a few months later.

ours (which we alwayes caryed wherever we went to audience) gladly; and without doubt that added to his cheer, which was very pleasant, as well as his countenance. He was set *Alla Turchesca*, with his feet cover'd and lapt with a course kind of linesay-woolsay blanket; the rest of his habit was no wayes distinguist from that of a common Turk. We were carryed into him, and he did not rise to my Ld., but onely bow'd; and my Ld. was placed on a stool just before him. He had three or 4 bookes lay'd by him, and round about the room on shelf lay severall more. His turbant in the middle being plain, and not in folds. We did not stay much above a quarter of an hour with him; soe we return'd to our old shop at Caragatch. Remember that these visits were in the height of the Plague; and several, I assure you, came amongst us with plague-sores running upon them at the Vizier's at our last audience, of which by and by. There was a fellow gave me a dish of coffee who had then about him 2 filthy sores; and after he had served us with coffee, by chance talking with some of our Merchants (that spoke Turkish) about the plague, told them that he had lost three children the week before, and that he had been sick unto death, but now his swellings were broke he was much better. The Turkes used no other antidote against the plague then multitudes of Issues, which really I count a most divine thing to that effect, though otherwise a plague in themselves.

I have above mentioned to you *Vani Effendi*, the great preacher amongst the Turkes.[1] I shall here insert some

---

[1] *Vani Effendi* was a celebrated preacher in the Court of Mahomed IV, and is said even to have brought the Emperor to tears. As in other parts of Europe, fanatical preaching was rife at this time, and in Turkey we find also Sabatai Sevi, who tried to make himself out to be the Messiah, and whose followers exist to this day. Vani attacked him

little notices of him. He is an old huncht-back man, very gray, a crabb'd countenance, yet his shrivel'd flesh is clear, not black or swarthy, but pale ; and Nature hath marked him in the face, for his right eye is lesse than his left, as if it were shrunk. He hath children at Brussa,[1] and is of such authority amongst the Turkes, as about 6 yeares since preach'd down all publick Tavernes and ale-houses, and the Dervises' publick meetings; yet I believe there is as much wine drunk (or more) and as many tavernes by connivance and bribery as ever there was. The fame of this old cox comb is more then a Pope amongst them ; he invited Sr. Thos. Baines to visite him ; therefore, sending one of our dragomen and *Renegado Boccareschi* to beg licence of him to come, he told them he should be wellcome. He is cal'd *Vani*, from a town of that name on the confines of Persia.[2] Sr. Tho. being come to him and set down, ask't liberty of discourse; he told him he might say what he pleased, nothing would be taken amiss.

Sr. Tho. 1st Quest. was: Whether all soules were equall of men, women, children ? After many shuffling answers, he said the prophet Mahomet was asked the same question, and answered it was *not yet revealed to him.*

2dly : Whether women shall be in Paradice ? Answr.: They shall have many there of those which were here and lived well and virtuously according to their law, and besides God will create them many others ; but of the two sortes, those that go from hence will be the better, because their obedience hath already been tryed and proved. He said that wicked men commonly drew their wives down to hell

---

furiously, and tried to convert the Jews to Mahommedanism. He was very instrumental in putting down the use of wine, and before the standard of the Turkish army he prayed with fanatical enthusiasm.

[1] Brusa, in Bithynia.   [2] Van, in Kourdistan.

with them; yet if the wife be virtuous she may goe to heaven, though the Man goes to Hell.

Now I understande one notion of my own. Being once with our chief Dragoman in company with a great Doctor of their law, I had the curiosity to ask (amongst other things) what use they should have of women in Paradise, whether for procreation or no? He told me that they shall conceive there for certain, but not by members of generation, but onely by intellectual seed and spiritually, to make a spirituall ofspring. *Vani* told Sr. Thos. that there is a middle life or place cal'd (as Sr. Tho. hath set it down) *Asaph* (it should be Aráf,[1] as in the chapter of Prisons, cap. 7), whither all that have lived a middle life shall goe; that is, sins and virtuous deeds being compared and weighed together.

3d: What people might be suffer'd to live amongst Turkes? Answr.: None but Jewes and Christians; all other are to be put to death. This toleration is given, because the Jewes had and yet have a true law, but most imperfect Christians have a true and perfecter law; but the onely perfect law is Mahomet's, which all now are bound to believe and follow; if they doe not, though they live never so well, they cannot be saved. There were two little boyes (by Christian slaves), and Sr. Tho. put this case: If you had lost (it had been better put if he had said hidden) a jewell, and should bid these two seek it, and tell them where abouts it was to be found; one being more successful then the other, finds it; the other notwithstanding being very industrious, and leaving no stone or stick unturned, perhaps finds onely a crisstall: shall this son be blamed for his ill successe, notwithstanding his indeavours were as much, perhaps more then the other? Here, saith Sr. Tho. B., the teares stood in his eyes, and he answered: Every body had heard of

---

[1] *Araf* is the Mohammedan form of Purgatory.

their law and their Prophet, and were bound to believe. Sr. Tho. B. said he had heard many things which he now found not truly reported of them, and he had read their Alcoran, which he now sees wrongly translated; both which rather prejudic'd him then furthered him in his belief, and many there are who never heard of it at all; suppose such a one (who never heard) to be a Christian and live well, whether he might be saved? He answer'd not close to the point. Sr. Tho. told what kind of Christian he was, viz., he would rather dye then worship either crosse, Pictures, Images, or the like. He adored onely one true God, and lived in his fear onely; he believed a Mussulman, living up to the height of his law, may be undoubtedly saved. He thought himselfe obliged (though it was never so absolutely in his power to do it) not to touch a hair of a Mussulman's head for his difference in religion, but rather to help, assist, relieve, and cherish them in every good office that he was able to doe for them. Here Sr. Th. B. saies he wept, and said he could not believe any Christian came so near true Musselmen, but that they all had been Idolaters; and the standers by (which were many) cryed out *E Adâm*[1]—he was a *Good Man*. You may imagine this was odde for a Greek (who worships all these things, and curses a Turk to the Divel) to say as Draggerman. *Vani* pressing the perfection of his law, and the necessity of turning to it, Sr. Tho. said he was now about 55 years of age, and his bones were dryed and hardened to their forme; and his understanding was in like manner settled by long practice of his own religion, and it would be a hard task, and of some long time, to unrivet his notions. Vani bad him welcome, desired more frequent converse, assuring him all security and freedome. The Dragoman told me he was afraid to speak, for though

---

[1] *Adam*, Turkish for "a man".

they might not touch Sr. Tho. B., yet they might chastise him for speaking anything about or against this Law.

Sr. Tho. Baines went no more; he sent to him severall questions by *Boccareschi*, till he was weary, first: To know if the soules of the dead (Men and Women) went immediately to heaven or hell, without any stay? Answr.: The blessed went not into Paradice till the day of Judgement, but had a continuall sight of it through a great windore. He said *Boccareschi* was not a fitting messenger, and desir'd, if he had any more questions, that he might set them down in writing, and he would answer in like manner. Sr. Th. B. left of. For my own part, I believe he might have given his first Answer to most of Sr. Th. B.'s questions, viz.: The Prophet (nor God himself) hath not revealed those things. He sent word by *Boccareschi* about Hell: 1st, there are 60 mountaines of fire, and millions of poysonous serpents and dragons to torment the damned. 2nd, that no Turke shall remaim there to eternity; infidells and Idolaters never get out.

Sept. 8th. My Ld. went for the capitulations to the Vizier, and, to take leave, we were caryed into the Khiá's (the Steward or Secretaryes) chamber, where we stay'd waiting two houres. We were treated in the mean time with coffee and sherbert. Mauro Cordato[1] (the Vizier's Dragoman), who has studied in Italy, and was at first a doctor of Physick, by nation a Greek, sat and bore my Ld. company. Amongst other discourse, he assured us that the first month (June) the plague began, there might die

---

[1] *Maurocordato*, the dragoman to Ahmed Kiuprili and the Ottoman Government, was a distinguished member of this Greek family in Scio. His mother was the daughter of a rich cattle merchant, Skarlato by name, and by this name he is perhaps better known. He studied medicine at Padua, and was Court physician as well as dragoman. He was employed on many important diplomatic missions, and signed the Peace of Carlowitz between the Porte and Austria.

from 60 to 100 per diem; the 2d month it increased to at least 250; this month (Sept.) dyed at least 600 per diem (but others talked much lighter), and after our coming away it increased to double the number. It is a very bad place for fruits, and this year worse than ever. He said that it was banisht the court. There were abundance of Turkes, and many of them sick (as is above said), intermixt with us. At last we were caryed into another room, and, after a little pause, came in the Vizier, and he and my Ld. sat as before. He spoke cheerfully, and proved in very good humour; yet his face, especially about the eyes, look'd very swel'd and reddish. We understood he had been soundly *keiph't* the night before.

The Vizier began, and told him the Capitulations were renewed according to his desire. My Ld. thankt him, and signifyed what high respect our king would have for him for his particular care in it; and he would see that he had particular thanks for it from him. The Vizier ask't what ships we had, and what were expected. Answer: Two dayly expected from Legorne, one generall ship in two months at Constantinople, 2 more at Smyrna. The Vizier ask't what newes? Answer: The last was that the two Armyes were within 2 or three leagues one of the other, and that Brandenburgh had routed the Swead; that the Ragusian Ambassador reported a battle to have been fought, wherein 12,000 French, with Turein[1] himself, kil'd. The Vizier said he had heard the like. We had 12 vests. My Ld. received the Capitulations, G. Sr.'s letter, and Vizier's letter to our king from his own hand, kissing them all, as the manner is. My host wish't the G. Sr. and Vizier a long life, and that the Vizier might have all

---

[1] Turenne. Louis XIV's campaign in 1676 resulted in the desolation of the Palatinate, and Turenne's victories continued till the peace of Nimeguen, 1678.

increase of honour and favour with the G. Sr. And so we came away.

Sept. 16*th.* My Ld. took leave of the Vizier's *Khia* and the *Rice effendi*, in whose familyes the plague was then very, very rife. Two men, with plague sores on them running, stood about a full quarter of an houre within a yard of him, yet God preserved both him and us. Onely, as is said, three or four servants dyed there. One or two had it all the way home to Stambole undiscovered, and there one, who allwayes was about my Ld. and Sr. Tho., dyed.

Sept. 19*th.* About 1 o'clock we set out for Stambole. Because the road was everywhere full of the plague, we every night lay in our Tents, which were caryed before us, and pitcht ready at every *condck*, and all our waggons and coaches were drawn round us, and a great fire being made. There were men watch't by turnes every night, for the road was very full of thieves. Not a day past but some newes or other came of their exploits. There were many in companyes, and if we had not had guards it would have been very easy cutting our throats. We made as many dayes coming home as we did going out, and pitcht under the same town sides; so that though we ourselves went not into Townes, most of our waggoners and servants did for wine, or women, or something or other, and so our danger was, in a manner, the same. I have been used to the fashion of the country of lying in my clothes, which I did both outwards and homewards, and once in a frolick to Brusa Baths I came not in a bed for 8 weekes together. Now I caryed a little sea bed with me, which I lay on at Adrianople, and upon the road. We first spread a carpet on the ground, and then lay'd our beds or quilts upon it, and so tumbled down upon them, booted, cloak't, etc., as we rode. I was a little ill at Caragatch, or else I enjoy'd my health very well all the time. I came with my Ld. and companye along to *Caresteran*. There

I left them with onely my man with me (wee were well arm'd) to go see *Misine*.[1] At Chiorlúh I met my Ld. and all the Company again.

Sept. 24*th.* Seeing the Sea from Chiorlúh, I thought it not much out of my way to goe to it, and thence to Selibria alongst the sea shore. I could perswade no man to accompany me for fear of Thieves, and a calf with a white face disheartened them all. Away went my man and I. There is from Chiorlúh, to your eye, a perfect streight valley to the Sea, which I thought was, at most within 5 miles, but I was horribly mistaken. Though in a right line it may be so, yet following a road that leads to it, by reason of a little rill that rises on the left hand out of the hills towards *Stambol*, which makes a moorish bottome, by windings and turnings I made it about as much more. This little rill, in most places, is so very narrow as I could easily step over it, and yet we reckon'd 7 or 8 Turkish mills upon it, so little water sufficing for each of them. In 2¼ houres we got to the sea, counting it at least 9 mile, all the hills on either side (especially the left) covered with vineyards, and they were then in the height of their vintage. We past severall very good fountaines in the way, and about a mile of the sea we past a little Turkish village. So soon as we arriv'd at the sea, we turn'd to the left hand for Heraclea. At the end of about 6 mile we met a good fountaine, which refresh't us well. The country all champion, and many little villages were to our left hand on the hanging hills. We arriv'd at Heraclea in 2½ houres. At our rate it was about 13 or 14 miles, the country still champion, onely some few trees thinly set about Heraclea. In the playnes are many hills raysed (as sepulchres, I suppose). One large one is by

---

[1] Doubtless the small village of Missinli, about three miles north of Karesteran. (Austrian Staff Map, 1829.)

T

the sea, upon a rising ground, not far from the town. It stands upon a peninsula. The Isthmus is on the N.W. side. To the sea is a pretty high cliff. On that upper ground stood the antient town, now inhabited most by Greekes. On the lower ground to the Isthmus live many Turkes, and have severall Moschés. There are yet standing, in all, 40 Greek churches, yet (as elsewhere) none deserve the name but the Metropole's, which is a good old odde fashion'd building. It hath a Cupola and half cupolas about it like Sta. Sophia.

They show there, within the Metropolis, the top stone of Sta. Gluceria's tomb, which they say was saved out of her monastery, which stood hard by, but was ruin'd and most part tumbled into the Sea. It is pure white marble, about a foot thick, most neatly covered and hollowed on the edges, with a coronite[1] round the head, and at the feet with two spires. At the head there is cut an archt hole, in which they say her head was kept; and there is a hole sideways of it which is like a saucer, and in the bottome of it is in another small one, out of which they say continually issued an holy oyle. All this arch't hole was cover'd with a plate of gold; the pins that fasten'd it yet remain. I assure you the whole thing is absolutely the curiosest piece of work that is to be found in Greece of so modern artifice. On the upper side, between the arch't hole and the bottome, rose an inscription in impure Iambick. It was wrote in a moderne character, which is very difficult to be read, and the latter end of each verse was wrote under the former part in very much smaller letters. I verily believe this whole thing was but a piece of Greekish monkery, and they might have some pretty contrivance to let oyl, or the like liquor, drop upon occasion, to work some miracle upon the credulous.

---

[1] Form of word showing derivation *coronetta*, *Ital.*, a little *corona*.

In the Greeks' Hierology they observe the 23d of May[1] as a great holy day to her memory, and say that she was martyrd in the times of Antoninus, by his Proconsul Sabinus; that she was torn apieces by wild beasts, and afterwards translated to Heraclea. I am sure the story and the inscription savours of no such antiquity. This church is dedicated to St. Peter and St. Paul, and is generally called τῶν μεγάλων ἀποστόλων. The Metropolite has very good accommodations there for himself and his *papas*. Below, in the cloyster, just at the foot of the staires going up to the Metropolite's apartment, lyes buryed Mr. Edward Wych, brother to Sr. Peter,[2] who was Embassadore here. He went with our chief Dragoman (yet living) to Scio to meet Sr. Peter's Lady, then coming out of England to her husband; and, coming back, he touched at Tenedos, where the plague was very rife, and he got it and dyed, and was brought here and buryed, 1628.

Coming out of the Greekes' apartment, we went into St. George's church (whome they call ἅγιος Γεώργιος), who is here reverenced as the greatest Saint imaginable, and they attribute many miracles to his image, which is a head cut flat in wood and trimm'd up with abundance of tinsel stuff; the candles have made it as black as soot. The chief thing he is famed for is the deliverance of poor mariners, and in the church was hang'd up to him infinites of ἀναθήματα, dedicated by poor creatures which had escaped shipwreck: most are little short pieces of halsers or cables, or smal ropes, having one end tipt with silver.

Upon the cliff to the S.E. stand 4 or 5 windmills im-

---

[1] Sta. Glyceria's Day is 10th of May. She suffered martyrdom at Trajanopolis, in Thrace, under Sabinus, A.D. 140, for publicly reproving the President at the sacrifices. She converted her gaoler, Laodicus.

[2] Sir Peter Wych was Ambassador to the Porte in 1632. Covel's date seems wrong.

moveable, and are driven onely by the Embaty,[1] which never failes in the daye time to come of from the sea.

I came from *Selibria* home with the rest. The Plague had been as hot at Stambol all last summer, and after our returne (which was Sept. 27th) it encreased. Upon the death of the foot boy in our house (of whom is above written), my Ld. and Sr. Tho., with 4 servants, withdrew to a house out of town. I took the opportunity at that time to go with some gentlemen of Smyrna (who had been at audience with us) as farre as Brusa, where the G. Sr. baths are; and indeed it is a brave place. I took some delight upon mount *Olympus Mysiæ*,[2] which is very, very high, and over looks the town; it is always cover'd with snowe, as it was then whilst we were on the top of it. I took notice of many fine plants, trees, and other curiosyties there, as likewise about the Town and at the baths; and should certainly have been highly pleased with my voyage, had not a sad accident embitter'd all to me. One of the gentlemen, my dear friend, fell sick of a very high feavor: we fear'd it was the Plague. All the rest of the company left me and my man alone with him; and after 13 dayes he dyed there. I was ill treated by the Turkes; but I got leave to bury him with much adoe; and, writing to my Ld., I had a Chiaus and Dragoman came and chastised those Rogues very handsomely. I spent a month there, and have made remarques of many things; but I must leave the story of that and all the rest to another time to tell you by letter or word of mouth.

I will see Nice,[3] Nicomedia, Cyzicus, Mount Athos, Lemnos, Lesbos, Chios, and what else lyes in my way before I leave the countrey, though I shall make Inscriptions and such knackes but onely my passe time. Here are every year

---

[1] The *Imbat* is a wind which blows every day in summer time.
[2] Bithynia.   [3] *I.e.*, Nicæa.

abundance of Whiflers[1] in those scraps of learning. Last year were here one Mr. Wheeler, a pretty ingenious youth, our countryman, and one Mr. Le Spòn,[2] a Frenchman, who certainely have made the best collection in the world, and intends to print them when he comes home. He hath gathered up and down at least 10,000 that never yet saw light in Greek or any other author. I have a very great intimacy with him, and maintein a strickt correspondency with him, and I shall certainely give him all I have which he wants; and I am sure I have one or two very rare, and not met with all by him. Here is now one Mr. Vernon (lately Secretary to Mr. Montague in France), who is mightily eager after all such things, and is going for Persia. So the main businesse will be caryed on by others, to the satisfaction of themselves, if not of others. For my own part, my heat and leachery after such things was soon over after I arrived in these places. But, when all is done, they goe but on the skirts of Asia all of them; whereas from hence to Aleppo, and all about Ancyra, and on the other side in Caria, etc., are the statelyest things in the world, and in very great numbers. He that thinks them worth his labour and expence and hazard, let him go fetch them; yet I confesse I have an itching after them, for I can assure you there are some things that will give great light to Church story, especially as to the Arians, Basilidians,[3] and other Hereticks. It is very troublesome to transcribe what I have collected; I must be pardoned herein till I see you. In the mean time, I joyn absolutely with you in your opinion of that part of learning, and in

---

[1] *Whifler*=a fickle person, a trifler.
[2] Spon and Wheeler, the authors of an excellent work on the Levant.
[3] Basilidians = the followers of Basilides, the founder of one of the semi-Christian sects commonly called Gnostics, which sprang up in the early part of the second century, A.D.

your censure of the professors of it. I have two or three pretty knackes which I have lighted upon very cheap, and yet I vallue them dear. I have a delicate cat's eye; two or three *Seraphims;* two little cupids holding a lyon, imbossed admirably in a *Cameo;* severall petrifyed mushroomes; tiles; etc.

In truth, I am now weary, and I believe so are you by this time. I cannot read these papers over to correct them. You are my Friend: for your sake I have scribbled them at full gallop; for my sake passe by whatever is amisse, or twice over, or rudely and carelessly done. I did all to testify what you shall ever find—Fidum pectus amicitiae. You must communicate them to Sam. Th.; and for others I leave it to your discretion who you shall admitte to see my levityes. It would be some passetime to T. Fairmeddow over a pot of ale; but use your discretion. I shall tell him I have wrote you at large. Now, Dear friend, the Mighty God of heaven and Earth watch over us for our good; and, if it be his blessed will, bring us together once more. I am,

Thy faithfull and affectionate friend,
J. C.

The two volumes of Dr. Covel's consecutive diary terminate with his visit to Adrianople. There are, however, several smaller diaries of different journeys, which would be too long to insert here. One is thus headed:

Feb. 16, 167$\frac{8}{9}$.—OUR VOYAGE TO NICOMEDIA, NICÆA, ETC.

Dr. Covel sailed up the Gulf of Ismidt, and, on arriving at the town of Ismidt (Nicomedia), he was "nobly lodged at the monastery by Greeks". He speaks in quaint terms of the numerous ἁγιάσματα, or sacred springs, at Ismidt, and describes more particularly one dedicated to St. Anne, and its supposed healing qualities.

"I saw", he writes, "a man who, last 2nd of February, went to St. Anne's ἁγίασμα for cure, being full of ulcers, and could receive no benefit otherwayes but washing all over. His ulcers were dryed up in less than a fortnight's time, which made me reflect upon the story of Naaman."

"*Feb.* 22. Got to Isnick (Nicæa), which is not now within the walls, a third part inhabited, or filled with houses, most being gardens or yards enclosed with mud walls. I do not remember that I saw one tolerably good house in the town; and most were intolerably bad, little, pittyfull, low, dirty hovels, instead of houses."

As usual, Dr. Covel's narrative is full of archæology, and as he only stopped one day at Nicæa, it is marvellous how much he saw and put down.

" If I had had any instrument in the world to have taken a plain angle withall, I should have plotted down everything exactly. Now I have done it by guesse and loose calculation, and let that suffice."

On his return journey he visited the islands of Prinkipo and Chalcis. He was on this latter on Feb. 25, and visited the celebrated monastery there.

"This monastery about 5 or 6 yeares since, was unfortunately burnt down, and Panagiotes[1] (the late Vizier's Dragoman), who lyes buryed here, rebuilt it at his own cost."

"Our first ambassador, Sir Edw. Barton, lyes buried without the outward gate, to the right hand. His armes

---

[1] Panagiotes was a Cypriote Greek, a linguist, astronomer, and mathematician, who, in his position as dragoman to the Grand Vizier Kiuprili, did more for the maintenance of Greek freedom than anyone else, and was the founder of the Phanariote league.

are rudely done, but I take them to be three stagges heads above. It was cut by a Turk, and thence came all the mistakes in the writing, and at the bottome are three Cypress trees, which are commonly put on the Turks' tombs."[1]

On April 2nd, 1677, Dr. Covel left Constantinople for good, and his return journey to England forms another MS. volume. He thus begins it:

"This day, in the year 1638, I was born at two o'clock in the morning, being Monday, and it pleased me to see so many things meet this day, whereby I might reckon it my second birth. Just at two o'clock Antonio called us to go to the Alloy. This day I left Stamboul, which, for many reasons, I may well liken to the prison of my mother's belly."

Dr. Covel and Sir John Finch, the ambassador, started together on the *Alloy*, and the new Grand Vizier, Kara Mustapha,[2] came to see them off, and brought them "large quantities of presents, and grand accompaniment."

The homeward diary is very much scamped and badly written, but there are interesting passages in it. He gives us a good description of Cyzicus and the temple of Nemesis therein, and his account of Mt. Athos is also valuable, though prolix. The ship *Alloy* then came to the island of Lemnos, "where we lay weather fast." Dr. Covel here gives us an interesting account of what he saw in connection with the *terra Sigillata* of Lemnos, the sacred earth with supposed curative properties, a superstition

---

[1] For particulars of Sir Edward Barton and his death, see Introduction.

[2] Kara-Mustapha, who succeeded Ahmed Kiuprili as Grand Vizier, was son-in-law of Sultan Mahomed IV. His career was most disastrous. He was defeated before Vienna, and eventually put to death, having done more towards the downfall of the Turkish Empire than anyone in its history.

which has survived since the days of Galen, and still exists, so I will give Dr. Covel's description in full.

"On the side hills, on the contrary side of the valley, directly over against the middle point betwixt this hill and Παναγιά κοτζινάτζ, is the place where they dig the *terra sigillata*'. At the foot of a hard rock of grey hard freestone enclining to marble is a little clear spring of most excellent water, which, falling down a little lower, looseth its water in a kind of milky bogge; on the East side of this spring, within a foot or my hand's breadth of it, they every year take out the earth on the 6th of August, about three houres after the sun. Several papas, as well as others, would fain have persuaded me that, at the time of our Saviour's transfiguration, this place was sanctifyed to have his virtuous earth, and that it is never to be found soft and unctuous, but always perfect rock, unlesse only that day, which they keep holy in remembrance of the Metamorphosis, and at that time when the priest hath said his liturgy; but I believe they take it onely that day, and set the greater price upon it by its Scarcenesse. Either it was the Venetian, or perhaps Turkish policy[1] for the Grand Signor to engrosse it all to himselfe, unless some little, which the Greckes steal; and they prefer no poor Greek to take any for his own occasions, for they count it an infallible cure of all agues taken in the beginning of the fit with water, and drank so two or three times. Their women drink it to hasten childbirth, and to stop the fluxes that are extraordinary; and they count it an excellent counter-poyson, and have got a story that no vessel made of it will hold poison, but immediately splinter in a thousand pieces. I have seen several finganes (Turkish cups)

---

[1] Lemnos was only regained from the Venetians in 1657, twenty years before Covel's visit.

made of it in Stamboul; we had a good store of it presented to us by Agathone and others, all incomparably good. We had some such as it is naturally dig'd out and not wash'd. (There is no such chappel nigh as Bel talked of, called Sobiranon, to be found, unless he took Παναγιά κοτζινάτζ for it.) Thus they take it out: before day they begin and digge a well about $1\frac{1}{2}$ yards wide, and a little above a man's height deep; and then the earth is taken out soft and loomy, some of it like butter, which the Greeks say, and the Turks believe, is turned out of rocky stone into soft clay by virtues of their mass. When they have taken out some 20 or 30 kintals for the Greeks' use, they fill it up again, and so leave it stop't without any guard in the world. . . . .

"We came down to a town called Hagiapate, where there is a great large fountain, where they wash and prepare the ἅγιον χώμα (sacred earth) for the Turkish seal. They first dissolve it in water, well working it with their hands; then let the water pass through a sive, and what remains they throw away. They let the water stand till settled, then take of the clear, and, when dry enough, they mould in their hands; and most of this we have is shaped from thence. It is all here white, yet I had some given me flesh-coloured. I enquired diligently about it, and they all told me it came out of the same pit; but I expect some of these fellows have found some other place which they conceal. We had some little quantity given us of several people, but very privately, for fear of the *Avaniás*. Agathone, being the Pasha's favourite, feared nothing, but gave us at least 20 okes before 20 people. They tell a story that the earth is hollow from the holy well, when dig'd, to the fountain, where they wash it; and that a duck once dived in the water there and was taken up here; but it seemed an impossible thing to me, there being not water enough in the first place to cover a duck, and the water in the bogge so very shallow, and the earth not sinuous."

Dr. Covel's remarks on the sacred earth of Lemnos are particularly valuable, as this is one of the clearest instances of a pagan superstition being carried on through the influence of Christianity down to our own times. Pliny mentions it (*Hist. Nat.*, 29, 5); also Dioscorides (*De Mater. Med.*, 5, 113); and Galen made an expedition to Lemnos on purpose to see it, and gives us an account of it (*De Simpl. Med.*, 9, 2, vol. xii). He mentions the disorders for which it was considered beneficial ; he also gives us the ceremonies and mode of operation ; on certain occasions a priestess of Artemis came, and, after certain rites, carried off a cartload to the city ; she mixed it with water, kneaded it, and strained off both the moisture and gritty particles, and, when it was like wax, she impressed it with the seal of Artemis. During the Middle Ages, the reputed virtues of this earth remained unimpaired as a remedy for the plague. Belon saw it in the sixteenth century (*Observations de plusieurs singulaires*, p. 51). Here we have Dr. Covel's account of it in the seventeenth century. Conze was able to buy specimens of it in 1858 ; but Dr. Tozer, who visited Lemnos three years ago, writes of it as an expiring superstition. In that year only twelve persons were present at the ceremony ; and the Turkish governor, seeing so small a prospect of revenue, has ceased to be present in person. Dr. Tozer could not even obtain a specimen in a chemist's shop ; but the superstitious in remote parts of the island still use it.

Proceeding from Lemnos, the *Alloy* went to Chios, where Dr. Covel gives us an account of the silk-trade carried on there, and the growth of the mastic, and the *avanias* thereon imposed by the Turkish Government. " The poor sort of Greek women dayly scold and quarrell, and pull one another's head gear of,[1] then in a fury run to Turkish justice; and, in conclusion, both pay soundly, though the richest purse always speeds best."

When passing between Chios and the island of Psara, Dr. Covel tells two curious nautical yarns. "*The Plymouth*, which caryed my Lord Winchilsea to Stambol, passing between these two islands, strook twice or thrice upon a blind rock, and a great peice broke of, and stuck in the keel of the ship, and continued in quite till she returned to England, and was found when she came to be carin'd. The peice is now kept in the king's closet. Captain Blake told me that a ship coming from the E. Indyes, the Doctor was very kind to a sick mariner, who thereupon made the Dr. his heir; he, tempted thereby, gave him something to sleep, and, taking opportunity, thrust in a small needle or bodkin under his ear, and kil'd him. He was thrown over board, and three days after, sayling with a very stiff gale, they spyed his body floting under the weather bow; as fast as the ship could make way, it kept pace. With wonder they took it up, and, after many consultations, the Captain came himself first and touch't it; when the Dr. came, the blood spirt out of the dead man's nose and the wound under his ear, upon him: he confest all, and was brought home and hang'd."

After rounding Cape Matapan, the *Alloy* sailed up the Adriatic to Venice, where Dr. Covel stayed some time and crossed Italy and France on his way to England.

"On Monday morning, Jan. 20th, 1679, we got over to Dover in four houres just; that night to Canterbury; next night to London."

At the end of his *Diary* there is this curious note on a London fog:—"Feb. 12, 1679, was Black Sunday; so

---

[1] The curious headgear of the women of Chios is still worn in the remoter villages.

dark about 9 or 10 o'clock for about $\frac{1}{2}$ an hour, as candles were lighted in most churches in London. It is thought it came partly from a misty thick air, partly from a very black, thick cloud, which, being low, hindered in the third place the smoke to rise high, which increased the thickness of the air. I am informed the like hath been often before. Mr. Standish was lighted home with a torch at 3 in the afternoon."

INDEX.

Abydos, castle at the mouth of the Hellespont, 50, 82, 143, 154
Abyla, rock on the African coast opposite Gibraltar, 106
Acrobats perform during the solemnities, 216
Actors perform during the solemnities, 215
Admiral (see Robinson, Captain)
Admiral of Turkish fleet demands a present of the Captain of the *Hector*, 47, 48; receives two chests, 49
Adrianople, gate, 81, 173; summer resort near, 188; country near, thinly populated, 188; reception of the English embassy at, 189; divination with Bible and key at, 191; many Roman Catholics in, 210; storm at, 212; fireworks at, during solemnities, 213; dancers at, during solemnities, 213; plays acted at, during the solemnities, 216; acrobatic performances at, during the solemnities, 216; jugglers at, during the solemnities, 220; plague in, 241; great mortality in, 242; indifference of the people to the plague in, 244; bridges at, 249; geography of neighbourhood of, 251; ceremony at, in honour of the audience, 258; divan at, 258
African Company, the, rise of, in the sixteenth century, ii
Aga of the Janizaries, a severe man, 232
Agathone, favourite of the Pasha, gives sacred earth to Covel, 284

Agazé Sultana, her dowry, 232; her attendants, 234; her procession, 235; views sports at the Mosaïf's house, 237
Ak-bonar, town near Adrianople, 248; Mahomed IV flies to, to avoid the plague, 248; fruitful country near, 249
Alama (Almeria), 95
Aldridge, William, English consul at Chios, 46; his anxiety respecting the organ, 58; and Jonas, in attendance during the presentation of the organ, 66
Aleppo, principal English mart, ix; Michael Locke, consul at, ix; he founds the factory at, ix; goods for, delayed by the Turkish army, 31; French consul at, dines on board the *Hector*, 31; letters carried to, from Scandaroon, by pigeons, 32
Algiers, description of, 13-15; Dallam arrives at, 13; early season in, 13; Moors, Jews, and Turks in, 14; behaviour of renegade Christians in, 15; King of, desires to see the organ, 15; King of, takes captain of the *Hector* prisoner, 15; releases him and makes him a present, 15
Allen, Sir Thomas, commander of the *Greenwich*, 101; in Cadiz harbour, 105; notice of, 105 *n*.
Amalfians, the, obtain capitulations, iii
Ambassador, the (see Lello, Henry)

U

INDEX.

Ambassadors to the Porte, list of, xlii (see *Addenda et Corrigenda*)

Amurath III, Sultan, alliance with, desired by Queen Elizabeth, vii; concludes charter-treaty, viii; promises assistance against the Spanish Armada, but breaks his word, ix; his present from Queen Elizabeth, x; his death, 194

Anne, St., sacred springs, near Nicomedia, 281

Antiparos, cave of, mass celebrated in, xxxi

Arab juggler imposes on the superstition of the people, 220

Arcadia, herds of swine in plains of, 87; sudden rain in, 88

Archipelago, Covel enters the, 138

Arda, course of the river, 250, 252; dirty state of, below Adrianople, 253

Argentiere (see **Kimolos**)

Argosies, origin of the name, vi

Argostoli, good harbour at, 18, 91

Arnold, Dr., of the Sorbonne, disputes with Covel on the doctrines of the Greek church, xxxi

Assumption, Feast of the, observed by the Greeks, 144

Assurance, the, a convoy vessel, 102

Audience, the, a mere hurried formality, 266; -chamber, magnificence of the, 267

Avanias, or unauthorised demands by the Turks, increase in the severity of, xxxv

Ayash, a town of Asia Minor, 33

Backstrevacui, on the Tondja, bricks made at, 249

Baines, Sir Thomas, his friendship with Sir John Finch, xxxii; physician to the Legation, xxxii; his death, xxxiii; travels in a double horse litter or takt-i-rovan, 171; lodges in the college at Ponte piccolo, 175; at Adrianople with Finch, 189; attends solemnity entertainment with Count Bocareschi, 227; moves about to avoid the plague, 242; visits Vani-Effendi, 269; discusses religious faith with him, 269; is urged by him to become a Mussulman, 271; sends messages to him by Boccareschi, 272

Bairam, a season of rejoicing among the Turks, 152

Baltimore, Lord, his daughter in a convent at Malaga, 111

Banquet in honour of the audience description of, 261-262; no knives and forks at, 261; news discussed at, 263; disorder in outer room during, 264

Barton, Sir Edward, first resident ambassador at Constantinople, x, xlii; takes out present to Sultan Amurath III, x; accompanies Sultan Mahomet III to Hungary, xi; biographical notice of, xi; his monument at Chalki, xii, 281

Bassa of Morea, son of Mahomed the Bosnian, story of, 184-185

Bat, believed to possess marvellous powers, 256

Bates, the case of, xxi

Baylye, Mr., comes from Constantinople to meet the organ, 50; is in attendance at the presentation of the organ, 66

Bendish, Sir T., is sent to displace Sir S. Crowe, xxiii

Biram (see **Bairam**)

Blacksmiths' Company, Dallam a liveryman of the, xvi; neglects his duty as a steward of, xvii

Blake, Captain, his story of the doctor and the sick mariner, 286

Bobbas-cui (see **Eski-Baba**)

Bocareschi, Count, his civility to Covel, 225; his character, 226; dies of the plague, 226; his rudeness to Marin Caboga, 227; carries messages between Sir Thomas Baines and Vani-Effendi, 272

Bodenham, Captain, goes to Chios, v
Bogathos (see Bojados)
Bojados, town near Silivri, 180
Bosnacui, *i.e.*, village of the Bosnians, a seat of the Marquis de Nointel, 250
Brèves, François Savary de, his controversy with Vizier Ibrahim, 80; bribes Ibrahim, 81
Bridegroom, present of, 227 (see Mosaif)
Bromwell, Captain, of the *Thomas and Frances*, 101
Brusa, description of the baths at, 278; deaths from plague at, 278
Bubuli, D. Hilarione, account of, 149; his comparison of the Greek and Roman churches, 150
Buckett, Rowland, organ painter to Dallam, 66
Burgas (see Lule-Bourgas)

Cable, Thomas, his death on board the *Hector*, 34
Cabóga, Marin, Ragusean ambassador at Adrianople, 190; visits Sir John Finch, 190; his belief in witchcraft, 190; his experience during the earthquake at Ragusa, 192; accompanies Covel during the solemnities, 226
Cadeleskier, or judge-advocate, his tent, 167
Calpe, rock on which Gibraltar stands, 106
Cambridge, King's College, organ at, constructed by Dallam, xvii
Candia, superstition of brazen man on, 26
Capitulations, or treaties for trading, ii; early origin of, ii; granted to Warings or Varangians of Scandinavia, ii; granted to Venetians, Amalfians, Genoese, and Pisans, iii; granted to French, iv; the first of the modern, iv; obtained by the Earl of Winchilsea, xxiv; Sir Paul Ricaut's book on, xxiv; obtained by Sir John Finch, xxxii, 272
Caragatch, the plague reaches, 242; church at, 243; junction of rivers Arda and Maritza at, 243; large carp at, 243; cheflicks, or country houses at, 244; wine trade in, 244; the parson of, a great vintner, 245; shows kindness to Covel, 245; loses his kinswoman in the plague, 245; great funeral at, 246; heat and unwholesomeness of, 246
Carles quoted as an authority by Covel, 127
Carlos, Signor, an Irishman at Malaga, 107
Carmesale, the vessel in which Dallam left Constantinople, 82
Carpathos, fowls that burrow like rabbits at, 27
Carpenter, Mr., secretary to Sir John Finch, 261; is present at the audience banquet, 261; enters the audience chamber with Finch, 265
Carthage, salt-making at, 121; Covel visits, 121; remains of ancient city at, 122; beauty of remains, 123; Queen Dido's tomb at, 123; treachery of dervishes at, 124
Castle Tornese, difficulty of approach to, 88; market at, 88
Castles, the (see Abydos and Sestos)
Cephalonia, good wine made at, 91
Cerigo, birthplace of Helen of Troy, 26
Cervi, old Greek peasant at, 131; description of, 132; treachery of mountaineers on, 133; encounter with ruffians on, 134-5; four seamen taken prisoners on, 135
Ceuta, pleasant situation of, 12
Chabbey, Eusine, entertains Covel, 139

U 2

INDEX.

Chalcedon, lighthouse at, 168
Chalcis (see Chalki), monastery at, 281; Panagiotes, dragoman, buried at, 281; Sir Edward Barton, ambassador, his tomb at, xi, 281
Chancie, Mr., surgeon on board the *Hector*, 13; goes on shore at Algiers, 13; lands at Scandaroon, 28
Charles II, letter to, from the Kaimacham, 150, from Mahomed IV, 151
Chiorloo (see Tchorlou)
Chios, an English consul established at, in 1513, v; Dallam lands at, 43; description of, 44; curiosity of people of, 45; food not to be bought on Sunday in, 45; dress of women of, 46; William Aldridge, English consul at, 46
Chora, great fertility of, 53
Chorlaye (Chorley), village in Lancashire, 84
Church, plottings in the Greek, 150
Circumcision performed on Prince Mustapha, 207; on 2,000 youths, 209
Company's Chancellor, the (see Cook, Mr.)
Conisbye, Humfrey, is in attendance during the presentation of the organ, 66; fords a river on horseback, 85; is about to cut off a Jew's head, 86; is restrained by Sir Paul Pindar, 86; regrets that he did not see the fire-ball, 87; drives away watermen at Zante, 90
Constantinople, Sir Edward Barton, first resident ambassador at, x; Dallam arrives at, 57; the *Hector's* salute on reaching, 59; Feast of Bairam at, 64; Covel arrives at, 144; great mist at, 162; Jacob's tomb near, 173; the plague at, 246
Cook, Mr., secretary, receives no present and is offended, 196; is present at the audience banquet, 261; enters the audience chamber with Finch, 265
Corojecui, village near Adrianople, 249; house of Mahomet IV at, 249
Corposans, or phantom lights, 126
Courtesy of Turks to Franks during the solemnities, 205, 212
Covel, Dr. John, profuse writings of, xxvi; his knowledge of Turkish music, xxvii; biographical account of, xxvii-xxxiii; his portrait at Cambridge, xxviii; poem by, xxviii; appointed chaplain to Sir Daniel Harvey, xxix; appointed chaplain to the Princess of Orange at the Hague, xxix; sent home in disgrace, xxx; his book, *The Interpreter of Words and Terms*, xxx; disputes with Dr. Arnold, xxxi; his book on the Greek Church, xxxi; his death, xxxii; starts for Constantinople, 101; takes his passage on the *London Merchant*, 102; passes the Land's End, 102; is attacked by sea-sickness, 102; dines on board the *Turkey Merchant*, 104; lands at Malaga, 107; visits the cathedral, 107; converses with the priests at Malaga, 108; is entertained by Rev. Father of San Domingo in Malaga, 109; meets English-speaking gentleman in Malaga, 110; is asked for presents, 111; spends a night at Malaga, 115; leaves Malaga, 117; dines on board the *Martin*, 117; arrives at Tunis, 119; visits Carthage, 121; leaves Tunis, 125; sees a corposan, 128; lands at Cervi, 131; meets old Greek peasant at, 131; enters the Archipelago, 138; arrives at Smyrna, 139; entertained by Eusine Chabbey, a Turk, 139; starts for Ephesus, 141; leaves Smyrna, 142; is attacked with ague, 142; enters

the Hellespont, 143; arrives at
Constantinople, 144; visits Sir
Daniel Harvey, 144; his illness,
148; is entertained by dervishes,
153; visits castle at the mouth of
the Hellespont, 154; accompanies
Sir Daniel Harvey's body to
Smyrna, 154; arrives at Mitiline,
154; puts Sir Daniel Harvey's
body on board the *Centurion* at
Smyrna, 155; dines on board the
Centurion, 155; runs ashore at
Tenedos, 156; is invited to dine
with the Patriarch of Constantinople, 158; attends sermon at St.
Francesco's, 159; sees Demetrius
Simon wash the feet of the brothers,
159; visits vaults under St. Sophia,
170; leaves Pera, 172; doubts
accuracy of maps of Ortelius, Ptolemy, Sansoin, etc., 173, 176;
arrives at Ponte piccolo, 174; at
Ponte grande, 177; at Tchorlou,
180; at Karitchtran, 183; at Lule
Bourgas, 184; at Eski-Baba, 186;
at Hafsa, 187; at Adrianople, 189;
accompanies Finch in his audience
with Achmet Kiuprili, 194; receives
a vest from Achmet Kiuprili, 196;
present at solemnities, 205, 212;
discovers the tricks of an Arab
juggler, 221; his adventure during
the fireworks, 226; accompanies
Marin Caboga to the solemnities,
226; is well treated during the
solemnities, 240; his dog desired
by the Vizier's aga, 241; goes to
Caragatch to avoid the plague,
242; visits Corojecui, 249; visits
Ortacui, 252; dines with the Marquis de Nointel, 255; caught in
severe storm near Ortacui, 256;
sits at the Dafterdar's table at the
audience banquet, 261; is disappointed of entering the audience
chamber, 265; leaves Adrianople,
274; visits Missinli, 275; travels
with tents on account of the plague,
274; goes to Erekli by sea-shore,
275; visits the baths at Brusa,
278; his curiosities, 280; visits
Nicomedia, 280; visits Nicæa, 281;
leaves Constantinople, 282; his
birthday, 282; embarks on the
Alloy for England, 282; visits
Chios, 285; visits Venice, 286;
crosses Italy and France to England, 286; reaches London, 286

Crowe, Sir S., ambassador at Constantinople, xxiii, xlii; his goods
confiscated by Parliament, xxiii;
imprisons English factors, xxiii;
superseded by Sir J. Bendish and
impeached by the Levant Company, xxiii

Cyprus, description of, 28

Cythera (see Cerigo)

Dafterdar, the, or High Treasurer,
his tents, 168; proxy for the bridegroom, 230; present at the audience
banquet, 261

Dallam, George, son of Thomas, his
addition to the organ in Hereford
Cathedral, xix

Dallam, Ralph, son of Thomas,
organs constructed by, xviii, xix

Dallam, Robert, son of Thomas,
organs constructed by, xviii; monument to, at Oxford, xviii

Dallam, Thomas, makes an organ to be
sent to Sultan Mahomed III, xv;
biographical notice of, xvi; organs
constructed by, xvii, xviii; his baggage, 1; leaves London, 4; goes
on board the *Hector* at Gravesend, 4; arrives at Dover, at Deal,
and at Sandwich, 5; enters Dartmouth harbour, 6; waits at Plymouth for wind, 7; enters the
Mediterranean Sea, 11; passes
Tarifa, 11; passes Marbella, Malaga, and Salobreña, 12; arrives at
Algiers, 13; questioned by king
at Algiers, 15; passes Dellys,
Bougie, and Tunis, 16; passes
Sicily and Malta, 17; arrives at

Zante, 18; passes through quarantine before entering, 19; desires to ascend mountain at Zante, 20; visits monastery on mount Scopo, 21; is well treated at monastery, 22, 23; pays a second visit to monastery, 25; departs from Zante, 26; passes by the Strophades, 26; passes by Candia, 26; sees the coast of Caramania, 27; lands at Scandaroon, 28; threatened by mountaineers at Scandaroon, 29; startled by large snake at Scandaroon, 30; visits Jonah's Pillar, 32; passes by Castellorosso, 33; plays on the virginals to governor of Rhodes, 35; lands at Rhodes and visits the town, 35; leaves Rhodes, 39; enters Ægean Sea, 40; goes on shore at Chios, 43; visits the Consul of Chios, 44; entertained by Consul of Chios, 45; lands at Troy, 47; lands on Cape Janissary, 49; takes piece of white marble pillar from Troy, 49; enters the Hellespont, 50; leaves the *Hector* and goes on board the ambassador's boat, 50; arrives at Gallipoli, 51; is entertained by the consul, 51; buys half a sheep at Gallipoli, 51; arrives at Ganos, 53; goes ashore at Erekli, 57; is well entertained, 57; lands at Selibria, 57; arrives at Constantinople, 57; takes organ to ambassador's house, 58; sets to work to put it together, 58; moves it to the seraglio, 61; begged to remain at Constantinople, 64; must expect nothing from Sultan Mahomed, 65; is called into the presence of Sultan Mahomed, 68; plays to Sultan Mahomed, 71; receives bag of sequins, 71; relates his adventures to Lello, 72; is begged to remain at the seraglio, 73; pretends he has wife and children in England, 73; is offered two wives by Sultan Mahomed, 73; is shown the riches of the seraglio, 74; watches Sultan Mahomed's concubines at play, 74; is to be left in Constantinople to remove the organ, 76; runs for his life, 79; visits Adrianople, 81; is attacked with fever, 81; joins company bound for England, 81; leaves Constantinople, 82; passes by Troy, 82; is in danger of shipwreck at Lemnos, 82; reaches Volo, 83; lodges miserably at Lamia, 83; commences ascent of mountains of Parnassus, 83; reaches Lepanto, 85; lodges comfortably in the house of a Jew, 86; reaches Patras, 86; arrives at Castle Tornese, 88; crosses to Zante, 88; takes leave of dragoman Finche, 89; in quarantine at Zante, 89; meets the *Hector* at Zante, 90; leaves Zante, 90; is becalmed between Malta and Sicily, 93; reaches Pantelaria, 93; passes Zembra and Porto Farina, 93; hears the cry of a mermaid in the Gulf of Lyons, 94; reaches Formentera, 94; is becalmed near Alicante, 94; passes Cape Palos and Cape de Gata, 94·5; is becalmed near Castel de Ferro, 95; lands in England, 98; travels to London, 98

Dam, Jaques von, Dutch consul at Smyrna, 140; his house at Sedjagui, 140

Dancers during the solemnities, 213; their dress, 213; their musical instruments, 214

Dartmouth, Dallam arrives at, 6

Day, Mr., Captain Wild's lieutenant, pursues rogues on Cervi, 136

Deal, Dallam arrives at, 5

Despotodagh, visible from Hafsa, 187; mountain due west of Adrianople, 253

INDEX. 295

Digby, Sir Kenelm, quarrels with the Venetian admiral, xxxvii
Dionysius, Archbishop of Larissa, is consecrated Patriarch, 145; his quarrels with Parthenius, 145; is deposed, but returns to office, 145; sermon preached at his consecration, 148; flies to the French ambassador, 151
Dover, Dallam arrives at, 5; Dallam lands at, on his return, 98
Dowry, the bride's, carried in the procession, 232
Dumb men in attendance on Mahomed III, 69
Dunkirkers, encounter with, 8; admiral of, comes on board the *Hector*, 9; declares himself to be a merchant, 10; is allowed to go by master of the *Hector*, 10
Durham, the Dallams' organ at, xviii
Dwarfs in attendance on Mahomed III, 70

Earlesman, Mr., English consul at Tunis, 124; disagreement with, 124
East India Company, the, rise of, in the sixteenth century, ii; its controversies with the Levant Company, xxii
Easter Eve, great storm on, off the African coast, 16
Edward Bonaventure, the, sails in company with the *Hector*, 90
Elizabeth, Queen, desires alliance with Sultan Amurath III, vii; concludes charter-treaty, viii; begs assistance from Sultan Amurath III against the Spanish Armada, ix; her present to Sultana Safiye, x; sends an organ to Sultan Mahomed III, xv
Ellis, Edward, his mission to Constantinople, vii
Elmo, St., fire of (see Corposans)

Ephesus, description of the road to, from Smyrna, 141
Erekli, the windmills at, 57; Dallam well entertained at, 57; the Bishop of, at the consecration of Dionysius, 147; monument to the dead near, 275; description of, 276; Sta. Gluceria's tomb at, 276; Wych, Edward, buried at, 277 St. George's Church at, 277; windmills near, 277
Ereklidia (see Relezea)
Eski-Baba, tomb in St. Nicholas' Church at, 186; bridge at, 186; point of divinity discussed at, 186; aqueduct being built at, 187; monument to the dead near, 187
Etna, Mount, description of, 17
Euripides, his opinion quoted by Covel, 133
Eyre, Sir John, ambassador at Constantinople, xlii

Faightes, or fightes, use of, 8, 97
Favourite, the (see Moutessarif)
Feast of the Assumption o' served by the Greeks, 144
Felton, John, dies on board the *Hector*, 47
Fez, the King of, visits Dallam at work, 58
Finch, Sir John, ambassador at Constantinople, xxxii, xlii; obtains capitulation during the plague at Adrianople, xxxii; biographical account of, xxxii; friendship with Thomas Baines, xxxii; death, xxxiii; travels in double horse litter, or takt-i-rovan, 171; beacons placed by tent of, 171; his coach, 172; lodges at the college in Ponte piccolo, 175; his reception at Adrianople, 189; his miserable lodgings at, 190; his audience with Achmet Kiuprili, 195; is presented with a vest by Achmet Kiuprili, 196; is visited by Count Kindsberg,

197; attends none of the solemnity sights, 227; presents a mastiff to Mahomed IV, 238; goes to Caragatch to avoid the plague, 242; returns to Adrianople, 242; his audience with Mahomed IV, 257; shares table with Kiuprili at the audience banquet, 260; enters the audience chamber, 264; promises Covel that he shall enter the audience chamber, 265; does not exchange a word with Mahomed IV at audience, 266; his interview with Kiuprili respecting the capitulations, 273; leaves Adrianople, 274; lives outside Constantinople on account of the plague, 278; embarks on the *Alloy* for England, 282

Finche, a dragoman, his fidelity, 84; takes leave of the English company, 89

Fire-ball seen in the Morea, 87

Fireworks during the solemnities, 222-224

Foot-ball, antiquity of the game of, 87

Foret, Sieur, obtains a capitulation for the French, iv

Formentera inhabited by banished men, 94; murdered man found at, 94

Francis I of France concludes a capitulation with Sultan Solyman I, iv

Franks well treated by Turks during the solemnities, 205, 212

French, the, obtain a capitulation, iv

French Ambassador, the (see Brèves and Nointel)

Friends taken for enemies, 130

Galata, Dervish Mustapha at, 168; music of the dervishes at, 169; Tekies, or monasteries at, 169; Arzeh Mahmet Effendi buried at, 169; Ismèl Effendi buried at, 169;
the vaults under Sta. Sophia at, visited by Covel, 170

Gallipoli, the consul at, a friar, 50; comes on board the *Hector*, 50; Dallam lands at, 51; Covel arrives at, 143

Ganos, wretched accommodation at, 53; much vermin at, 54; a garter taken for a serpent at, 55; disturbed night at, 56

Garret, Stephen and William, original members of the Levant Company, viii

Genoese, the, obtain capitulations, iii

Ghosts, belief of the Greeks in, 257

Gibraltar, description of, 11, 106; heat on entering the Straits of, 12; many whales near, 96

Giole-babba, lake at Corojecui, 249

Glover, Sir Thomas, ambassador at Constantinople, xx, xlii; meets the organ in the Hellespont, 50; makes restitution to Greeks, 52; is in attendance during the presentation of the organ, 66

Grand Seignor (see Mahomed)

Grand Vizier (see Kiuprili)

Great Susan, the, ship sent to the Levant, viii

Greek and Roman churches, the, compared, 150

Greenwich, the, convoy vessel, 101; formerly commanded by Sir Thos. Allen, 101

Grerách basha, chief surgeon to Mahomed IV, 206; circumcises Prince Mustapha, 207; his character, 208

Gyllius, P., his accuracy doubted by Covel, 173

Hafsa, called Capsia by Ortelius, 187; description of, 187; Mount Despotodagh visible from, 187

Hale, Edmund, a coachman, accompanies Dallam to monastery at

Zante, 20; foolish behaviour of, in chapel, 23; would not eat or drink at monastery, 24

Harebone, William, his mission to Constantinople, vii; first ambassador from England to the Ottoman Porte, viii, xlii; assisted by Sokolli Vizier and Seadedin, historian, viii

Harvey, Sir Daniel, ambassador at Constantinople, xlii, 144; his death, 154; his body taken to Smyrna, 154; his body put on board the *Centurion*, 155

Harvie, John, lands at Scandaroon, 28; visits Jonah's Pillar, 33; accompanies Dallam to the seraglio for the presentation of the organ, 66; lands in England with Dallam, 98

Hawking in Asia, 240

Hayward, captain of the *Plymouth*, xxiv

Hector, the, the master of, warned of Dunkirkers, 7; allows them to depart, 10; gives chase to a ship, 17; master of, receives presents, 17; lets ship go, 18; boards a Marseilles vessel, 18; master of, refuses to land passenger at Candia, 27; carries him to Cyprus, 27; the French consul at Aleppo dines on board, 31; anchors off Rhodes, 34; Turks of Rhodes come on board, 34; captain of, makes a present of cloth to the deputy governor of Rhodes, 35; captain of, and merchants land at Rhodes to demand Mr. Mayo, 38; runs aground on the coast of Samos, 42; chased by galleys off Samos, 42; disobliging ways of captain of, 44; accosted by Turkish frigates, 47; meets Turkish fleet, 48; captain of, gives tobacco to captain of Turkish galley, 49; suspicion of plague on board, 51; arrives at the Seven Towers near Constantinople, 57;

salutes Sultan Mahomed, 59; carpenter of, killed by sound of the guns, 59; sailor killed by explosion in gun, 60; inspected by Sultan Mahomed, 60; inspected by Sultana Safiya, 60; takes up Dallam at Zante, 90; seizes a Maltese wheat ship, 92; and the rest of the company fight two men of war, 97

Hellespont, the two castles at the mouth of the, 154

Heraclea (see **Erekli**)

Heraclissa (see **Relezea**)

Hercules, Pillars of (see **Abyla** and **Calpe**)

Hill, Captain John, of the *London Merchant*, 101; his competency, and kindness to Covel, 102; his friendship with a nun at Malaga, 112; his quarrel with a Roman Catholic, 113; is present at the embarkation of Sir Daniel Harvey's body, 155

Holy Cross, the, makes a voyage to Crete and Chios, v

Hungary, Mahomed III's wars in, xi

Huntingdon, Mr., converses with priests at Malaga, 108

Hyet, Mr., the oldest merchant in Adrianople, is present at the audience banquet, 261; enters the audience chamber with Sir John Finch, 265

Ibrahim, basha, General of the Turkish army, constructor of the aqueduct at Eski-Baba, 186

Ibrahim, vizier, his controversy with Brèves, 80; account of, 80 *n.*

Ilderim, a suburb of Adrianople, 248

Iman, or learned man, speaks the prayers in the Mosque, 211

Ishék-cui, village, origin of the name of, 251

Iviza, a strong castle at, 94; present of goats and fruit from, 94

Jacob's tomb near Constantinople, 173

Jamovary, town near Smyrna, description of, 141

Janizaries, the, wear no weapons at festivals, 199; feed on bread and pilan, 250

Jebbatore (see Gibraltar)

Jemoglans try to persuade Dallam to remain at Constantinople, 64, 73, 77, 80; friendly behaviour of, 78; show Dallam kiosk for the organ, 78

Jenkinson, Anthony, goes to Aleppo, v

Job's Tomb, mausoleum near Constantinople, 173

John the Quaker, ill-treatment of, at Constantinople, xxv

John and Francis, the, carries Turks and Jews to Alexandria, 93

Jonah's Pillar visited by Dallam, 33; samphire growing on, 33

Judas, meetings to shoot at the figure of, 158

Jüpe, origin of name, 173; Mahomed the Bosnian buried at, 187

Kaimacham, the, his letter to Charles II, 150

Kalenderis, a sect of dervishes, 153

Karakongilas, or Kalkagari, evil spirits believed in by the Greeks, 257

Kara-Mustapha, successor to Kiuprili, 282

Karitchtran, description of, 183

Kerington, Captain, of the *Levant Merchant*, 101

Khanoum-cui, town near Caragatch, 247

Khavsa (see Hafsa)

Khiderleh, seraglio near Caragatch, 248; or St. George, Covel's view of origin of name, 248

Kimolos, a halting port for ships, 138

Kindsberg, Count Giovanni Christophoro, German ambassador at Adrianople, visits Sir John Finch, 197; notice of, 197; his belief in gold found in grapes, 198

King's College, Cambridge, organ at, constructed by Dallam, xvii

Kinnekleh (see Ginekly)

Kiuprili, Achmet, vizier, his success in war, xxv; wins Crete for the Turks, 161; description of his tent, 167; his audience with Sir John Finch, 195; personal description of, 195; his death, 195 *n*.; presents vests to English embassy, 196; goes to Sultan Selim's mosque on Prince Mustapha's birthday, 205; notice of, 205 *n*.; makes monthly payments before the audience, 259; shares table with Finch at the audience banquet, 260; his death, 267; his interview with Finch respecting the capitulations, 273

Kiuprili, the viziers, men of great ability, xxiv

Knill, John, death of, on board the *Hector*, 41

Knolles, the historian, referred to, 206

Koomburgas, town near Silivri, 179

Kos, or Lango, description of, 40

Kuzleraga, the, proxy for the bride, 230

Lamberte, Mr., leaves Ganos for Constantinople, 57

Lamia, or Zeitoun, miserable accommodation at, 83; danger of living in, 83

Land's End, distance of, from Scandaroon, 3

Lango, or Kos, description of, 40

Lanneret, the pinnace to the *Hector*, 5; is lost in a storm, 5; is run ashore at Falmouth, 6; is recovered at Plymouth, 6

INDEX. 299

Lello, Henry, ambassador at Constantinople, xlii ; succeeds Sir E. Barton, xii ; his quarrel with the French ambassador, xii ; his letter to Sir Robert Cecil, xii-xv ; has room built for organ, 58 ; his instructions to Dallam, 64 ; is in attendance during the presentation of organ, 66 ; gives entertainment on board the *Hector*, 73 ; his kindness to Dallam, 77 ; dismisses Dallam's dragoman for having deserted him, 79 ; forbids Dallam to work on Sunday, 80 ; is unwilling that Dallam should leave, 81

Lemnos, great storm off, 82 ; regained from the Venetians, 283 ; sacred earth of, 283 ; prepared for use at Hagiapate, 284 ; some given to Covel by Agathone, 284 ; authorities respecting, 285

Leo Africanus quoted as an authority by Covel, 124

Lepanto, Dallam arrives at, 84 ; description of, 85 ; ingenious water-mills at, 85 ; much fruit grown at, 85

Leslie, Walter de, German ambassador to the Porte, 197

Levant Company, rise of, in sixteenth century, ii, vii, x ; first charter, viii ; original members of, viii ; sends out its first ship, viii ; second charter, ix ; letters patent granted to, by James I, xx ; monopoly of, clearly established, xxi ; crest and arms of, xxi ; controversies with East India Company, xxii ; privileges granted to, xxii ; impeaches Sir S. Crowe, xxiii ; strict regulations of, xxiii ; petitions Parliament against East India Company, xxxvi ; prosperity of, in eighteenth century, xxxvii ; loses money through quarrel of Sir Kenelm Digby and the Venetian admiral, xxxvii ; charter remodelled by Parliament, xxxviii ; builds many consulates, xxxviii ; builds embassy at Constantinople, xxxviii ; British Government assumes much of the work of, xxxix ; dissolved, xxxix ; excellent work done by, xl

Levant Merchant, the, vessel bound for Smyrna, 101

Levantine families in Turkish empire, origin of, xxxv

Livy quoted as authority by Covel, 121

Lixure, a town of Cephalonia, 91

Locke, Michael, consul at Aleppo, ix ; founds factory at Aleppo, ix

London, fig in, 287

London Merchant, the, bound for Smyrna and Constantinople, 101 ; Covel takes his passage in, 102 ; has a collision with the *Pearl*, 106 ; runs aground in the Hellespont, 143

Lucian, his knowledge of corposans, 127

Lukium, or Lookioom, mortar, how made, 182

Lule-Bourgas, 183 ; monument of the dead near, 184 ; description of town of, 184 ; tobacco-pipe heads made at, 184 ; mill at, 185 ; description of the country near, 185 ; industry of the Greeks at a village near, 185

Lyons, Gulf of, the cry of a mermaid heard in, 94

Mahomed III, Sultan, succeeds his father Amurath III, x ; notice of, x ; puts nineteen of his brothers to death, xi, 62 *n.* ; his letter to Queen Elizabeth, xi ; inspects the *Hector*, 60 ; goes to visit his mother, 60 ; description of his attendants, 69 ; offers Dallam two wives, if he will stay, 73 ; description of his concubines, 74 ; forbids the departure of the *Hector*, 75 ;

and his concubines visit kiosk, 79 ;
desires to see Dallam at work, 80
Mahomed IV, a weak man, xxiv ;
description of his tents, 163 ; dress
of his attendants, 199; desires
actors from Venice to attend circumcision solemnities, 202 ; goes
to Sultan Selim's mosque on
Prince Mustapha's birthday, 205 ;
description of, 206; his love of
hunting, 207 ; notice of, 207 ;
attends festivities in honour of his
daughter's marriage, 208 ; receives
daily presents, 208 ; attends sports
at the Mosaif's house, 237 ; personal appearance of, 240 ; goes to
Ak-bonar to avoid the plague,
248 ; his seraglio at Khiderleh,
248 ; his house at Corojecui, 249 ;
his audience with Sir John Finch,
257
Mahomed the Bosnian (known as
Sokolli) assists Sir W. Harebone in
obtaining capitulations, viii ; story
of his son, 184, 185; buried at Jüpe,
187 ; repaired many bridges, and
built many mosques, 187, 188 ;
was vizier for forty years, 188
Mahomet, Vizierarem (see **Mahomed the Bosnian**)
Malaga, Covel lands at, 107 ; description of the cathedral at, 107 ;
young man hesitates to enter cathedral at, 107 ; convent of Sta.
Victoria at, 108 ; convent of San
Domingo at, 109 ; convent of
San Domingo at, picture in, 110 ;
Lord Baltimore's daughter in convent at, 111 ; life in convents at,
111 ; Captain Hill's friendship with
a nun at, 112 ; his quarrel with a
Roman Catholic at, 113 ; foundling
hospital at, 114 ; ordinary diet at,
114 ; prices of food at, 115 ; vermin
at, 115 ; description of, 117
Malta in the hands of the Knights
of Rhodes, 17

Maras, a town near Caragatch, 247;
healing earth at, 247
Maritza, course of the river, 250
Martel, Monsieur, his squadron by
Tunis and Tripoli, 117
Mary and Martha, the, bound for
Smyrna, 101
Matthew Gonson, the, makes a voyage
to Crete and Chios, v
Maunday Thursday, observance of,
156
Maurocordato, Dr. Alexander,
Kiuprili's dragoman, attends Dr.
Covel in his illness, 149 ; is present
at the audience, 259, 263 ; has the
impudence to sit by Sir John Finch,
264; account of, 272 ; gives statistics of the plague, 273
Maye, Mr. Chaplain, taken prisoner
at Rhodes, 37 ; ill-treatment of, at
Rhodes, 38 ; is restored to the
merchants, 39 ; goes on board the
ambassador's boat, 50
Mediterranean, Dallam enters the,
11
Mermaid, the cry of one heard, 94
Mestages, or fire carriers, 171, 172
Methodius brought out by Parthenius, 145
Michel, Waivode of Moldavia, built
a bridge at Adrianople, 249 ; notice
of, 249 *n.*
Mist at Constantinople, 162
Monuments to the dead at Lule-Bourgas, 184 ; near Hafsa, 187
Morea, 86 ; the weather very hot in
the, 87 ; desolate country in the, 87
Mortar, preparation of (see **Lukium**)
Mosaif (see **Moutessarif**)
Moscovy Company, the, rise of, in
the sixteenth century, ii
Moutessarif, the, sub-governor of a
province, favourite of Mahomed IV,
167 ; description of his tent, 167 ;
in the circumcision procession,
200 ; solemnities in honour of his
marriage, 208 ; his present to the

INDEX. 301

bride, 227 ; his marriage, by proxy, with the daughter of Mahomed IV, 230 ; sports at his house, 237
Muctary, Turkish town near Lule-Bourgas, 185
Mufti, the chief lawyer, his tent, 167 ; is visited by Sir John Finch, 267 ; description of, 267
Musical Instruments, description of, 211
Mustapha, first Turkish envoy to England, xi ; his mention of Sir E. Barton, xi
Mustapha, dervish, at Galata, 168
Mustapha, Prince, solemnities in honour of his circumcision, 198 ; notice of, 198 *n.*; magnificent horse trappings of, 202 ; his personal appearance, 203 ; his dress, 203 ; is circumcised, 207
My Lord (see Harvey, Sir Daniel) ; (see Finch, Sir John)
My Lord's Secretary (see Carpenter, Mr.)

Naculs, paper pyramids, carried in processions, 200, 228, 233 ; description of, 201
Natalis Comes quoted as an authority by Covel, 127
Nicæa, description of, 281
Nischardji-baschi, or Secretary of State, 258 ; and at audience banquet, 261
Nointel, Marquis de, favours union of Eastern and Western Churches, xxxi ; celebrates Mass in the cave of Antiparos, xxxi ; entertains Covel, 255 ; exposes a Turkish soothsayer, 255
North, Sir Dudley, goes to Smyrna, xxxiv ; his frugality and energy, xxxiv ; is appointed treasurer to the Levant Company, xxxv ; his account of the *avanias*, xxxv ; remains in Adrianople during the plague, 244 ; is present at the audience banquet, 261 ; enters the audience chamber with Sir John Finch, 265
North, Montagu, of Aleppo, joins his brother Dudley at Constantinople, xxxiv

Organ, made by Dallam, xv ; taken to ambassador's house, 58 ; greatly injured by voyage, 58 ; put together in Lello's house, 60 ; viewed by Turkish officials, 60 ; moved to the seraglio, 61 ; presented to Sultan Mahomed IV, 67 ; description of, 67
Orta-cui, village near the Arda, 252 ; description of, 252 ; good fish at, 253 ; houses built of wood at, 253 ; prosperity of inhabitants of, 254 ; manner of threshing at, 254 ; severe storm near, 256
Ortelius, his accuracy doubted by Covel, 173, 176, 178

Paget, Lord, ambassador at Constantinople, xlii
Pain, Captain, of the *Speedwell*, 101
Panagiotes, dragoman to Kiuprili, account of, 281 ; his tomb at Chalki, 281
Parnassus, hills of, bad weather on, 83 ; danger of travelling on, 84 ; village women go barefoot on, 84
Parthenius disobliges many Greek Metropolitans, 145 ; abolishes temporary unions of Greek women with Turks, 145
Partridge, Captain, of the *Turkey Merchant*, 101 ; declines to enter Tunis, 119 ; his want of courtesy towards Captain Robinson, 129
Passaro, Cape, great storm at, 93
Patras, description of, 86
Patriarch, the, his manner of blessing, 159 (see Dionysius and Parthenius)

302   INDEX.

Paulo, a Greek, laughs at the miracles of Sta. Victoria, 108
Pearl, the, bound for Smyrna, 101 ; has a collision with the *London Merchant*, 106
Pentloe, Mr., case of, xxxvi ; Mrs., is seized by the Turkish Government, xxxvi
Pickering, Dr., physician to the factory at Smyrna, 142 ; is caught in a storm near Orta-cui, 256 ; is present at the audience banquet, 261
Pigeons, letters carried by, from Aleppo to Scandaroon, 32
Pindar, Sir Paul, ambassador at Constantinople, xxi, xlii ; secretary to Sir Henry Lello, 63 ; brings present to Sultana Safiye, 63 ; mention of, 63 *n*. ; is in attendance during the presentation of organ, 66 ; fords a river on horseback, 85 ; prevents Conisby from attacking a Jew, 86
Pisans, the, obtain capitulations, iii
Pliny quoted as an authority by Covel, 116, 121, 122, 126
Plymouth, the, accident to, between Chios and Psara, 286
Plymouth, Dallam arrives at, 6
Polybius quoted as an authority by Covel, 121
Ponte grande, description of road to, 177 ; pleasure-garden near, 177 ; description of, 177 ; bridges at, 178 ; dirty condition of lake at, 178 ; villages near, 179
Ponte piccolo, description of, 174 ; college at, 175 ; bridges at, 176 ; Greek villages near, 176
Porpoises come about the ship, 11 ; near the coast of Spain, 96
Porte, the, list of ambassadors to, xlii
Porter, Sir James, his work on the policy and government of the Turkish people, xl
Present, the (see Organ)

Quaker, John the, ill-treatment of, at Constantinople, xxv

Ragusa, the earthquake at, 193
Ragusan Ambassador, the (see Caboga, Marin)
Rebecca, the, takes leave of the company, 96 ; returns pursued by men-of-war, 97
Rejoicings at the birth of a prince, 152
Relezea, or Ereklidia, encounter with Greeks at, 51 ; description of the governor of, 52
Rhodes, the Knights of, at Malta, 17 ; description of the island of, 34 ; deputy governor of the town of, visits the *Hector*, 34 ; Dallam lands at, 35 ; description of the town of, 35, 39 ; ill-treatment of Mr. Maye at, 38 ; covetousness of the deputy governor of, 39
Rhodope (see Despotodagh)
Ricaut, Sir Paul, secretary to Lord Winchilsea, v ; consul at Smyrna, vi, 140, 155 ; his book on Greek and Armenian Churches, vi ; and on the state of the Turkish Empire, vi, xl, 140 ; his book on the capitulations, xxiv ; entertains Covel at his house at Sedjagui, 140 ; quoted as an authority, 70 *n*., 145, 153, 228, 252 *n*. ; his boat at the embarkation of Sir Daniel Harvey's body, 155
Rimbault, Dr., his authority quoted, xvi
Ritz, Valentine, his portrait of Covel, xxviii
Robinson, Captain, of the *Greenwich*, Admiral of the convoy, 101 ; tells the news to the sailors, 103 ; dines on board the *London Merchant*, 104, 117 ; gives instructions in case of encountering enemies, 117 ; doubts as to his genuineness, 118 ; is offended with Mr. Earlesman, 125 ; takes his leave, 128

INDEX. 303

Roe, Sir T., ambassador at Constantinople, xxi, xlii
Roles, Captain Dier, of the *Mary and Martha*, 101
Roman and Greek churches compared, 150
Roman Catholics, many in Adrianople, 210
Rope-walking, very remarkable, 238, 239; accident during, 239
Rushout, Sir James, ambassador at Constantinople, xlii

Sacred earth of Lemnos, 283, 284, 285
Safiye, Sultana, Queen Elizabeth's present to, x; mother of Mahomed III, x; inspects the *Hector*, 60; receives Sir Henry Lello's present, 63; is pleased with Sir Paul Pindar, 63
Sailors, the, entertain the officers and passengers, 104; their custom of ducking, 105, 106
Salter, Mr., receives no present, and is offended, 196
Samos, birthplace of Pythagoras, 40; terror of inhabitants of, at the sight of the *Hector*, 40; captain of, brings present to the *Hector*, 41; millet grown on island of, 41; the *Hector* runs aground on the shores of, 42
Sandwich, Dallam arrives at, 5
Santons, or holy men, 153, 166
Scandaroon, halting port for vessels, x; distance of, from Land's End, 3; Dallam lands at, 28; wild appearance of, 28; traces of ancient city at, 30; lizards on ruins of city at, 30; large snake at, 30; bad accommodation at, 31; letters carried to, from Aleppo by pigeons, 32; the *Hector* leaves, 33
Scopo, hill at Zante, 20; monastery on, 21

Scutari, gardens at, 168
Seadedin, the historian, assists Sir W. Harebone to obtain capitulations, viii
Sea-sickness, Covel and other passengers attacked by, 102; treatment for, 103
Sedjagui, summer residence near Smyrna, 140; Sir Paul Ricaut's house at, 140; Jaques von Dam's house at, 140; opium eater at, 140
Selibria (see Silivri)
Seneca quoted as an authority by Covel, 121
Seraglio, the, description of, at Constantinople, 61, 63; gates kept shut in, 61; lovely gardens and fruit at, 62
Sestos, castle at the mouth of the Hellespont, 50, 82, 143, 154
Shark, a, follows the *Hector*, 95
Sharpe, Mr., leaves Ganos for Constantinople, 57
Sicily, description of, 17; communication by watch-tower lights in, 92
Sikibaba, Eski-Baba, so called by Ortelius, 186
Silivri, large melons grown at, 57; description of road to, from Ponte grande, 179; description of country near, 180
Simon, Demetrius, washes the feet of the brothers at St. Francisco's, 159
Sinekly, Turkish town near Silivri, 181
Sistos (see Sestos)
Smith, Thomas, an original member of the Levant Company, viii
Smyrna, Sir Paul Ricaut consul at, vi; embarkation of Sir Daniel Harvey's body at, 155
Sokolli (see Mahomed the Bosnian)
Solemnities, procession during the, 198; festivities during the, 208; fireworks during the, 213, 222-24;

dancers, 213; actors, 215; plays acted, 216; acrobats, 216, jugglers, 220; wrestlers, 221
Solyman I, Sultan, concludes a capitulation with Francis I of France, iv
Sophia, Sta., at Galata, the vaults under, visited by Covel, 170
Soorano (see Argostoli)
Speedwell, the, bound for Smyrna and Constantinople, 101
Spon and Wheeler, their authority quoted, 142, 207, 279
Sporca, Sultana, account of, 160; the story of her dancing girl, 161
Sposa, the (see Agazé, Sultana)
Sposo, the (see Moutessarif)
Stamboul (see Constantinople)
Stanco, or Kos, description of, 40
Staple, Richard, his mission to Constantinople, vii
Stoey, Captain, of the *Pearl*, bound for Smyrna, 101
Strabo quoted as an authority by Covel, 121-122
Straits of Gibraltar, custom of ducking at the, 105
Strophades, the, monastery on, 26; no women on the island of, 26
Sultan, the (see Amurath III, Mahomed III, Mahomed IV, Solyman I)
Superstitions of the Turks, 255
Surgeon, the, of the *London Merchant*, and some gentlemen, injured in a storm, 104
Susan, the, in the harbour at Argostoli, 91
Swallow, the, in company with the *Hector*, 90

Tarifa, pleasant situation of, 11
Tarrefe (see Tarifa)
Tarsus, market at, 32
Tchorlou, or Chiorlóo, description of, 181; aqueduct at, 181; country near, 183

Temple, Mr., of Smyrna, brings wine on board the *Centurion*, 155; entertains Covel at his house, 156
Tenedos, Aga of, sends a present of fish, 142; Aga of, begs for glass bottles, 143; dress of the Greeks at, 156; no church at, 156
Testerdore (see Dafterdar)
Thomas and Frances, the, bound for Smyrna and Scandaroon, 101
Timur, origin of the name, 243
Tobacco presented to the captain of a galley, 49
Tondja, the river by Adrianople, 249; its course, 250
Tooloonjés, or police, keep order in the streets, 204, 212
Tradesmen, their procession during the solemnities, 232
Troy, Dallam visits, 49
Trumbull, Sir William, ambassador at Constantinople, xlii
Trumpeter left behind at Deal, 5
Tunis, the Turkish fleet at, 17; difficulties about entering, 119; Captain Partridge declines to enter, 119; abundance of provisions at, 120; fish at, 121; Mr. Earlesman, English consul at, 124; the *Martin* left behind at, 125
Turkey, method of reckoning distance by navigators in, 171; discomforts of travelling in, 174; wretchedness of the buildings in, 179; manner of building tombs in, 187
Turkey Merchant, the, bound for Scandaroon, 101
Turkey Merchants (see Levant Company)
Turks renew capitulations granted by the Greeks, iii; trade by means of Greek vessels, iii; their civility to the Franks during the solemnities, 205, 212; their reverence at prayer time, 210; their fondness

for wine, 245; their superstitions, 255; use no silver dishes, 263

Vani-Effendi, the preacher, notice of, 268; invites Sir Thomas Baines to visit him, 269; discusses matters of faith with Sir Thomas Baines, 269
Varangians (see **Warings**)
Velutelli, Acerbo, obtains patent for importing currants, vii
Venetians, the, obtain capitulations, iii; conduct the trade between the Levant and England, v; decline to sail in English seas, vi
Venice, the Baily of, at Constantinople, entertained by Sir Henry Lello, 73
Vernon, Mr., collects information in Turkey and Persia, 279
Vice-Admiral (see **Wild**, Captain)
Virginals taken on board the *Hector* by Dallam, 4
Vizier, the (see **Ibrahim** and **Kiuprili**)
Von Hammer, his authority quoted, viii, xxix, 80, 145, 192

Waist, the, a portion of a ship, 103 n., 126
Warings, or Varangians, from Scandinavia, obtain capitulations, ii
Watson, Myghell, Dallam's joiner, 20; accompanies him on expedition at Zante, 20; fright of, 20; remains hiding in a bush, 24; is ashamed of his cowardice, 24; accompanies Dallam to the seraglio for presentation of the organ, 66

Whale-spawn near the coast of Spain, 95
Whales come about the ship, 11; in calm water near Gibraltar, 96
Wheeler, Sir George, his authority quoted, xxvii, (see **Spon** and **Wheeler**)
Wight, the Isle of, wreck of Venetian argosy off, vi
Wild, Captain, of the *Assurance*, Vice-Admiral of the convoy, 102; dines on board the *London Merchant*, 104, 117, 129; gives signal to the fleet to prepare for fight, 129; at Smyrna, 155
Winchilsea, Earl of, ambassador at Constantinople, xxiv, xlii; obtains further capitulations from Vizier Kiuprili, xxiv
Witches, belief of Greeks in, 257
Worcester Cathedral, additions to the organ in, by Dallam, xvii
Wrestlers at the solemnities, 221
Wych, Edward, brother to Sir Peter, buried at Erekli, 277; Sir Peter, ambassador at Constantinople, xlii

Zante, description of, 18-19; is governed by the Duke of Venice, 19; fruit cultivation by Greeks in, 19; quarantine at, 19, 89; Dallam lands at, 20; monastery at, description of, 21; monastery at, chapel of, 23; monastery at, richly-attired women in, 23; many sweet flowers at, 24; monastery at, visited by merchants, 25; games at, 25-26; miserable weather at, 126; many earthquakes at, 126;
Zeitoun (see **Lamia**)

LONDON: CHAS. J. CLARK, 4, LINCOLN'S INN FIELDS, W.C.

www.ingramcontent.com/pod-product-compliance
Lightning Source LLC
Chambersburg PA
CBHW030743250426
43672CB00028B/387